VICTOR
HUGO

VICTOR HUGO WITH HIS SON,
FRANÇOIS-VICTOR

From the portrait by A. de Chatillon in
the Musée Victor Hugo.

VICTOR HUGO

BY

MADAME DUCLAUX

KENNIKAT PRESS
Port Washington, N. Y./London

VICTOR HUGO

First published in 1921
Reissued in 1972 by Kennikat Press
Library of Congress Catalog Card No: 70-153903
ISBN 0-8046-1594-2

Manufactured by Taylor Publishing Company   Dallas, Texas

PREFATORY NOTE

By the General Editor

MME. DUCLAUX wrote to me six months after the beginning of the War that during September 1914 she did some work on *Victor Hugo* within sound of the cannon of the Marne ; but, as one may well believe of such a lover of the great poet, she soon found that her country's life and death struggle made any other thought but that of helping her people in their war out of the question. For, as we remember, even the old poet shouldered his rifle and clamoured to be made use of in 1870. And now that the triumph, which would have consoled him for the anguish of those days, has come, here comes this book to remind us of what we owe to France, not only for her arms but still more for her great poets, her great torch-bearers for liberty. It would be impertinent in me to add anything more to what Mme. Duclaux has said about Victor Hugo, except to suggest how timely is such a book at a moment when the hope of the world still depends so largely on a sympathetic understanding by France and England of all that is best and most permanent in the spirit of the other. Victor Hugo is perhaps the type of Frenchman most unlike the Englishman, especially in that glorious swagger, which comes not from vanity and emptiness as it might with us, but from that abounding enthusiasm and zest in the immediate task which cannot halt to consider a possibly absurd aspect.

vii

Mme. Duclaux, English by birth and French by long association, has interpreted her poet with a tenderness and a sense of humour which makes us understand and sympathize even with his excesses and feel some of the Frenchman's joy in his finest work.

BASIL WILLIAMS.

July 1920.

CONTENTS

XVIII. THE "COUP D'ÉTAT"   169

   XIX. A VOLCANO IN ERUPTION   180

   XX. CONTEMPLATION   189

   XXI. THE ZENITH 201

 XXII. THE CLOSE OF A CHAPTER   218

XXIII. THE EXILE'S RETURN   228

XXIV. THE LAST SHEAF OF HARVEST   .   .   . 241

  XXV. THE BUDDHA ON THE BRACKET   .   .   . 251

        BIBLIOGRAPHY 261

        INDEX 263

CHRONOLOGICAL TABLE

1802. Victor Hugo is born.
1807. He spends a year in Italy.
1808. Education in Paris.
1812. At the College of Nobles at Madrid.
1814. His father places him at M. Cordier's school in Paris preparatory to l'École Polytechnique.
Restoration of the Bourbon Monarchy in France. The Comte d'Artois sends the Décoration du Lys to Victor Hugo and his elder brother.
1819. He founds with his brother Abel a literary review, *Le Conservateur Littéraire*.
1820. He is named Maître ès Jeux Floraux by the Academy of Toulouse.
He composes an Ode on the death of the Duke of Berry which arouses public, and even Royal, attention.
1821. Death of Victor Hugo's mother.
1822. Marriage of Victor Hugo. The King grants him a pension.
1827. Victor Hugo secedes from the ranks of the Ultras and takes up his position in the Liberal camp.
1830. Production of *Hernani* at the Théâtre Français.
A Revolution in France disperses the legitimate Monarchy, and raises to the throne Louis-Philippe, Duke of Orleans.
Domestic difficulties distress Victor Hugo's hitherto happy home.
1831. A coolness divides the poet from his friend Sainte-Beuve.
He publishes *Notre-Dame de Paris* and *Feuilles d'automne*.
Victor Hugo sees a possible Saviour of Society in Napoleon's son, the Duke of Reichstadt.
1832. Death of the Duke of Reichstadt.
1833. Grave revolutionary unrest in Paris. (The recollection of these times will later on inspire *Les Misérables*.)
Victor Hugo forms a *liaison*, destined to endure for nearly fifty years, with Juliette Drouet.
1835. *Chants du crépuscule.*
1837. A second violent quarrel with Sainte-Beuve.
Victor Hugo makes the acquaintance of the heir to the throne ; under his influence, and especially that of the Duchess of Orleans, he comes round to the Monarchy of Louis-Philippe.
1838. He publishes *Ruy Blas*.
1841. He is elected a Member of the French Academy.
1842. His journey to the Rhine, and his view of the Rhine from the double standpoint of poetry and politics.
Sudden death of the Duke of Orleans. Shall the Duchess be Regent-Presumptive ?

1843.   Marriage and accidental death of Hugo's daughter Léopoldine.
1845.   Victor Hugo is created, by Louis-Philippe, a Peer of France.
1848.   A Revolution in France sends Louis-Philippe into exile. Victor
        Hugo proclaims the Regency of the Duchess of Orleans, but,
        finding that impossible, is easily gained to the cause of the
        Republic.
        In December, Victor Hugo votes for the election of Prince Louis-
        Napoleon Bonaparte to the Presidency of the Republic.
1851.   In December, the Prince President seizes the supreme power by a
        coup d'État.
        Resistance of Victor Hugo as an active member of the Committee
        of Insurrection.
        All being lost, he escapes to Brussels.
1852.   Victor Hugo, with his wife, family (and Madame Drouet) settles in
        Jersey.
1853.   And publishes Les Châtiments.
1854.   Outbreak of the Crimean War. Hugo hopes it will be fatal to
        the Empire.
1855.   He is expelled from Jersey, and settles definitely in Guernsey,
        where he shortly afterwards buys Hauteville House.
1856.   He publishes Les Contemplations.
1859.   The first volume of the Légende des siècles.
1862.   Les Misérables.
1865.   Chansons des rues et des bois.
1866.   Les Travailleurs de la mer.
1868.   Death of Madame Victor Hugo.
1869.   Victor Hugo publishes l'Homme qui rit.
1870.   Outbreak of war between France and Prussia. On the 4th Septem-
        ber, after the capitulation of Sedan, the French Republic is estab-
        lished. Victor Hugo immediately returns to Paris, and remains
        there during the siege.
1871.   28th January. Capitulation of Paris.
        In February, Victor Hugo is elected Member for Paris in the
        National Assembly, and proceeds to Bordeaux to arrange terms
        of peace with Prussia.
        13th March. Death of Charles Hugo at Bordeaux.
        18th March. Public funeral of Charles Hugo in Paris.
        18th March. Outbreak of the revolt of the Commune.
        Victor Hugo retires to Brussels.
        27th May. His house is attacked by a hostile mob.
        29th May. He is expelled from Belgium as an abettor of the
        Commune of Paris.
1873.   After a year in Guernsey, Victor Hugo settles in Paris, where, at
        Christmas, his son François-Victor dies.
        Victor Hugo publishes his Quatre-vingt-treize.
1876.   Hugo is elected a Senator for the Department of the Seine.
1877.   L'Art d'être grandpère.
1881.   Les Quatre Vents de l'Esprit.
1882.   Torquemada. Margarita.
1883.   Death of Madame Drouet.
        Victor Hugo publishes the third volume of the Légende des siècles.
1885.   22nd May. Death of Victor Hugo.

CHAPTER I

CHILDHOOD

THE France into which Victor Hugo was born was not unlike our recent world of the Great War. The armies of the Republic, having repelled the invaders, had seethed over her borders into Holland, into Italy. All Europe was in ebullition, and felt the dread of the triumphant conqueror who led the armies of France.

[1] Eighteen Hundred and Two. Sparta gives way to Rome.
Napoleon begins to bud in Bonaparte.
Now where the Emperor's forehead presses home
The mask of the First Consul bursts apart.
'Twas in Besançon,[2] an old Spanish city,
A child was born, by chance,—a wind-swept grain
Whose double root was Brittany, Lorraine,—
Mute, sightless, pale was he, a thing to pity,

---

[1] Ce siècle avait deux ans. Rome remplaçait Sparte,
Déjà Napoléon perçait sous Bonaparte,
Et du Premier Consul déjà, par maint endroit,
Le front de l'Empereur brisait le masque étroit.
Alors dans Besançon, vieille ville espagnole.
Jeté comme la graine au gré de l'air qui vole,
Naquit d'un sang breton et lorrain à la fois
Un enfant sans couleur, sans regard et sans voix ;
Si débile qu'il fut, ainsi qu'une chimère
Abandonné de tous excepté de sa mère,
Et que son cou ployé comme un frêle roseau
Fit faire en même temps sa bière et son berceau.
Cet enfant que la Vie effaçait de son livre,
Et qui n'avait pas même un lendemain à vivre
C'est moi.
                                        Les Feuilles d'automne.

[2] Besançon, the capital of Franche-Comté, the subject of long disputes between France and the Empire, for thirty years was incorporated into the Spanish dominions—between 1648 and 1678.

So faint, so frail, no baby but a ghost,
All, save his mother, gave him up for lost.
His fragile neck fell sideways like a reed,
His cradle and his coffin came together :
This child whose name Life would not write or read,
This dying child that could not hope to weather
The morrow of his birth—'Tis I !

Victor was but six weeks old when his father, Commandant Joseph Léopold Sigisbert Hugo, was sent from Besançon to Marseilles, and thence to Corsica, to Elba, accompanied in all these changes of garrison by his wife and his three little boys : Victor had two elder brothers, Abel and Eugène. But this hard and roving life tried too severely the feeble health of the youngest-born. When, in 1804, the Major was ordered to Italy, to the front, the young mother felt that her place was not on a battlefield. She parted from her husband, took her babies to Paris, and devoted herself to the care of them. Not till October 1807 did she take them to rejoin their father, now Colonel Hugo, Governor of the province of Avellino and the right hand of Joseph Bonaparte, King of Naples. Napoleon's Roman peace had settled on the reluctant conquered country, and the Governor of Avellino thought to offer his family a settled and illustrious home.

Of that long journey Victor, who was but five years old, remembered little : a sledge-ride on the snow of the Alps ; the grey, piled roofs of Susa, a flood at Parma, the bridge of Saint-Angelo at Rome, and the barracks :

où mon père, jeune homme,
Nous regardait jouer dans la caserne à Rome,
A cheval sur la grande épée, tout petits,

and Naples shining in the sunshine with the sea at her feet ; the child said that the city wore a white dress fringed with blue.

Naples was a glimpse, an unforgettable vision, and the little band went still farther south. They stopped at Avellino, where the Governor of the province, Colonel Hugo, in full uniform, stood waiting to greet them on the steps of a great marble palace, fissured by earthquakes. The child remembered of Italy what a child can grasp : the vast room in which he slept alone, with a rift in the wall through which he saw the changing landscape outside; the brilliance of the air, the golden sunshine, the burning heat, the general splendour of the scene; but especially the precipices, filled with nut-bushes that, in the eyes of a little boy, made the peculiar charm of that great landscape. The nuts of Avellino are famous the world over; their oval "avelines", are larger than any other hazels; and when the Hugo children discovered that Victor, by a fortunate idiosyncrasy, was insensible to giddiness, they saw that he spent most of his time clambering about the almost perpendicular walls of those ravines gathering nuts. I have often wondered whether the poet's frequent use of the metaphors or images, "abîme," "gouffre," "préci-pice," and even "la bouche d'ombre," may not be due to that early experience; he had felt the attraction of the abyss at an age when most children stray not far beyond the kitchen-garden. At five years old he observed and remembered. And Colonel Hugo, writing to his mother in Burgundy, remarked that the child was already unusually sedate and deliberate.

Abel is the most amiable of boys, tall, polite, more deliberate than children are generally at his age, and, like his brothers, very good-tempered.
Eugène has the handsomest face in the world, and is as lively as quicksilver—less inclined, I fancy, to study than his brothers.
Victor, the youngest, shows a great aptitude for learning. He is as deliberate as his elder brother and very thoughtful. He speaks little, and always to the purpose. His reflections have often struck me. He has a very sweet face.[1]

This sweet but solemn baby showed already one of the chief qualities of the future poet's genius : the faculty of absorption, of reflection, of an extraordinary retentiveness. Already in this early journey he acquired the first elements of that sense of glory which in later years enabled him to represent with such splendour in his verse the great adven-ture and the nomadic triumphs of the Empire. As he was to sing in his *Odes et Ballades* (" Mon Enfance "), in an early poem still embued with the stiff, almost stilted, quality of Napoleon's epoch :

[1] *Victor Hugo raconté . . .*

My childhood in the world of war was spent
'Mid the piled arms, the dusty wains, the tent—
   I've slept upon the gun-carriage o' nights.
I loved the fiery chargers and their manes,
   The stirrup's creaking where the bright spur bites.

I loved the thundering forts with lofty flanks,
The drawn sword of the chief leading the ranks,
   The mounted sentry in a lonely glade,
The tried battalions marching through the towns
   With a torn banner, all its wounds displayed.

My envious soul admired the swift hussar,
His breast embroidered with the gold of war,
   The lancer, all his snowy plumes a-stir,
The tall dragoon whose Scythian helmet flaunts
   A mare's tail mingled with a tiger's fur.[1]

Victor's wanderings were far from finished. His father's
chief, Joseph Bonaparte, was barely settled on his throne
in Naples, contented with his lot and determined to con-
ciliate his people, when Napoleon decided to create him
King of Spain. This meant leaving Italy and conquering
an unwilling and unwanted crown. Spain was in no
humour to recognize the monarch thrust upon her ; Spain,
like King Joseph, would rather matters had remained as
they were, but it was impossible to gainsay the glorious
tyrant who shaped Europe as it suited his fancy. Joseph
with a sigh left the sunny Chiaja and set out at the head of
his troops. The Governor of Avellino felt in honour bound
to accompany his patron upon his dangerous expedition,

[1] Parmi les chars poudreux, les armes éclatantes,
   Une muse des camps m'emporta sous les tentes,
     Je dormis sur l'affût des canons meurtriers,
   J'aimai les fiers coursiers aux crinières flottantes,
     Et l'éperon froissant les rauques étriers.

J'aimai les forts tonnants, aux abords difficiles,
Le glaive nu des chefs guidant les rangs dociles,
     La vedette, perdue en un bois isolé
Et les vieux bataillons qui passaient dans les villes
     Avec un drapeau mutilé.

Mon envie admirait et le hussard rapide,
Parant de gerbes d'or sa poitrine intrépide,
     Et le panache blanc des agiles lanciers,
Et les dragons, mêlant sur leur casque gépide
     Le poil taché du tigre aux crins noirs des coursiers.
                      ("Mon Enfance.")

but it was naturally impossible to undertake the Peninsular War in the company of a young wife and her babies. Madame Hugo and the little boys were regretfully sent back to Paris after a brief year's visit, leaving in the future poet's imagination no accurate image but

> Un vague faisceau de lueurs incertaines,

a wandering cluster of uncertain gleams. Farewell to blue seas and marble palaces rent by earthquakes ! Italy counts for little in the formation of Victor Hugo—he was but six years old when he left it !—he perceived of all that grandeur and beauty just such a haunting glimpse as he caught of the landscape of Avellino through the rift in his bedroom wall.

When Madame Hugo brought her two younger boys, Eugène and Victor, to Paris in 1808, she took a temporary lodging in the rue de Clichy ; but, after the palace at Avellino, how cramped and narrow seemed the Parisian flat ! Madame Hugo was no townswoman. At fifteen years of age, during the civil war in Vendée, she had scoured the woods of the *Bocage* with Madame de la Rochejacquelein ; as a woman of thirty she still loved air, space, and a noble adventure. She was to find them all in a roomy old house with a garden on the southern side of the Seine. It was a portion of the ancient convent of the Feuillantines left untouched by the Revolution :—Impasse des Feuillantines, No. 12—an isolated mansion in a deserted quarter of the left bank of the Seine. The garden had long since run wild, it was full of trees and birds, with in one corner a ruined chapel, less a town garden than a park, deep and vast, shut in by high walls, almost a field in the middle, at the edges almost a wood. Paris had many such gardens in 1808, and has some still ; one such waves its unpruned loose-hanging branches below my balcony even as I write. When Madame Hugo took her little lads to inspect this fairyland they greeted it with shouts of delight, rushing here and there like wild things : here at last was the equivalent of the abyss of Avellino ! Their eyes were not large enough nor their legs long enough to take in all its possibilities.

" See what I've found ! "

" Oh, that's nothing.   Look here ! "

" Oh ! Oh !   A swing ! "

" An avenue of horse-chestnuts ! "

" A cistern gone dry !   A fort !   It'll make a fort ! "

" I say !   Come here ! "

" Apples !   Oh, and pears ! oh, and a trellis of grapes ! "

" And they're ripe ! " [1]

I doubt if the future poet in his career of perhaps un-paralleled glory was ever to know happier hours.

> Three brothers ; each was but a little lad ;
> Our mother bade us play, but she forbad
> The ladders and the flower-beds in the grass ;
>
> Three brothers—I the youngest of the three—
> We munched our crusts with such a hungry glee
> The women laughed aloud to see us pass.[2]

Madame Hugo was not very sensitive to the charms of Nature ; she cared little enough for mountains and land-scapes, but she loved a garden, and, more than anything, she loved the health and happiness of her boys : those years in the Impasse des Feuillantines were probably the pleasantest of her life.

We know all about that garden—not only from Victor Hugo's poetry, though more than once he has described that early Eden—but also from the author of *Victor Hugo raconté par un témoin de sa vie*, in later years the poet's wife, but in those early times a little playmate, a comrade, one year younger than Victor, who shared all their fun, stormed their forts with the boys, and sometimes, with bandaged eyes, was driven in the wheelbarrow from end to end of their domain, and not let free until she had guessed the exact spot where she stood.   There was the swing,

---

[1] *Victor Hugo raconté* . . .

[2] Mes deux frères et moi, nous étions tout enfants.
Notre mère disait ; Jouez, mais je défends
Qu'on marche dans les fleurs et qu'on monte aux échelles ;

Abel était l'aîné, j'étais le plus petit.
Nous mangions notre pain de si bon appétit,
Que les femmes riaient quand nous passions près d'elles.
Les Contemplations, " Aux Feuillantines."

too ; Adèle Foucher, trembling and protesting, was launched high in the air by three vigorous pairs of arms ; but none of the boys could swing himself so high as Victor—right up into the branches of the trees, as though he never meant to come down !

The garden was so full of trees and flowers and birds and rabbits, that one scarcely knew which to prefer : the first lilacs and crocuses in spring, the long summer evenings, the apples and grapes of autumn or the snowballs in winter ; the garden was not only our poet's fairyland, but his school. He had, however, another master. Madame Hugo was a Royalist ; she discovered in the neighbourhood an ex-priest of the Oratory, the Père de La Rivière, nominally married (in order to put the hounds of the recent Revolution off the scent) to an old housekeeper of his, who waited on him still. The " Père de La Rivière," ex-priest, ex-aristocrat, had become the " Père Larivière " (or, as we might say, Daddy Rivers), who taught reading and writing to the shopkeepers' children of the quarter. He furbished up his half-forgotten Greek and Latin for the little Hugos ; and the poet always retained a kind remembrance of this early tutor, " naïf comme un savant, malin comme un enfant." Three-and-forty years after, in an hour of deadly peril, when he had to escape from Paris under a feigned name (which while hiding his identity might still be recognized by his wife), he chose the name of his old master, the Père Larivière.

This old hedge-schoolmaster of the Paris streets was not Victor Hugo's principal tutor. It so fell out that a more important part of his education was to be undertaken by his godfather—an unknown godfather whom the child had rarely seen. General Lahorie had been a comrade of General Hugo's when both were young, during the campaign in Vendée. Since then Lahorie had fallen upon evil days. He was one of those old captains of the First Republic who in their hearts had never accepted General Bonaparte's elevation to the Empire. They were Republicans, these old soldiers ; but if it were shown that a monarchy was a necessity of State, they would have preferred a legitimate king, their born superior, to a fortunate comrade-

at-arms. In disgust of Napoleon, Lahorie had conspired
with General Moreau to restore the Bourbons. Moreau's
plot had been discovered in 1804 and the two Generals had
been condemned to death, but had contrived to escape—
Moreau out of France, Lahorie into hiding, travelling as it
were underground from one friend's house to another. By
1808 he had pretty well worn out his welcome, his old haunts
were all known to the police, a price was on his head ; he
was at his wits' end where to go. It was then that Madame
Hugo discovered the deserted convent and the abandoned
garden of the rue des Feuillantines. The brave lady took
into her charge the man who was her Victor's godfather
and sheltered him for a year and a half. Even the children
at first did not know of the refugee, who took up his quarters
in an abandoned chapel, converted into a sort of tool-house,
in the grounds—the one spot, the one forbidden Blue-
beard's chamber, where they were not allowed to penetrate : their mother kept the key. But, of course, at last
these intrepid little marauders discovered the General ; they
were sworn to secrecy, and thenceforth he was their companion. " Il comprenait les jeux." He told them wonderful stories ; he served camp-dinners on the garden-steps ;
he read Tacitus with Victor and gave him all Voltaire's
plays. His godson never forgot certain of his phrases—
the solemn way, for instance, in which he once said,
" Avant tout, la liberté ! " Victor had been accustomed to
hear more often of " la gloire." . . . In the eyes of General
Lahorie the friends of liberty were generally the enemies
of Napoleon. Despite his seclusion, he had resumed his
plotting and his planning with the partisans of the Bourbons.
Madame Hugo, as I have said, was a Royalist ; and I cannot
help wondering whether she were not an aider and abettor
in some of these conspiracies—whether, perhaps, her real
aim in taking the roomy solitary house and forsaken garden
of the Impasse des Feuillantines were not the facility which
they afforded for secret comings and goings. There, at
any rate, Lahorie lived in safety, undiscovered, invisible
and happy. At last, one day in 1810, the Minister of Police
having assured a common friend that so belated a conspirator ran no risk of arrest and that the General might

walk the streets of Paris a free man, Lahorie left that enchanted garden. His little playmates were never to see him again ! On the morrow he was again arrested and thrown into prison—a prison which he was to leave but for one day, in 1812.

Meanwhile Victor Hugo began to appreciate Napoleon.

In the case of so retentive a nature we cannot exaggerate the importance of first impressions.

One which was always to remain with Victor Hugo was that of the Strong Man, silent and still, unmoved by the stir that his glory awakes in an attentive and enthusiastic world, dominating his environment in an Olympian calm.

One of his earliest memories was the illumination of all Paris for the birth of the King of Rome in 1811. " J'avais sept ans," he says ; but he was really nine. The triumph and festival that irradiated all the city penetrated even the garden of the Feuillantines, and Victor, excited, exalted, escaped from his mother's care (she hated to see her boys running after soldiers) and followed the crowd to the neighbouring Place du Panthéon. There was such a throng as the child had never seen, soldiers, citizens, all singing at the top of their voices : " Veillons au salut de l'Empire." The sides of the square and all the neighbouring streets were packed with troops, and in the middle there was a space of glory, hedged round by the Old Guard, where, followed by a train of kings and princes, appeared Napoleon. He alone was apparently unmoved. He stood there mute, grave, rather shabby, in his old cocked hat and legendary grey great-coat that seemed to mock the dazzling uniforms of his satellites.

Victor was puzzled : Why was the Emperor so much less splendid ? Are splendour, noise, applause, a form of homage rendered by inferiors ?

For some reason, General Hugo was in Paris. The children seldom saw their father,

Ce héros au sourire si doux,

whom they were to learn to love in after life ; but they revered him as a supreme court of appeal. On the morrow,

therefore, as father and son were walking on the slope of
Saint Geneviève's Hill, the child put the question to his
father : Why were the kings, the generals, and even the
soldiers, so noisy and so splendid, and the Emperor so
shabby and so calm ? The sun was setting and all the
western sky was aflame while the town at their feet looked
grey and still. The General thought a moment, and then
replied, " You must never go by appearances ! There is
more flame in the centre of that grey earth than in those
fiery clouds ! The Emperor, too, is full of secret fire and
unevident splendours :

> " Ainsi travaille, enfant, l'âme active et féconde
> Du poète qui crée et du soldat qui fonde,
> Mais ils n'en font rien voir." [1]

This vision of the Emperor and this explanation of his
father's crystallized in the child's mind. At seven years
old—or rather at nine years old—they inspired him with
the idea of a dignity inherent in itself and superior to
circumstance—a first conception of the Olympian.

The impression was soon to be deepened and
strengthened by a long visit to Spain. There was a certain
affinity of nature between the little boy who, at five years
old, had been described as " sedate and deliberate " and
the Spanish conception of the Hidalgo : Something austere,
and yet a little emphatic ; reserved, but magnificent ; and
grandiose perhaps rather than simply great. Above all,
the spectacle of a conquered country resisting in every
fibre the dominion of the conqueror, and esteeming itself
vastly superior to that conqueror, enforced in the child's
mind the sense, already conceived, that exterior success
and triumph should not be considered as essential goods.
Self-approval, self-esteem are more important than the
applause of others. Dignity, perseverance, strength of will,
and even obstinacy, are arms sufficient, with which a valiant
soul may achieve its true victory in this world. . . .

General Hugo was King Joseph's right-hand man in
Spain ; he was Governor of Madrid and Count of the Empire,
and was admirably lodged in the splendid palace of Prince

---

[1] *Les Feuilles d'automne*, " Souvenir d'Enfance."

Masserano. But he had little leisure to enjoy its magnificence. Spain was in a state of seething unrest. The French army of occupation was incessantly harassed. The General was absent when his wife and children arrived in Madrid, and for six delightful weeks the three little lads ran wild in palace and patio, saturated with sunshine, with beauty and splendour, with the delicious brilliant *far-niente* of the South. But at last the father came home ; and the General (if he had thought his labours at an end for a while as an imposer of discipline) found at home new worlds to conquer. On the following Monday Eugène and Victor were sent to school ; Abel, the eldest, being twelve years of age, was reserved for the glory of a Royal Page at Court.

The school which opened its immense and heavy gates to receive the two little French brothers was the College of Nobles. The masters were monks ; the pupils were Spaniards of the bluest blood, inwardly disdainful of the sons of the invader. These young hidalgos addressed each other by their titles : " Count," " Marquis." They were full of arrogance and pride. They knew to a nicety the value of a title or a coat of arms, and doubtless were aware that Don Eugenio de Hugo and Don Bittor de Hugo were viscounts, and indeed nobles, of a very recent date. Between these newcomers and their environment a secret hostility was intensified by an impulsive act of Madame Hugo's. Mistrustful of the sombre passion inherent in Spanish Catholicism, and aware of the vibrating delicacy of her children's nervous constitution, she had declared to the deep-eyed monk who took her sons in charge that they were Protestants—in order to secure them against his religious instruction. Her Voltairean equanimity had not realized the full measure of the disfavour to which she exposed her little boys : Conquerors, heretics, enemy aliens, the young Hugos were not loved. Eugène bore in his cheek the mark of a stab, dealt (with a pair of scissors) by the hand of Frasco, Count of Belverano, a warrior of his own age. Victor had his own troubles with another pupil called Elespuru. He neither forgave nor forgot ; years later, de Belverano was to figure as the least sympathetic personage in *Lucrezia Borgia*, and Elespuru as one of the quartet of fools in *Cromwell*.

This severe and claustral education was perhaps, on the whole, a beneficial change from the charming riot and gay liberty that attended Madame Hugo's system of free natural growth and expansion. The children learned the meaning of self-control, discipline; they acquired a high ideal of courtesy. A certain gravity and ceremonial in these young Spaniards attracted Victor. For one of them he formed a friendship which, with his customary fidelity, he was never to forget; and, fifteen years later, Ramon, Duke of Benavente—pensive, intellectual, condemned to a life of solitude and sorrow—figured as the subject of one of our poet's Odes. Grafted on the trunk of Spain, the fresh French young shoot appeared to prosper, when again the upheaval of Europe changed the shaping destiny of a child. Victor was now ten years of age. We are in 1812. . . .

1812—the turning-point of Napoleon's fortunes. The defeat of his armies in Russia was for him more than an overwhelming disaster—it was, in Talleyrand's phrase, " the beginning of the end." From East to West the vanquished nations began to lift their suffocated heads; a breath of hope and life stirred in the air like a waft of spring, and nowhere more irresistibly than in Spain—in proud, bitter, injured, trampled Spain.

CHAPTER II

1812 announced the universal revenge of the nations. From Russia to Spain the electric current thrilled and rang and everywhere a secret force vibrated in response. The rule of the French in Spain had always been uneasy; the Spaniards still considered the kidnapped Ferdinand their lawful king and Joseph Bonaparte a foreign invader; five years of constant effort had not established him securely on his throne despite an army of 300,000 men occupying the Peninsula under Massena, Soult, and Marmont, Napoleon's famous marshals.

And now the success of Wellington in Portugal revived the hopes of the Spaniards; while Napoleon in Russia suffered an epical defeat. In May 1813 Wellington marched on Madrid, driving the French back towards the Pyrenees— past the Pyrenees; then, in his turn, crossing the frontier and invading France! Napoleon, beaten in Russia, beaten in Prussia, beaten in Spain, reluctantly gave back his crown to Ferdinand VII. and sent him from Valençay to Madrid.

These world-shaking events had had their repercussion in the family circle of General Hugo. In the spring of 1812, Abel, already a young second lieutenant of fifteen under his father's orders, had taken part in the hard-fought battle of Salamanca, and had suffered the crushing reverse of Vittoria. In March, Madame Hugo and her two younger sons hastily left Madrid for France; in the first days of April they were in Paris. The garden of the Feuillantines was full of spring flowers; the sheets were spread on the beds; the roast hung before the fire; the cloth was laid; the weary travellers entered their home as though they had left it a few

hours before for some country walk. Madame Larivière
had taken care of it all. M. Larivière, with a Latin classic
in his yawning pocket, stood there waiting for his pupils to
begin to construe. And again the boys took their lessons
in the old charming free-and-easy style, working under the
spreading trees in the garden, or in their bedrooms, or not
at all, as the fancy took them. It was a world away from
Madrid, the College of Nobles—the monks with their discipline, and the young Spanish counts and marquises full
of insolent disdain and humiliated pride. The delight of
this home-coming prevented the boys from seizing the full
national significance of their retreat from the Peninsula.
But they found a new Paris, exhaling a grave unrest. It was
no longer the splendid triumphant capital of 1809, full of
kings and soldiers, where the glad crowds shouted when
Napoleon went by in his old grey coat, " Vive l'Empereur ! "
and sang in chorus, " Veillons au salut de l'Empire."

Napoleon had restored the prestige and re-established the
finances of ruined and devastated France ; but that was
already a long time ago. He had conciliated the Church.
He had given his country a civil code so supple and so
strong that for fourscore years it was to serve with scarce
a change, and even to-day supports solidly all our recent
superstructures, while it stands as a basis for the modern
conception of social organization in Europe. He had
widened the limits of France and enlarged her boundaries
to include the Scheldt, the Elbe, the Rhine, the Arno, the
Tiber, and the Isonzo. But everything had been sacrificed
to this dream of glory. There was a party in France which
longed to resume—after the huge interruption of the Revolution and the Empire—the tasks and experiments in
letters, science, industry which had occupied the France of
1789. The world had not stood still while France achieved
her military triumphs. The steamboat existed already in
America. George Stephenson in England was framing his
iron horse, James Watt was a candidate to the French
Académie des Sciences. There was a France intensely
occupied with spinning-jennies and chemical experiments
that dreamed of vast factories and the renewal of the world
by organized industry. There was a France, expressed by

Chateaubriand and Madame de Staël, that knew itself capable of a magnificent revival of letters—a France that felt itself the equal of the Classic Age, although so long curbed, and stifled, and silenced by the mailed fist of the Emperor. And there was a France of men and women who looked on their growing sons and trembled, knowing the price of universal victory, and noting the number of mourners in the streets, and all the halt and maimed and blind among their young acquaintances. Madame Hugo was of this latter party :

> Ma mère aux doux yeux, qui souvent s'effrayait
> En m'entendant parler guerre, assauts et bataille.[1]

Brief—there was a party for peace at any price.

And there were the dissatisfied generals : the soldiers of the Republic who had fought for liberty, had snatched freedom and glory from the Coalition of Sovereigns, and now found that they had vanquished the dynasts of Europe only to found a syndicate of tyranny : a Bonaparte Emperor of France, a Bonaparte King of Holland, a Bonaparte King of Spain, a Bonaparte Queen of Naples, a Bonaparte Grand-Duchess in Tuscany. In their eyes Napoleon appeared no demigod, but a monstrous monopolizer.

Three of these generals, imprisoned on a charge of treason, plotted continually behind their bolts and bars, and so successfully that for one day—the 24th of October 1812—they found themselves the masters of Paris. They had spread a report that Napoleon was among the killed in Russia. And Paris realized the fragility of the Empire, and, seeing France without a chief, turned towards the exiled Bourbons. Had Louis XVIII. been less gouty and less indolent, had his brother shown a more martial resolution, the *coup d'État* of General Malet might have succeeded. As it was, he founded by surprise a Provisional Government which lasted barely four-and-twenty hours. But this was near enough success to infuriate Napoleon, who saw in the rash attempt a sign of public disaffection— a lack of loyal attachment to his dynasty. He rushed back to Paris from Smolensk, vowing vengeance on his enemies.

---

[1] " Souvenir d'Enfance."

He found them condemned and executed. The first moment of surprise and stupor having passed, the Governor of Paris had seized the persons of General Malet and his confederates, General Guidal and General Lahorie. This last was Victor Hugo's godfather—that friend whom Madame Hugo had so long concealed in the abandoned chapel of her great wild garden of the Feuillantines. She tried once more to come to the rescue. She had some influence at the headquarters of the Court Martial, not only as the wife of General Count Léopold Hugo and the sister-in-law of General Louis Hugo, the hero of Eylau, but as the intimate friend of a family called Foucher. M. Foucher, an old crony of the General's long before either of them had married, was head clerk of the Board of Recruitment, and was lodged in the Hôtel de Toulouse (a handsome seventeenth-century mansion only recently destroyed) in the rue du Cherche-Midi, which was the seat of the Councils of War. Madame Hugo obstinately haunted that tribunal of military justice ; she besieged with her appeals M. Foucher, his brother-in-law M. Asseline, Clerk to the Council, and another friend of hers, M. Delon, Reporter to the Committee. The dauntless woman gave no thought to the risk she ran in crossing the path of Napoleon's vengeance, nor to the effect that her action might produce on her husband's career. These officials received her with perfunctory politeness, some kindly, some coldly : M. Delon, an ardent Bonapartist, was more than cold. They could hold out but little hope of mercy. It was intolerable that three generals, confined in three different prisons, should have contrived so nearly to upset the most despotic of governments. They could expect nothing but anger from the police whom they had fooled. The day of judgement dawned. And all day long Madame Hugo sat, hoping against hope, in Madame Foucher's parlour. The three conspirators were condemned to death and were shot before sundown.

The next day—it was the 29th of October—Madame Hugo's two boys were strolling past the Church of Saint-Jacques-du-Haut-Pas. Victor noticed a new bill placarded on the wall and went up to read it, being attracted, child-like, by a familiar word printed in large capitals : *Soulier*.

For once it had nothing to do with boots or shoes ; it was the name of the Governor of Paris. Victor read out :

EMPIRE FRANÇAIS—Par conseil de Guerre, ont été fusillés en plaine de Grenelle, pour crime de conspiration contre l'empire et l'empereur, les trois généraux Malet, Guidal, et Lahorie.

The names meant nothing to Eugène and Victor. They had known the refugee of their garden under a feigned name, the pseudonym he used during those years of concealment. But, just then, their mother came up and, pointing to the last word on the list, she said to Victor, " Lahorie. That was your godfather ! "

And the child remembered the chapel in the garden, and the friend who used to share their games and studies, the warm pressure of his hand upon the little shoulder, and the ring of his voice as he said, " Avant tout, la Liberté."

Madame Hugo had never greatly loved the splendours of the Empire. She was Countess Hugo on the address of her letters, and there began and ended her grandeur. A woman of an ardent, virile type of character, she was happiest in retirement, sowing and planting in her garden or superintending the education of her sons. After the death of Lahorie she appears to have withdrawn still more from social life. Her boys and a few tried old friends sufficed her. Her austere, reserved, yet tender devotedness was masked by an imperious manner ; she was intimate with few people, familiar with none ; she brought up her sons with the utmost freedom as to details, relying on their honour and obedience in a way which we consider more English than French, but with a strict and absolute discipline in essentials : her word was law. Although a Royalist in politics, there was little of the Catholic about her ; like many women whose girlhood had been passed under the shadow of the Revolution, her religious opinions were as vague as her morality was sincere. Her creed, if she had one, was a Deism, in the manner of Rousseau or Voltaire. She encouraged her boys in a great latitude of reading, debating with them the most serious and difficult subjects. Such was the vigilant guardian whose eager and absolute love, if it brooded passionately over all three brothers, was concentrated yet more tenderly on the youngest, the most fragile, the most gifted, Victor Hugo.

CHAPTER III

ROYALIST PARIS

MADAME HUGO never forgave that Bonapartist official who had refused to extenuate the crime of General Lahorie. She struck the name of Delon from her visiting-list ; she forbade Eugène and Victor to have any further dealings with young Delon, a fine lad, who had been one of their favourite friends—a dozen years later he was to die in Greece commanding Lord Byron's artillery. On the other hand, she felt a closer bond linking her to the Fouchers, who had shown themselves helpful and compassionate. She became a frequent visitor at the official mansion that sheltered the Councils of War : the old Hôtel de Toulouse in the rue du Cherche-Midi. The Fouchers like herself were Royalists by birth, tradition, and training, Imperialists merely by default, as preferring any form of order to a revolution. For years Madame Hugo had choked down her political opinions, stifling their expression out of deference to her husband and regard for his prospects ; besides a monarchy had seemed a beautiful myth of a bygone world, as remote from reality as the Golden Age. But, after the execution of Victor's godfather, the ardent woman turned in loathing and contempt from the despotism of the Emperor, and all her loyalty revived towards the king across the water. By the Fouchers' friendly fireside she could tell her stories of the war in Vendée ; could make her boys and Madame Foucher's weep for pity of the poor lad named Louis the Seventeenth ; could inflame them with enthusiasm for her own girlish and heroic adventures :

18

. . . ma mère en Vendée autrefois
Sauva, dans un seul jour, la vie à douze prêtres.
Les Contemplations, v. 3.   *Écrit en 1846.*

Madame Hugo had never been of the same opinion in
politics as her husband : Victor Hugo loved to point out
the antithesis between

Mon père, vieux soldat, ma mère, Vendéenne.[1]

And doubtless these dynastic antagonisms helped to
swell the sense of differences, of small hostilities and diver-
gences, that gradually separated the absent husband from
his wife.   General Hugo was a brave soldier, something of
a martinet, with a soldier's weakness for a petticoat.
Madame Hugo, ardent, implacable, high-minded, full of
views and ideals, was not the woman to make allowances
or concessions.   Little by little, absence ended in a complete
estrangement.

The hour was unfavourable to the glory of Napoleon.
For eighteen years all had gone well with his armies—the
French invaded or annexed Belgium, Holland, Germany,
Austria, Italy, Spain, Portugal, Russia.   It seemed unthink-
able that France could be invaded in her turn, while Napoleon
was alive at the head of his troops.   But here were the Allies
on all her frontiers, in the proportion of four to one, and
the country found itself unprepared, insufficiently protected,
beaten.   In 1814, by the last days of March, the foreign
armies were in Paris, and on the 12th of April the Count of
Artois made his solemn entry into the capital of his brother,
King Louis XVIII., still in England.   The Uhlan sentries
stood on guard before the Louvre ; the Cossacks watered
their horses in the fountains of the Tuileries Gardens ;
General Blücher proposed to blow up the Jena Bridge,
named in memory of a Prussian defeat ; and the Royalists
of Paris cried " Vive le Roi ! " for the return of the Bourbons
brought peace.

The Royalist Party in France was not composed entirely
of Royalists.   Naturally, the *Émigrés*, who little by little
had filtered through the frontiers, were the nucleus ; but
Napoleon's persecution of the kidnapped Pope had added a

[1] *Feuilles d'automne*, " Ce siècle avait deux ans."

large contingent of indignant Catholics, who were anti-Bonapartists rather than Monarchists ; and after 1807, when the Emperor suppressed the civil courts of law and refused to convoke the legislative bodies, composing the national budget and levying rates and taxes by his own authority and at his own sweet will—after 1807, I repeat, these acts of despotism estranged the Liberals and many families of the professional classes. Even among the Imperial officials there were those who thought, with Talleyrand, that the Emperor was mad, and many more who considered that, at least, his day was done and that it would be wise to leave the sinking ship. The increasing disaffection of all that was intellectual in France, inspired by Napoleon's growing autocracy, prepared for 1814 the unkindest cut of all, which was the treachery of the Marshals. Marmont, Soult, and Ney compelled their master to abdicate and made for themselves friends of the Mammon of the morrow.

Thus, on the 11th of April, the Emperor, perforce, bade a sad farewell to his Old Guard in tears, and left Fontainebleau for his new possessions, no longer Master of Europe, but Emperor of Elba. Louis XVIII. was King of France. And little Victor Hugo, while he rejoiced in all his mother's royalism, was perplexed, and rather humiliated, to find himself the subject, no longer of " L'Empereur," but merely of a king : it seemed a come-down. The upheaval of a world shook the Hugos' modest hearthstone. King Joseph's crown had been the first to fall of all those Corsican royalties, soon to be reduced to exile. After a terrible battle at Vittoria, at which Abel Hugo had fought under his father's orders, all had been lost in Spain. General Hugo, with his son, returned to France, but he did not linger in the capital, merely passing through it on his way to Lorraine, where he had been charged by Napoleon with the defence of the frontier-fortress, Thionville. The defence of a small fortress like Thionville was a modest office for the man who had administered Madrid, but the General's pride was of the sort that accepts any task if it be possible to accomplish it in perfection. France had fallen, peace was signed, and Thionville still held out ; when at last General Hugo was compelled to negotiate (since obviously Thionville is not in the domains of the Emperor of Elba), he left his citadel a free man, his sword at his side, with all the honours of war.

A year later, when Napoleon's return from Elba brought his old officers back to their allegiance, General Hugo hurried to Paris, and speedily was again in Thionville, defending that place for the Emperor. The Hundred Days hurtled by in a clatter of war ; peace was restored, and Napoleon Bonaparte dispatched to the island of St. Helena. And still, like Casabianca, Leopold Hugo refused to quit the fortress that had been entrusted to him. The troops besieging Thionville were Hessian and Prussian ; the General would not surrender to Germans. He hoisted the white flag of the Bourbons, but he refused to budge. At last King Louis sent him a Royal command to hand over the keys of the fortress to the German general on the 20th of September. On the 13th of the month Hugo decamped, incapable of surrendering to a foreign commander.

During his stay at Thionville the General had received a visit from his wife in August. Now that the couple had decided to dwell apart there were matters of interest which it was necessary for them to decide together. While she was at Thionville, Madame Hugo received letters from her children. And here we find the first letter of Victor Hugo's.

2 August 1815.

À Madame la Comtesse Hugo, à Thionville.

MY DEAR MAMMA—Since you went away we are very dull here. We often go to see M. Foucher, as you told us to do. He suggested that we should share his son's lessons ; we have declined with thanks. Every morning we work at our Latin and mathematics. M. Foucher has been kind enough to take us to visit the museum of Natural History.

. . . . .

Come back soon ! Without you, we don't know what to do or what to say ; everything is uncertain and difficult. We never cease thinking of you. Mamma ! Mamma !—Your respectful son, VICTOR.

I find this little letter touching—especially that final cry :

" Nous ne cessons de penser à toi Maman ! Maman ! "
Madame Hugo soon returned to her little brood, and they
were doubtless happy together although their days of
poverty had dawned. General Hugo's obstinate defence
of Thionville had ruined his chances at Court ; he was a
marked man, dismissed from active service on the half-pay
of a retiring pension, requested to settle at a certain
distance from the capital. Blois was suggested, and the
General bought a square white house on a hill above the
Loire, and a small estate and shooting-box in the neighbouring marshes of Sologne, consoled in his retirement by
the presence of a lady to whom he had transferred those
domestic affections which the continued absence of Madame
Hugo had too long left unemployed.

The General was a poor man. His estates, as Count of
Cifuentes and Marquis of Siguenza, with King Joseph's gift
of a million francs, remained on the farther side the Pyrenees,
confiscated ; all his Imperial emoluments expired with the
Empire ; the Government of Louis XVIII. did not even
recognize his rank as a General of Division ; he had obtained that rank in Spain in the service of King Joseph.
In his disgrace at Blois the ex-governor of Madrid
received the half-pay of a French major's retiring pension,
which at that time was something under forty pounds a
year.

Naturally this state of affairs affected the situation of
Madame Hugo. On his return from Spain, the General had
made her an annual allowance of 18,000 francs—£720—
which in the Paris of 1812 was a comfortable income. Her
portion was now diminished, and narrowed means no longer
permitted her to rent the house and garden of the Impasse
des Feuillantines—the garden, indeed, was expropriated by
the town of Paris ; the present rue d'Ulm occupies the
site.

On the first fall of the Empire she had rented a ground
floor and garden opposite the Hotel of the Councils of War,
where the Fouchers had their home, in the rue du Cherche-
Midi ; and, after a few years, a still smaller apartment on
a third floor in the rue des Petits Augustins, which is now
called the rue Bonaparte. In spite of many cares, Madame

Hugo was not wholly an unhappy woman. Her unfaithful
husband left her in full possession of her beloved sons. The
restoration of the Bourbons filled her with delight. Little
Adèle Foucher never forgot that feverish and overweening
gladness ; many years later, when she undertook to write
an account of Victor Hugo, she described the attitude of
his mother during those early years of the Restoration :

> The restoration of the Bourbons was for Madame Hugo an
> exceeding joy. Her hatred of Napoleon, long contained by the
> dread of injuring her husband, now burst forth unrestricted.
> He was no longer the Emperor, only " Buonaparte." He had
> no sort of genius—not even a talent for military affairs. He
> had been beaten all over Europe—in Russia, in France. He
> was a coward. He had run away from Egypt and again from
> Russia, leaving to the tender mercies of the plague, or the
> snows, the unlucky soldiers whom his ambition had dragged so
> far from home ; he had blubbered like a child at Fontainebleau
> when he took leave of his Old Guard ; he had murdered the Duke
> of Enghien in cold blood.
> But the Bourbons had every merit and every grace.
> The monarchy revived the memory of her early days, of her
> beloved Brittany. And in fact she seemed to have suddenly
> become quite young. She missed no one of the rejoicings and
> festivities that marked the accession of Louis XVIII. Her
> dress was the flag of her opinions—all white—pure white. A
> white cotton gown and a white straw hat trimmed with tuberoses.
> The fashion of the hour was to wear green shoes so as to tread
> the Imperial colour underfoot. All Madame Hugo's shoes were
> green.[1]

On the day of the Royal entry the Count of Artois—the
third of those three brothers, all destined to be kings of
France, of whom the eldest was Louis XVI. and the
second the newly restored monarch—had sent to the three
young Hugos the emblems of the Royal Order of the
Flower-de-Luce, with a diploma signed by his own hand ;
the lily was in silver and hung from a white moiré ribbon.
Who was so proud as Victor Hugo, twelve years of age,
when he entered the Church of Notre Dame for the solemn
rejoicings of the Royal Te Deum, with this decoration
pendent from his button-hole and pretty Adèle Foucher
hanging on his arm ?

[1] *Victor Hugo raconté* . . .

From this date the young Hugos were almost completely separated from their father. The General interfered from time to time in order to maintain some sort of discipline and routine in their education. But they seldom saw him ; they were more and more englobed in the orbit of their devoted mother, and they moved, with her, in the system of Royalist society.

Victor Hugo has left an admirable sketch of that society in the Third Part of *Les Misérables*. It was a little world, quite devoid of the glory and the grandeur of Napoleon's Empire, but with traditions of its own, a courteous urbanity, a charming impertinence, a delicate raillery. The *Émigrés* of the Revolution had not yet received their indemnity, so that most of the persons composing this society were narrowly circumstanced ; and indeed they had so long been poor in exile that the patent evidence of wealth appeared to them as a rule in rather dubious taste. But in those scantily furnished and shabby drawing-rooms there reigned an exquisite refinement of tone ; no one was loud, coarse, obsequious, emphatic, rank, or rude ; and the dukes and marshals of the " Corsican Ogre," if they could have penetrated there, would have appeared as strayed revellers from the servants' hall. It was not a bad world to be bred in.

Nowhere (wrote Chateaubriand in his *Mémoires d'outre-tombe*), nowhere else could one find gathered together so many persons, equally distinguished although different in rank, whose conversation was as delightful in recounting the details of everyday life as it was elevated in its loftier flights, being marked by a simplicity which sprang from a fine selection and not from lack of means, and inspired by a courteousness that good breeding and long usage had transformed into a mode of feeling—into a part of the character.

Not all the members of that little society were of noble origin : the sharply-defined differences of rank which ten years later under Charles X. will pigeon-hole Paris in compartments of rigorous strictness were gracefully veiled by the similarity of political or religious opinions. Men like the Marquis de C. d'E.—to whom Victor will address his retractation in 1846—captains from Coblentz, pages of their lamented Marie-Antoinette, admirers of the Comte

d'Artois, mingled with men of the upper middle class, like
M. Foucher, like M. Gillenormand, dignified old *bourgeois*
who felt no lessening of their own importance implied in
the acknowledgement of a neighbour's superior rank.   And
of course there was a sprinkling of abbés—though the
Countess Hugo was not particularly pious, rather lax and
Voltairean in her views.   But then, perhaps, so were the
abbés !

Among them all, no woman appeared more interesting
than Madame Hugo—still young, so fervent a Royalist, the
mother of those three gifted and handsome boys, deserted by
her husband—"one of B.P.'s Generals, my dear."   It was
the thing to call Napoleon B.P.—the short for Buona Parte.
And we remember the murmur of sympathy that greeted
little Marius (the hero of *Les Misérables*) as he stirred among
the circle of ancient dowagers seated round the fire—we
remember the hushed comment of refined and interested
voices :

" Such a pretty boy ! "

" Poor child ! "

They called him poor child because his father was a
monster, a bandit, the man at Blois.   " Ce sabreur."   " Ce
brigand de la Loire."

These time-worn ladies in their garments of another
age ; these good-natured old *Émigrés* with a bonbonnière
bigger than their snuffbox, in which there was always a
pastille for Victor, were fossils, no doubt, but very charming old fossils—loyal, brave, chivalrous, devoted, warm of
heart.   If the poet of *Les Contemplations*, if the author of
Les Misérables, smiles sometimes as he retraces their image,
it is with a lingering affectionate smile.   The young Jacobite
of 1819 will become the Liberal of 1829, the Jacobin of 1848,
the demagogue of 1852, but he will never find a word of
reproach for that world of his youth—save that he had
outgrown it.   It was a good and charming world—for a child,

Quand j'étais royaliste, et quand j'étais petit.

Tenderly, nobly, it had sheltered his youth.   It was his
mother's circle—

Et, souvenir sacré ! ma mère rayonnait.

A world one might smile at, yet not without its dignity and moral grandeur. " C'était la France d'autrefois ! "

The France of yesterday ! The France that one day Victor Hugo's genius will endeavour to transform ; a classic traditional France, in which he was to grow up, so different, so humanitarian, so romantic ; a France whose inheritance was a certain exquisite self-effacement ; a France whose acquirements were taste, culture, order, vivacity, a penetrating common sense—admirable qualities which Victor Hugo certainly appreciated, but which he was never to acquire.

Good heavens, what would have been the future of Olympio had he not known at least those years of delicate social discipline in the old-fashioned aristocratic drawing-rooms of Royalist Paris !

CHAPTER IV

THE FIRST GLEAMS OF GLORY

GENERAL HUGO had interrupted the pleasant easy-going lessons with M. de La Rivière and had insisted that his two younger sons should enter as boarders in a large boys' school : the Pension Cordier. Eugène was fifteen, Victor thirteen years of age ; they were infinitely more original, brilliant, travelled, and amusing than their school-fellows ; they had the honour and glory of a room to themselves, whereas the common herd slept in the dormitories. Soon they were the kings of the school—the rival kings—and the Pension Cordier was divided into two nations perpetually at war : " les Veaux," who owed allegiance to Eugène ; and " les Chiens," who were Victor's people.

One day a " Calf " in a particularly boisterous game threw a stone at the king of the " Dogs," which struck his knee, resulted in synovitis, and our Victor is laid on his back for weeks, if not months, to enjoy the lonely privilege of a bedroom to one's self :

Et que faire en un gîte à moins que l'on ne songe ?

In similar case, La Fontaine's hare was plunged " dans un sombre ennui " ; but Victor Hugo amused his interminable convalescence by reading and re-reading, with the delightful unwearied patience of a child, the whole collection of Voltaire's Tragedies which had been given him years ago by his godfather, General Lahorie. Thus Voltaire, who had stimulated the poetic gift of Lamartine, now fired the poetic genius of Hugo. For when the lad knew these plays almost by heart, he thought he might try his hand at an imitation. It is interesting to note his age : thirteen.

I do not mean to suggest that the origin of genius may be organic and glandular, that sexual development is at the back of its creative force. I am sure that explanation is too short and simple to account for the most mysterious and divine of gifts. Yet it is certain that, from first to last, the poetic faculty of Victor Hugo was intimately connected with his sexual sensibility. Not consciously so at first. Until some while after his twentieth year, no youth was ever purer or more severe than Victor Hugo.

Hitherto the methods of the Pension Cordier had left him little time to dream and muse. But now that blessed stone had lodged him safely on Parnassus. The habit of verse grew upon him, became a second nature—he had discovered an invaluable resource against dullness, distress, despair. Even when restored to health and Euclid he continued to write poetry with unabated joy. During the three years (1815–1818) that he remained at the school in the rue Sainte-Marguerite he tried his prentice hand at every possible form of verse : odes, satires, epistles, poems, tragedies, elegies, idylls ; imitations of Ossian ; translations of Virgil, Horace, Lucan, Ausonius, Martial ; fables, tales, romances, epigrams, madrigals, acrostics, charades, enigmas, impromptus, and even a comic opera. He read them all to his appreciative mother, to Eugène, to any one who would lend an ear. This is the poet's own account (Victor Hugo collaborated largely in the confection of *Victor Hugo raconté* . . .), and he has taken us so far into his confidence as to afford us a glimpse of some of these " bêtises que je faisais avant ma naissance "—some of this nonsense that I talked (he says) before I was born. Other poems have been exhumed by M. Gustave Simon. These first essays of Victor Hugo's are no more remarkable in themselves than the earliest poems of Shelley. They indicate a bent ; and the habit of verse-making encouraged an extraordinary aptitude. From the very first they reveal a methodical system of work, a clearness of purpose, a vividness of representation—of *mise-en-scène*— which will always characterize our poet. M. Gustave Simon, who has had the golden opportunity of comparing two long poems on the Deluge, one composed by Victor, one by Eugène, in the same year, 1816, notices, as the chief difference, this faculty of representation, peculiar to Victor. But, so far at least as one can judge from the fragments and the analyses that he gives in his *Enfance de Victor Hugo* (Paris, 1904), I should be inclined to say that Eugène—poor Eugène—shows a more romantic fancy, though of a nervous nightmarish sort. While Victor describes the spectacle of Nature—the tempest—the procession of animals entering the Ark, Eugène shows the earth opening in a vomit of fire, terrible phantoms issuing from their sepulchre, while the angels sound their inexorable trumpets, and the earth sinks in the abyss of the Flood. It is at once the Deluge and the Last Judgement—horror piled upon horror.

Genius is a bird that makes its nest before it lays its egg. In these early poems, brilliant, facile, and elegant as they are, there is nothing that bears the stamp of our modern Euripides ; nothing of that prophetic imagination, that romantic touch, those revelations of cosmic grandeur, those sudden passages of tender simplicity—nothing, in short, of those qualities which—new and fresh and strong as a wind from the sea—were to revive and invigorate the poetry of France. But the child of fifteen knows how to express himself with clearness and facility ; how to draw out a plan, how to develop it, dispose the scene and combine the effects ; he has acquired the technical management of verse ; he has cultivated a critical faculty which reviews every line and weighs the value of every word ; he is master of a method, and already knows how to look at his subject as a whole before putting pen to paper. The Victor Hugo of 1816 has pondered all these things in his heart, knows how to meditate, how to reflect. Already he sees his goal ; and on the 10th of July 1816, writes in one of his copybooks : " I will be Chateaubriand or nothing "— " Je veux être Chateaubriand ou rien." Victor Hugo is preparing to become a great writer. But poetry is still for him a task, an exercise in virtuosity, a canvas to embroider, a test of skill, not the deep impulse of an interior spirit, not the rending of the veil of the Temple and the flash of the eternal flame behind. But the child who, in the years of his manhood, was to write that the secret of all triumph is resumed in one word, *Perseverando*, had learned already the use of a long patience. Day and night he toiled at his craft of verse-making. And he does not neglect his duties at school. His exercises in Philosophy and Physics for the year 1817 show the care and regularity with which he pursued his studies. He was, in fact, preparing two careers at the same time. He hoped to be a great poet, a dramatic poet ; his mother was in the secret and gave him all her sympathy. But Victor's long head had calculated that he might miss that supreme ambition ; so, in a sort of under-study, he got up the examinations of the Polytechnic School in order, if all else failed, to become an artillery officer, as General Hugo wished. Science, algebra, mathematics alternate with Virgil and Chateaubriand in the busy round of his schooldays. Nor were these severe studies in the least against his bent. Victor Hugo possessed in the highest degree the principal quality of the geometrician—which is the faculty of imagining figures in space with exact precision, whether they be on the instant invented or recalled by a sort of intuitive remembrance. The algebrist, like the poet, is a visionary, and Euclid no less than Aeschylus sees the unreal objects of his thoughts painted on the air before him—ὡς ἐν γραφαῖς. Doubtless, if he had been less gifted with the dramatic sense, with the passion and music of the lyrist, the son of General Hugo would have been a great Polytechnician ; an eminent philosopher (Charles Renouvier) has declared that France lost in him " un géomètre de première ligne."

But those first gleams of glory which are sweeter than the flush of dawn were streaming on him already from another orient. He had sent one play to a humble theatre, the " Panorama Dramatique," and the manager had accepted it : great joy ! But man cannot escape his destiny, and Victor Hugo, fated to wage a lifelong war with the censor, began the unequal contest at fifteen years of age, for the Government refused him the right to produce his little piece. The lad was not discouraged. In 1817 the French Academy offered, for its annual prize of poetry (the French Newdigate), a competition on the theme : " The happiness procured by study in all conditions of life." Victor Hugo, fifteen years of age, seated before his desk in M. Cordier's

school, felt his fingers itch to take up a pen and try his
luck. The verses were soon written ; the crux was how to
get them to the office of the secretary at the Institute. At
last the youthful poet resolved to take into his confidence
a certain M. Biscarrat, an usher in the school, who was fond
of poetry. They framed a deep-laid plot : twice a week,
on Sundays and on Thursdays, the schoolboys were escorted
through the streets of Paris in solemn procession, ranked in
a double file, like the animals entering the Ark. The following Thursday, which was the last day on which the competition for the prize remained open, Biscarrat was to personally conduct the Pension Cordier on this expedition, and
the monument that he decided to offer to the boys' admiration was the Institute of France. There are lions at the
gates of the Institute, carved stone lions. In a paroxysm
of feigned ecstasy at the beauty of these placable animals,
Biscarrat besought his young charges to examine them
closely and with care ; meanwhile he and Victor dashed
across the court, breathless, trembling, and laid the manuscript on the sacred table of the astonished secretary. In
less time than it takes to tell, Victor's poem was in the
hands of the Immortals. A few weeks later the poet learned
his fate. He had not been crowned ; the prize was not his ;
but he had received an honourable mention ; some of the
Academicians expressed a wish to make his acquaintance,
and an amiable doubt that so accomplished a poet could be
really only fifteen. One Immortal, a certain M. Campenon,
compared the lad to the glorious Malfilâtre

Pour des vers pleins d'âme et de grâce.

Another proclaimed him " the worthy successor of François
de Neufchâteau." Across the hundred years that separate
us from that France of the Restoration the praise rings
quaintly ; but François de Neufchâteau and Malfilâtre were
personages in their day. Their praise filled with pride and
glory the heart of a young poet and proved the critical
acumen of the French Academy. Already in 1817 that
society of Immortals was accused of an excessive tradi-
tionalism, a humdrum classic taste that discovered no new
thing. The Academy of the young—the *Prix Goncourt* of

those days—did not hold its sessions under the dome of the Institute, but far away at Toulouse. The *Académie des Jeux Floraux* was the pre-Romantic organ, enterprising, adventurous, sallying forth, in its quest for young geniuses, into the highways and the byways and compelling them to come in. Yet the Académie Française discovered Victor Hugo before the Floral Games of Toulouse awarded him its Golden Amaranth, in September 1818, for a poem called *Les Vierges de Verdun*, and its supremest honour, the Golden Lily, for another ode. Victor's closest rival in this contest had been his brother Eugène, who carried off more than one honourable mention, and the charming sympathetic President of the Gascon Academy wrote to Victor :

We have not crowns enough for the two brothers ! Your seventeen years fill us with admiration and, almost, with incredulity. You are an enigma to which the Muses know the answer.

Victor's fame soon spread its wings and left the narrow limits of academies. In 1820, the assassination of the Duke of Berry inspired him with an ode which the old king himself recited, with dimmed eyes, before a mournful circle of intimates. Louis XVIII., who had the reputation of writing the prettiest notes in Europe, had a delicate taste in poetry : henceforth he will follow and protect the career of the gifted schoolboy. And not only the king of France, but the monarch of letters, Chateaubriand, was heard by an academician to call the lad an " enfant sublime." Next morning the phrase was quoted in a panegyric on the young poet which appeared in the Royalist organ, the *Drapeau Blanc*.

So that, one morning in February 1820, Victor Hugo awoke and found himself famous. He was eighteen years of age.

CHAPTER V

THE Duke of Berry's murder, which was the occasion of
Victor's Ode, was a political event of the first importance.
It imperilled the future of the Crown. For Louis XVIII.
had no children ; his brother, the Comte d'Artois, was
his heir ; and Artois' elder son was childless, married to
that poor victim, the daughter of Louis XVI. and Marie
Antoinette, sole rescued among the Royal captives of the
Temple, withered since her youth, and now, no longer
young, incapable of bearing children. The murdered man
had been Artois' second son, the hope of the race, recently
married to a high-spirited young Neapolitan princess ; he
also left no heir. The next in the line of succession was
the bugbear of the Bourbons, the idol of the Liberals, Louis
Philippe, Duke of Orleans, the son of the man who had
voted the death of his kinsman, the King of France.

The journeyman saddler who stabbed to the heart a
jovial, good-natured prince against whom he had no quarrel
believed that he was accomplishing a patriotic act, since, at
the cost of one life, he was ridding France of all the Bourbons
and opening the way to a free, democratic future. Everything had conspired to favour his crime. On Sunday the
13th of February 1820 the Duke and Duchess of Berry
were at the Opera-house in Paris, when the young wife,
overcome by a sudden giddiness, was obliged to leave the
theatre. As the Duke was escorting the fainting lady to
her carriage that angry workman, Louvel, jostled against
the Royal couple and swiftly plunged a long thin knife into
the Duke's right breast. But that crime of Louvel's was
frustrated by the simple course of Nature. The Duchess's
indisposition had been an ordinary symptom of her state of

health. And seven months later Victor Hugo was inspired
to write another Ode, still more enthusiastically Royalist,
in honour of the birth of the Duke of Bordeaux, *l'Enfant du
Miracle*—as he was rather absurdly called—whom the older
generation of to-day can remember as the Comte de Cham-
bord.

The crime of Louvel did not deprive the Bourbons of an
heir, but it upset the nice adjustment of French politics.
There were two parties at the Tuileries, or rather there was
the King at the Tuileries : a disenchanted, sceptical old
gentleman, who had not lived so long in Buckinghamshire
for nothing ; he was full of semi-Liberal ideas and believed
in the virtues of compromise.   And, in a wing of the Tuileries,
at the Pavillon de Marsan, there was the King's brother,
the Comte d'Artois, far more vehement, romantic, and
passionate than he, and, as the phrase went, " plus royaliste
que le Roi." For Louis XVIII. was determined not to set
his gouty feet again upon the stony paths of exile.   His
idea, as he expressed it, was " to royalize the nation and to
nationalize the Crown."   He had given his word to respect
the Charter and he meant to respect it, governing with the
party of the Liberal Monarchists and the Ministry of his
open-minded young favourite, the Duke Decazes.   The
King was a gifted old man with a long head for politics,
but he had come to his own too late ; in 1820 he was an
aged invalid.   The murder of his heir startled his delicate
nerves, horrified him, and threw him off the balance.   The
reactionary party—the Ultras, as they were called—came
into power on a great wave of national anger and fervour.
The Liberal Duke Decazes was disgraced and treated almost
as though he had been a party to the murder.   The man of
the hour was Chateaubriand, the greatest writer then living
in France and the founder of the Romantic movement.
He was the hero of Victor Hugo ; it was Chateaubriand
who had pronounced the boy an " enfant sublime."   When a
little later the illustrious statesman was appointed French
Ambassador to the Court of St. James, he proposed taking
our young poet with him to London as his secretary.   But
already an irresistible, a predominant interest retained
Victor Hugo in France.

Victor Hugo would not leave Paris because of an affair of the heart! But he was scarcely less passionately absorbed in politics; I doubt if he could have torn himself away. His father was a Bonapartist and a Liberal; his mother an " Ultra "; the young man espoused his mother's cause. One day his father, passing through Paris, met the lad at General Lucotte's. Victor, very high and mighty, was vapouring away, giving vent to all his young enthusiasm. The General, who had entered unperceived, listened awhile, saying nothing. When Victor had finished his harangue, the father turned to his old comrade-at-arms and remarked :

" Well! Well! Time will show! The lad thinks like his mother, the man will think like me."

I do not know if Victor replied. Probably not. That stern little traditionalist, Madame Hugo, had educated him in the severest courtly school of manners. All sympathy and ardour for her sons' intellectual pursuits, sacrificing all her tastes and commodities to their needs, she was strictness itself on all questions of discipline, obedience, and respect. She gave them a free run of the library, but she kept the purse-strings very tight. Victor's nascent fame excused no slackening of rules. Invited to great houses, he had expressed a timid wish for a fashionable, high-waisted swallow-tail coat like Abel's. But Madame Hugo would have none of that nonsense ; she bade him wear out his shabby schoolboy suit while he was still small enough and slim enough to make use of those childish garments, and told him that his fine friends would judge him by his brains and not by the clothes on his back.

Abel by this time was grown up. He had left the army and gone into business, and, though not over-prosperous, had money of his own. He had always belonged to the General in that divided household. The younger lads seldom saw their father. Victor, at any rate, felt a secret rancour against the parent who only appeared in their lives at distant intervals and to change the course of their training, always in the direction of a normal, conventional, practical issue, far less enchanting than their mother's system of liberty and poetry. Still, without General Hugo

would our poet have had any grounding at all ?   The trail
of the self-taught amateur lies over all the vast and shallow
surface of his ill-regulated studies.

If we examine their portraits (which are preserved in
the Musée Victor Hugo in Paris), we should imagine the
General—with his fresh, good-natured, rather German face
and tall fine frame—less terrible a martinet than Sophie
Trébuchet, Countess Hugo, very pretty, but as stubborn and
proud of aspect as a Breton can be.   But the boys were
all for their mother.   They adored her.   And doubtless
part of their grievance against the General sprang from the
fact that he neglected her and, indeed, had put another
woman in her place.   For there was at Blois an imitation
Madame Hugo.   " Mon admirable et malheureuse mère,"
wrote Victor.   Yet, in her narrow lodging of the rue des
Petits Augustins, in the summer of 1818, she was a happy
woman when her two boys came back from school and set
up house with her.

Most evenings after dinner, between five and six o'clock,
Madame Hugo would tie on her bonnet and drape over her
amaranth merino gown her yellow cashmere shawl with the
palms, and she would set forth with Victor and Eugène to
pay a call on the Fouchers in the rue du Cherche-Midi.   In
those days as in these, light and fuel were scarce and dear
in Paris.   The Fouchers, who lived in the Hôtel des Conseils de Guerre, had both supplied by the State ;   and
doubtless to either household it seemed reasonable that the
friends should spend the long evenings together.   Madame
Foucher received them in her bedroom, a large comfortable
chamber with the bed stowed away in an alcove and no
visible dressing appurtenances, according to the fashion of
those days.   They would find her sitting with her son and
daughter at a round table placed in front of the wood fire,
the two ladies busy with their needlework and Victor Foucher
with his lessons.   Monsieur Foucher, who was in poor health,
would be plunged in his book and his deep armchair on one
side of the hearth, his snuff-box and a candle on a little
shelf at his side.   A second easy-chair in the opposite
chimney-corner would be placed ready to receive Madame
Hugo, and she would sink into it with a sigh, without

waiting to remove either shawl or bonnet, take her work
out of her reticule and silently begin to sew.

What was there so entrancing in these quiet evenings ?
Very often scarcely a word would be exchanged. M.
Foucher was absorbed in his book, the three women in
their needlework, and the three boys, on their hard chairs,
sat mum as mice. Every now and then Madame Hugo
would let her work fall on her lap and gaze silently at the
fire lost in a brown study. And sometimes she would take
out her snuff-box, reach across the hearth towards her old
friend, and say :

" Will you take a pinch, Monsieur Foucher ? "

He would answer " Yes " or " No," and that, very
likely, would be the sum of the evening's conversation.

Yet, for no entertainment in Paris would Victor (or
indeed Eugène) have missed one of these monotonous visits.

Monsieur and Madame Foucher were honourable bourgeois, slaves to their idea of duty, faithful in friendship, but
naturally silent, the most conventional of mortals. Victor
Foucher was a schoolboy too well brought up to speak in
the presence of his elders. The charm lay with Adèle.

In the spring of 1819 Adèle Foucher was not quite sixteen years of age—a year younger than Victor Hugo. She
was just emerging from the gawky stage into the beautiful
creature whose many portraits fill the portfolios and hang
on the walls of the Musée Victor Hugo. She was rather
tall for a Frenchwoman of that period, and slight, with a
long neck, long limbs, a round head, rather large, covered
with a quantity of very fine, shortish, naturally curly,
brown-black hair. Her moon-like forehead, singularly
beautiful in shape and very white, was set in these lightly
curling, misty, dusky locks   Her black eyes were rather
far apart under very long and fine eyebrows ; they had the
most innocent, ingenuous, and yet almost solemn expression ;
sometimes a light seemed to flash behind them and to emit
a ray. Her mouth was perhaps her most exquisite feature :
the most delicate lips, fading into the cheek, on which a
smile seemed to flower mysteriously ; the contrast between
the great grave eyes and the flashing smile sometimes gave
a wild beauty to the face as of a startled nymph. It was

(thought Victor Hugo) more beautiful still when grave :
the head of a Bellini Madonna on the long swan-like neck of
one of Jean Goujon's Dianas.   The nose alone was not
regular, though very pretty :   a neat well-defined little nose
of no orthodox shape, depressed at the base between the
eyebrows, delicately prominent at the bridge ; a faint, feminine
attenuation of a Wellington nose, perhaps, giving a grace
and an originality of its own to the profile.   The complexion was rosy and pale, and the very long dark brown
lashes showed on it becomingly when the eyes were drooped.
The shape of the face was round and shortish, and, as a
flower exhales its perfume, it emitted a look of innocence,
serenity, and dreamy unconscious passion.

With her long limbs, long neck, her indolent grace, her
lovely little hands with such taper fingers, Adèle Foucher
incarnated the ideal of Romantic beauty.   She would have
seemed more at home swinging in a hammock at Port-au-
Prince than demurely sewing by her mother's fire in the
rue du Cherche-Midi.   And none of the three parents had
as yet remarked her beauty !   In their eyes Adèle was still
a growing girl, lanky and sallow, too absurdly thin to be
pretty, but with great staring eyes that might soften into
beauty later on.   They thought her at the awkward age :
fifteen ;   the age of Juliet !   And of course they could not
imagine that young Hugo was already head over ears in
love with her.   Neither party would have approved the
match.   Victor was, in Madame Hugo's eyes, at once a
baby and an " enfant sublime," promised to the most
glorious destinies ;   while the Fouchers thought it a thousand
pities that their friend should bring up her two nice lads to
no regular profession :   what was the use of a title with
no fortune to support it ?   So all winter, unremarked,
Victor gazed at Adèle, and she stole rarer shy glances at
Victor, and thought how wonderful it was that he should
be such a prince of poets.

One day, by a rare chance, they found themselves alone
in the room.   Victor was gazing silently at Adèle when she
looked up and said :

" Victor, tell me your greatest secret ! "

" I love you ! " said Victor.

" And so do I love you," she replied.

And they were engaged.   It was the 26th of April 1819, momentous date !   They were secretly affianced, suddenly grown up, plunged into a wonderful world of feeling and remorse, for Adèle, at all events, suffered terrible qualms at the thought of deceiving her kind parents ; sometimes in her letters she breaks out into wails of childlike despair : " J'aurais tant de plaisir à te voir autorisé par Maman ! "

But what could Victor propose to an anxious parent as the basis of a future establishment ?   Those first gleams of glory are fairy gold and do not line the pocket.   He has nothing in view which a future father-in-law could prudently consider as a suitable prospect for a marriageable man. And also he knows, with a sinking of the heart, that, in his mother's eyes, Victor-Marie, Baron Hugo, already a member of the Academy of Toulouse, and Laureate of the French Academy, son of General Count Hugo, entitled, potentially if not probably (since it depends on a restoration of the Bonapartes), to a share in a fortune of a million in Spain, and, in any case, an " enfant sublime," is no sort of a husband for humble Adèle Foucher.

> Quant à la femme, elle est ce qu'elle est.   Je devine
> Que la vilaine est jeune, adorable, divine,
> Qu'elle a charmé mon fils sans penser au profit,
> Qu'elle a mille vertus, et cela, me suffit,
> Je n'en veux pas !   Beauté, soit !   Vénus dans sa conque
> Viendrait, ayant pour père un échevin quelconque,
> Que je dirais : Allez être belle plus loin !
> Vous n'êtes point ma bru.
> > Lui, vivre dans ce coin !
> > *(Le Théâtre en Liberté.   La Grand'mère.)*

Madame la Comtesse Hugo looked higher. . . .

Let us glance at this Victor Hugo of 1820.   The delicate boy has grown into a handsome little fellow.   He is short, not small, well and sturdily built, with broad shoulders and fine small hands and feet.   He has a very large and handsome head.   The forehead, which is finely moulded, occupies nearly half the face and, even in youth, the hair grows far off it and falls backward thick and lank in an immense shock of strong, handsome, rather coarse nut-brown flakes and locks.

Tes blonds cheveux épars et d'un blond plus doré
Comme ceux que Rubens et Rembrandt à leurs anges
Donnent en leurs tableaux par des teintes étranges,

says Sainte-Beuve in his quaint verses.

These straight locks or flakes of hair are ruffled tumultu-ously and romantically above the high white forehead. The frontal arch is exceptionally fine ; deep under it are set the bright grey-blue eyes, which will keep, until the winter of extreme old age, the fire, the depth, the weight of their glance. The eyelids are rather red and fringed with long blond eyelashes. The complexion is as changeable as a girl's, sometimes very pale, but more often as fresh and rosy as one of those Flemish angels to whom his friend Sainte-Beuve was so aptly to compare him. The line of the eyebrows is absolutely straight. The features are fine, but short and rather wide ; the nose almost as long from the tip to the crease where the nostril joins the cheek as from the tip to the base. The charming oval chin distracts our attention from the structure of the jaw, which is short and square beneath the dome of the enormous brow ; the mouth is singularly delicate, with pursed and chiselled lips. These features, which are very good, are of a type rather German or Flemish than French, and Victor Hugo doubt-less owed them to his Lorraine ancestry. What is neither French nor German is the contemplative gaze of the eyes, the brooding serenity of the mouth, the power of that vast forehead, which, in the early portraits, recall the dreamy ideality of Shelley. Hugo, too, was a citizen of Nephelo-coccygia.

Victor Hugo was very handsome. " An archangel from a stained-glass window," said the companions of his youth. He looked very young for his age, and at twenty the arch-angel was crossed by the schoolboy. A pinch of the nostrils indicated that he might be irritable ; a pout of the lip hinted at a ready disdain ; and, beneath its angelic grace and blondness, the structure of the jaw revealed a strong and sensual temperament if any admirer had been cold-hearted enough to spell the signs. There was certainly no trace of such a strain in his conduct. He was grave and austere, contemptuous of human frailty. If we compare the Marius of *Les Misérables* to the author of the *Lettres à la Fiancée*, we see the two profiles of the same young enthusiast. " C'était un garçon ardent et froid ; noble, généreux, fier, religieux, exalté ; digne jusqu'à la dureté ; pur jusqu'à la sauvagerie." For the first time in his life he had a corner in his heart closed to the mother he adored. But love, like murder, will out.

Monsieur and Madame Foucher were more perspicacious than their friend. The mother told her girl she showed her feelings too clearly, and Adèle wept bitterly, shaken with shame and remorse. The scolding did not clear Madame Foucher's conscience ; she would not for worlds that the Hugos should suppose they were encouraging Victor ! What did Madame Hugo think of this youthful flirtation ? Either she was aware of it, and her opinion would be worth having, or she had noticed nothing, and, in that case, her eyes ought to be opened. So, on the 26th of April 1820—just one year after the children's mutual avowal—Monsieur and Madame Foucher set out to call on their old friend, who was already established for the summer months in her little villa at Issy.

Madame Hugo received them most affectionately. But, when they came to the motive of their visit, a change came over the spirit of her dream. What ? Victor in love ? Victor, that child ! The idea was ridiculous. With a maternal lack of logic, Madame Hugo looked on her youngest son as at once an infant and a person of considerable importance : a baby from the point of view of love and marriage, but a man of too much magnitude to mate with an Adèle Foucher "—a good little girl, no doubt, but . . ." And at this point the excited mother's feelings carried her away. She evidently considered her friends' daughter a very humble little person : " Victor n'avait pas de fortune mais il avait du talent, et Adèle était dans une situation modeste." The Fouchers, wounded to the quick, listened in silence—as surprised as we generally are when some accident shows us how we appear to our own familiar friend. Madame Hugo, nervous and out of health, was now in that state of mind when an angry woman can no longer stay the torrents of her eloquence : " Never ! Never ! Never ! So long as I am above ground ! " she declared. When at last she sank silent, while the Fouchers took their leave, a coolness, if not a rupture, estranged the two families ; and Victor had given his word not to cross the Fouchers' threshold.

It is at this moment that we get our first conception of Victor's force of resistance : that pertinacity, that strength of will, that formed so important an element in his character and even in his genius. He had no one to rely on but himself. His mother was against him ; Adèle's parents also ; his father barely existed for him. For Victor Hugo misunderstood the positive, sanguine, good-humoured General as completely as Marius Pontmercy the " Brigand de la Loire." In later days we shall see with what affection he will surround—

> Mon père, ce héros au sourire si doux,

but in his early youth he would as soon have asked for sympathy from a panoply of arms. And though Madame Hugo overwhelmed him with her anxious tenderness, he knew she would never give way.

" Elle m'a rendu bien longtemps malheureux parce que elle poussait trop loin le désir de me voir heureux," he confessed to Adèle in November 1821. From Adèle herself he was utterly separated. Yet he was convinced that a firm mind can frame its own destiny.

Years after, in the *Travailleurs de la Mer*, he will tell us that the secret of moral grandeur is a certain obstinacy in pursuing what we deem to be the best. " Open a great heart and you will find graven there the one word, *Perseverando !* The final triumph is generally assured to the man who never disputes his conscience or lets his will relax, disarmed." These maxims of Hugo's old age were the examples of his youth.

The months dragged on ; the year wore out. Once or twice in the street or at church the lovers caught sight of each other. But their real communication was a secret correspondence which was always to remain one of the joys and triumphs of Victor's life, those *Lettres à la Fiancée*, which inaugurate the volumes of his Correspondence.

In those days, Victor, one would suppose, must have lived with a pen in his hand, for, in addition to these almost daily love-letters, he was busy with more than one literary project. In order to conquer fame, independence, and Adèle, what would he not attempt ? In 1819 he had founded, in conjunction with his brother Abel, a weekly review, *Le Conservateur Littéraire*, of which he wrote the greater part himself, publishing in it his poems and many remarkable pages of criticism. One is surprised to find that Victor Hugo possessed the critical faculty, but nothing better has been written on Chénier than the review with which he greeted the appearance of those wonderful poems that issued, in 1819, from the long-closed grave of a murdered poet like a handful of lilies suddenly burst into miraculous flower. He was also occupied with a romantic novel, *Han d'Islande*, conceived in the manner of Sir Walter Scott, in which he dramatized his passion for Adèle and the diffi- / culties that prevented true love from running smooth. After all these years, and despite the completest change of fashion, we can still read *Han d'Islande*, not for the satanic dwarf and his terrible adventures, not for the Scandinavian scenery, but partly because it is really remarkably well written, and especially for the character of Ethel—Adèle (the two names are almost the same in a Gallic mouth), so ardent and so pure, so ingenuously confiding, hanging on the arm of her morose old father as Cosette enlaced the rugged Jean Valjean—as Adèle showered her attentions on the melancholy Monsieur Foucher in that grim old house of the Councils of War, transformed in the novel into a State prison on a romantic and fortified island. And if Adèle is the heroine, Adèle just as she was, who is the hero, Ordener, but Victor Hugo, as he would be ? A grave young lover, virginal and pure, wise beyond his years, prudent, magnanimous, and resolute.

This was how Victor appeared to himself. I fear that to his doting mother the solemn youth seemed obstinate and moody. She trembled for his health. And all her fears were not for him : what had come over the spirit of Eugène ? The bright handsome lad had lost his cheerful beauty, was odd, full of queer fancies, absences, and silences, withdrawn into himself even more than Victor. Sport was not as yet invented, at least not in Paris, but Madame Hugo's motherly good sense hit on an equivalent. In 1821 she moved from her little flat in the rue des Petits Augustins and rented a larger one in the rue de Mézières, where there was a garden. Her chest was weak; she told her sons that an open-air life would fortify her health; and all that spring, in her little plot, she kept them as hard at work as if they had been journeymen gardeners, delving, digging, planting, sowing, grafting, pruning, and toiled herself no less than they. She loved a garden, and doubtless she thought that a hard and active life was good for amorous youth; her love of flowers and her love for her fellow-workers prevented her from feeling her fatigue. She should have had more mercy on her own fragility. In the early spring she broke down, and before the first of her blossoms had bloomed the poor consumptive lady was in bed with an attack of inflammation on the lungs. Eugène and Victor were her faithful nurses, and pulled her through her illness by Easter. But it was a treacherous convalescence; by the end of May she was in bed again. This time the fever was harder to conquer; still, some five weeks later, hope began to revive. On the 27th of June she seemed to be sleeping sweetly. " Her best night," said Eugène. " She has not wakened since midnight." It was noon. Victor, vaguely alarmed, stooped over their mother. She was dead.

The General did not come from Blois to the funeral. The Fouchers made no sign; perhaps they were not informed. The poor lady went to her grave in the cimetière Montparnasse attended by her three sons, a few rare friends, and some literary admirers of Victor's nascent genius. The poor boys felt to the full their unfriendedness. Late in the evening, Victor, half-mad with misery, rushed to the rue du Cherche-Midi. There were lights in the windows of the office of the Councils of War. A sound of music. He had forgotten that it was Monsieur Foucher's birthday. The young people had got up in his honour some simple private theatricals followed by a dance. Victor dashed up the stairs, slipped into an unlit, empty closet whose glass door communicated with the drawing-room, and saw Adèle dancing, with flowers in her hair. Oh, Despair!

Life, in its course, was to bring Victor Hugo all that

he then dreamed of or prayed for : Genius, Love, and Fame. But the dust of fifty years will not fill the hole in his heart made by his mother's grave. He will become a renegade to all their joint convictions : a Republican instead of a Royalist ; a transfuge from the class that she esteemed ; and Adèle Foucher's husband. Yet, in the secret of his soul, Victor Hugo will never cease to take counsel with the memory of his mother ; will believe that it is she who inspires him to turn into courses so contrary to her own ; and it is in all sincerity that he will affirm that, thanks to her, his conscience has remained unaltered through all the changes and chances of his days :

> Car j'aperçois toujours,—conseil lointain, lumière,
> Dans le bruit, dans le vent orageux qui m'emporte,
> Dans l'aube, dans la nuit, l'œil de ma mère morte.[1]

---

[1] *Les Contemplations.*

CHAPTER VI

THE BRIDEGROOM AND HIS BROTHER

The letter which Victor Hugo sent to Blois to inform his father of Madame Hugo's death contains a postscript in Abel's handwriting : " Eugène n'est pas dans le cas de t'écrire " (Eugène is not able to write).

Eugène had been a handsome, vivacious youth with much force of imagination ; in 1818 he had obtained a prize at the Floral Games of Toulouse, where, only second to Victor, he ranked as a poetical prodigy. " Toulouse has not crowns enough for the two brothers," exclaimed the President of the Gascon Academy. And at school, no less than Victor, he had been a leader and a champion among his companions. The two boys had always been rivals and inseparable friends, tenderly attached, yet stung sometimes by that strange fraternal jealousy which so often embitters the tenacious affection of brothers.

When Victor fell in love with Adèle Foucher, was Eugène again his rival ? Beautiful Adèle, almost the only girl they knew at all intimately, tall, sweet, confiding, whose black eyes flashed so brilliantly, or dreamed so gently, in her southern face ? Nothing is more probable than that she was Eugène's first love. Friends of the brothers—not very intimate friends—(Soulié, Gaspard de Pons) have recorded their conviction that Eugène's life was wrecked by his untold love for the girl who only thought of his younger brother. And it is possible, of course, that the secret exaltation and brooding ecstasy of a hidden passion may have been the cause of the change which came over Eugène in his one-and-twentieth year, turning the lively imaginative lad into a taciturn, melancholy, capricious

46

invalid. The recent biographers of Victor Hugo have all accepted this theory which M. Louis Barthou mentions as a fact. Yet no line in the Correspondence of Victor Hugo, not even in the romantic and often untrustworthy *Victor Hugo raconté* . . ., gives any warrant for an assertion which is based on the gossip of acquaintances.

Certain at least it is that, towards 1820, Eugène became " capricieux et bizarre." In a letter written to General Hugo in April 1822—a most important and characteristic letter, not to be found in the Correspondence, but published for the first time in 1919 by M. Louis Barthou in his *Amours d'un poète*—Victor Hugo, reviewing the progress of his brother's malady, mentions the distress which it had caused his mother in the last painful days of her much harassed life :

His sombre humour, his odd ways, his strange fancies, made our dear mother cruelly anxious about him during her last illness. If we had not led so quiet a life, we might have supposed that some violent crisis was disturbing the existence of Eugène.

Victor imagined that his brother had perhaps been caught in the net of one of the innumerable political societies of the times. Never had there been so many plots, secret societies, Republican or Bonapartist conspiracies, as in that very year 1821, which is the date of the " Charbonnerie " —an association of half-pay officers, Liberal students of the University, old soldiers fervent for their Emperor, peasants alarmed lest the return of the *Émigrés* should result in the confiscation of the lands they had bought so cheap from the Revolution, any one, in fact, who desired the overthrow of the Bourbons. Affiliation was easy ; nothing was asked of the members save to possess a rifle, a few cartridges, and to pay an annual subscription of some twelve francs. Like many another student, Eugène Hugo may have belonged to the Charbonnerie. At any rate, Victor, the young Royalist, the disciple of Chateaubriand, seems to have suspected no other disturbing factor.

He continues :

After the loss of our dear mother, Eugène ceased to show us, or any of his friends, any sign of affection. . . . We noticed that he would leave the house at the most unlikely hours ; he would borrow our money, and often more than once in the same day, and he used to write letters which he never showed us, though we had no secrets from him. . . .

Perhaps Eugène, who seems to have been led away by undesirable companions, may emerge unstained from the abyss into which we fear that he has fallen. But why did he leave us without a word of kindness ?

Victor was a jealous lover. Had he suspected an unhappy attachment for Adèle he would have shown some sign of his displeasure, not necessarily in this letter, but in his correspondence with her. And there is nothing of the sort. True, Victor, though kind, magnanimous, forbearing, was not a sensitive soul, or at least not sensitive to any pains but his own, nor suspicious, nor easily anxious about other people. All the great moral dramas of his existence will take place under his nose, and he till the last unaware of them and surprised by a catastrophe. His nature, often sublime, was very simple, self-sufficing, unobservant. And one day Sainte-Beuve will dub him " l'homme grossier." " A genius can be stupid ; look at Victor Hugo ! " So, in his turn, the caustic Baudelaire remarked, " Victor Hugo ! an inspired donkey ! "

That was later. Meanwhile the two brothers were constantly together. After their mother's death the large ground-floor in the rue de Mézières, with its entresol and garden, was too expensive for their means. With a cousin from Nantes—a young Trébuchet come to Paris to study law—they moved into a little flat of two rooms on a top floor in the rue du Dragon, where they continued to edit the *Conservateur Littéraire*, in connection with Abel, who had rooms hard by. Some pages signed E.—not the least remarkable—are all that is left of the melancholy, anxious, critical spirit of Eugène. In one of these he likens the difficult beginnings of genius, often uncouth and obscure, to the fledglings of the eagle that crawl before they rise and spread their wings. Alas, poor Eugène, he was never to soar sunward !

After his wife's death, General Hugo offered to supply his sons with a sufficient allowance if they would quit their literary venture and undertake some regular profession. Abel and Eugène appear to have accepted; Victor, who had saved about thirty pounds out of his earnings, determined to continue writing, and on this capital and his slender gains he contrived to exist for a year; always neat and clean, if a little old-fashioned and shabby, in appearance; often hungry, but no man's parasite; disinterested and magnificently ambitious. In his belvedere of the rue du Dragon, high above the attic windows, Victor Hugo lived the simple life—and lived it with a vengeance. If he suffered no one knew it at the time; he made no confidences until fifty years later, when he showed us, in the struggles of Marius, an image of his own hard and independent youth.

Life can be a horrible thing, containing days without bread, nights without sleep, winter evenings with no candle and a hearth without a fire; weeks out of work, a future bereft of hope, a coat out at elbows and a shocking bad hat that a girl cannot look at without laughing; the front door locked at night, because last month's rent was not paid, an insolent porter, the gibes of neighbours, and a waiter at the tavern who serves you with a hostile grin; humiliations small and great, wounded dignity, useless tasks accepted for the pence they bring, bitterness, utter lassitude. Marius learned how a man may devour all that—and indeed have very little else to devour. At the hour of his life when a man's pride is most easily hurt, because he is so sensitive to love, Marius felt himself a laughing-stock, badly-dressed, ridiculous, because he was poor.[1]

Like Marius, Victor Hugo was borne up in this long effort by Love and Poetry, " two great wings sustaining an iron will which nothing could ever turn from its appointed goal " (as his friend Saint-Valry, in a remarkable phrase, said of our poet). It never occurred to him to give up the career of letters any more than to renounce his love. If genius is made up of will and intuition, the motor power in Victor Hugo was strength of will. In 1821, he is already the man whom, a dozen years later, his friend and enemy, Sainte-Beuve, will declare to be compact of rock and iron—" un misérable dont l'âme sans lien est faite de granit et de fer."

A man with an iron will turns everything to his purpose.

[1] *Les Misérables.*

The *Conservateur Littéraire* became a formidable engine to attack the resistance of Monsieur Foucher. When that worthy official issued a *Manual of Recruiting for the Army*, what a long and literary review proclaimed his mastery of the subject ! Human nature is human nature ; Monsieur Foucher was pleased. The Fouchers subscribed to the little review. Victor guessed that Adèle read his poems. So he wrote one on Raymond d'Ascoli, a young mediaeval poet separated from the lady of his love, who was extraordinarily like Mademoiselle Foucher, the very same dark beauty, and, more remarkable still, with a little brother of just the same age as hers. But Victor was not satisfied by these intellectual stratagems. When summer came, and the Fouchers bore off their daughter further than they had ever flown before—quite a considerable journey, in fact !— to Dreux on the verge of Normandy, Victor, nothing daunted, followed on foot, and at the end of a three days' tramp found himself, dusty but resolute, in the Grand' Rue of the town, face to face with M. Foucher, to whom he exclaimed on the happy chance that had united them, so far from home, and, striking the iron while it was hot, asked the astonished parent for his daughter's hand.

The Fouchers were not very cruel parents. They agreed to a conditional engagement, a sort of trial trip, unofficial until the General's consent should have been formally conferred—weekly meetings in the presence of the family ; occasional correspondence ; no intimacy that could make the neighbours talk. And now it was Victor who appeared reluctant to unburden his heart to his father. His mother's deserted death-bed, her unattended funeral, were still too near. Victor thought his father a hard man, and, in the event of his refusal, the law of France forbade the banns. From month to month he put off risking his last chance. The months drifted into a year. Sometimes he strives to reassure himself.

Mon père est un homme faible mais réellement bon. Pourquoi ne cherchera-t-il pas à réparer ses torts d'un seul mot ?

At last Adèle upbraids him. They have been plighted nearly three years.

How can I believe you really love me and wish to marry me, when, in the eyes of other people, you appear to do nothing to forward our marriage ?

Victor is furious, and replies :

I do nothing ?   I am proud and shy, and I ask favours of the great.   I wish to ennoble literature and I work for a wage. I love and respect the memory of my mother, and I forget her since I am going to write to my father.

So he writes to the Brigand de la Loire.   Who knows ? With one word he may be glad to wipe off old scores ? And the General consents so amiably that in a moment he gains for ever the heart of his son.   And we find Victor writing on Wednesday, 13th March 1822 :

Adèle, my Adèle, I am beside myself with joy.   My first thought is for thee !   All the week I have been stringing myself up to bear a blow.   And it is not sorrow but happiness that arrives !   There is but one cloud. . . .

The cloud was the news that the General, three weeks after Madame Hugo's death, had married the lady for whom he had forsaken her ; he had not hitherto announced this event to his sons.   But he made no opposition to Victor's marriage, and indeed spoke kindly enough of his old friend Foucher.   That opening of the gates of Paradise consoled Victor for the " cloud."   On the other hand, Eugène, from the moment that the news arrived, went steadily down the hill.   He took the news in the spirit of Hamlet.   And he threatened to send to Blois a letter of congratulation that should make his father wince.

A few days later the unhappy lad disappeared, and Victor takes up his pen to acquaint the General with their anxiety.   Eugène has left no trace beyond a cold little note—

Informing us that unforeseen circumstances compelled him to leave at a moment's notice but that he may return some day. . . . We had already noticed his strange moods and ways.   We regret that this last mad freak forces us to acquaint you with what we would have wished you never to suspect—so as to spare you at least one of our dear mother's sad preoccupations.

The young grandiloquence of this letter covered an

intense anxiety. Eugène returned, but still violent, unreasonable, and, as Victor remarks in September, " un peu fou." It was a carking care that underlay all the happy schemes and pleasant calculations that prepared the wedding of Victor and Adèle.

For the marriage was possible. The King promised a magnificent pension of a thousand francs ; forty pounds a year ! Victor felt a man of means.

Years later Victor knew to what circumstance he owed that pension. He thought it was a recompense due to his Ode on the Death of the Duke of Berry, which Louis XVIII. had much admired. But the true story is charming, and as it redounds equally to the credit of King and poet, I will repeat it here.

Perhaps my readers remember that young Delon—that friend of Victor's childhood, son of the Imperialist Reporter of the Councils of War, whom Madame Hugo had forbidden her boys to see after the execution of General Lahorie ? As the years went on, the rift deepened. The Hugos became more and more Ultra, the Delons more and more Bonapartist ; and in 1822, young Delon, compromised in the conspiracy of Saumur, was sentenced to death by default, for the young man was in hiding. At that moment Victor was in the throes of moving from the rue de Mézières to the rue du Dragon, and had two flats at his disposal. He wrote to Madame Delon, the mother, offering the rooms unoccupied as a hiding-place for his old play-fellow. " I am so good a Royalist, Madame, that the police would never think of coming to look for him under my roof."

Two years later the poet was dining with a M. Roger, Superintendent of the Post Office, who twitted him, laughingly, with being no conspirator. " You write to a political malefactor and put your letter in the pillar-box." On the same evening the letter had been unsealed by the secret service of the Post Office and put under the eyes of Louis XVIII., who delighted in the secret details of police. The King read the letter and said :

I know the young man. He is a fine young fellow. He has behaved like a man of honour. He shall have the first pension vacant in the Civil List.

And Victor received his pension: forty pounds! His book of Royalist Odes—those which had been appearing in *Le Conservateur Littéraire,* now published under the title of *Odes et Poésies diverses,* and identical with the first book of *Odes et Ballades*—was published, and brought in another thirty pounds, which the eager lover spent to the last penny in the purchase of a cashmere shawl for his beautiful Adèle. She must have looked very well in that shawl, with her tall, graceful figure, her abundant black curls, her languid grace, and that flashing glance of Doña Sol's.

> La flamme de ses yeux dont l'éclair est ma joie.

The two fathers had exchanged letters. The General rather touchingly says that his roving career has not allowed him to know his children thoroughly as other fathers do. Yet he thinks he can answer for Victor:

> Je connais à Victor une sensibilité exquise, un excellent cœur, et tout me porte à croire que ses autres qualités morales répondent à celles-là.

Has not Victor, unaided, in order to offer " an acceptable position to Mademoiselle Adèle, opened out for himself a brilliant career with the rarest distinction?" And the General goes on to say that " if the Government keep the stipulations made in the treaty of 1814, and accord an old soldier his promised indemnity, then Victor shall receive from his father the means of maintaining a modest household."

M. Foucher, on his side, says nothing about an exquisite sensibility—and indeed " exquisite " is a term that ill suits with our conception of Victor Hugo; he praises his son-in-law because he is " grave, orderly, disinterested "—by orderly the French generally mean economical. And it is a quality which the young couple will do well to cultivate. The King's forty pounds, later on increased to eighty pounds, are their principal resource. But M. Foucher proposes to lodge them rent-free in the Hôtel des Conseils de Guerre. And Victor has shown that he can maintain himself by the fruit of his pen. The General, for his part, has promised that if ever he gets his rights and his full pension, Victor shall profit by his good luck. And on the 12th of October 1822 the marriage took place in the same chapel at Saint-

Sulpice where, fifteen months before, Victor had prayed above his mother's coffin. The General, who had not come to the funeral, did not appear at the wedding.

Victor's best men (in France you have two) were the great poet, Alfred de Vigny, and Biscarrat, the poet usher from M. Cordier's school. Biscarrat had known Eugène from a boy. In the middle of the wedding-banquet he noticed the poor young man's strange looks and words and, confiding his suspicions to Abel Hugo, got him to lead his brother from the room. The kind usher stayed all night with his former pupil, who, after midnight, was seized with a fit of delirium so violent that, at dawn, Biscarrat went to fetch the bridegroom. They found the poor madman ranting in his bedroom, all the candles alight. He had discovered a sword, and with shouts and cries was hacking the walls, the tables, and the chairs, as mad as Ajax. From this attack Eugène recovered. But two months later, at Christmas-time, the brain-fever returned, and Victor, writing to his father, describes his brother as growing " steadily worse," in a state of moody solitude that alternated with agitation. The General, alarmed, came to Paris, placed his son under a doctor's care, and, when some degree of reason appeared to be restored, took the young man home with him to his quiet retreat at Blois. Eugène appeared the most placable of mortals—a drowsing sheep !—" un mouton endormi," wrote his sister-in-law. But one day at table, starting from his reverie, he suddenly flung himself upon the Countess Hugo and, brandishing a knife, attempted to stab his stepmother to the heart. It was impossible to keep the invalid at home. Nor could the great Dr. Esquirol, in whose asylum he was placed, do anything for him. He believed himself imprisoned for a political crime, the murder of the Duchess of Berry, and told Victor that the " cries of the female prisoners who were butchered in the cellars disturbed his rest at nights." After a while he was removed to the great State madhouse at Charenton, and there, sometimes better—able to read and receive visitors, feebly interested in Victor's fame—and sometimes sunk in despair and agitation, he lingered until he faded out of life at the age of thirty-seven.

CHAPTER VII

LIFE IS AN ODE

EUGÈNE'S madness, the General's scandalous re-marriage, the loss of his mother, were sorrows that Victor Hugo had felt to the full. But in the deep happiness of married lovers there is a core of peace that no grief can touch : a magic inner world safe and sure, a plane of existence beyond contact with any other mode of life. Passion and joy filled at last the cup which, for three years, his obstinate hand had reached out for in vain. And the first draught was delicious.

Life was an ode, solemn, musical, enraptured. " There is an Angel in my night ! " sang the poet. He walked, like Tobit, like Hippolytus, his earthly ways in a more than mortal companionship. Love opened to his soul and also to his senses a new world. He had gone to his marriage as pure as a girl, half unaware of the prodigious temperament which his strong will had contained. Adèle's virgin knight was transformed into an amorous husband.

Their first child was born, day for day, nine months after their wedding, and died on the anniversary of their marriage. For the next eight years young Madame Hugo, beautiful, adored, admired, and happy, will seldom know the simpler blessing of good health, for the burden of child-bearing was not easy in her case ; she suffered in all her maternal functions, was continually hampered either by a child who was coming or a baby at the breast, and often perplexed, in this delicate situation, by the problems of an insufficient income. Yet, notwithstanding some natural flaws, some pangs and many anxieties, their happiness, I think, was as nearly perfect as human beings may hope to find. Victor's Odes breathe a rapt adoration for his lovely wife, and also the tenderest affection.

> I love thee like a soul from holier spheres,
>   A wise old granny provident and sage,
> An anxious sister, tender to my tears,
>   And like the last babe born to our old age.[1]

Adèle was a very simple person, passionate and timid, but full of practical good sense, and with a generous and gentle disposition that to the end of her life kept its charm. She was a lively talker, too ; and if she was not much of a thinker, if as time went on Victor would sometimes bewail the narrow limits of their happiness, the round so quickly paced, in which, like a squirrel in a cage, the bliss of mortals is confined—

> Et ce cercle dont l'homme a si tôt fait le tour :
> L'innocence, la foi, la prière, et l'amour [2]—

he never ceased to admire, to cherish the lovely wife whom he had so passionately idolised in the years of his youth.

" Victor est toujours un ange et fait toujours de belles Odes," wrote Adèle. She took the beauty of her husband's Odes on trust, being to the end of her days incapable of appreciating the music or the value of a verse. She had loyally confessed this deficiency to Victor during their long engagement. " Virtue also is poetry," Victor had grandiloquently replied : " cette poésie, Adèle, tu la comprends toujours parce que tu es bonne, douce, noble et simple." Noble, simple, sweet, and kind she was ; ardently in love with her young poet ; and beautiful. It is not surprising that in these first years of marriage there seemed no lack, no flaw, in their wedded happiness. Twenty years later, after the cruellest crisis, he still will find her " parfaitement belle, bonne, douce, et charmante." And in these first years the high tides of a satisfied passion covered the rocks and shoals which the ebb sometimes lays bare. When, in June 1824 (Victor having received a second pension of

---

[1] Je t'aime comme un être au-dessus de ma vie,
    Comme une antique aïeule aux prévoyants discours,
  Comme une sœur craintive à mes maux asservie,
    Comme un dernier enfant qu'on a dans ses vieux jours.
[2] *Feuilles d'automne*.

forty pounds from the King), our young couple moved into
a tiny flat, over a carpenter's workshop, what a delight was
the setting up house in a home of their own, at number
Ninety rue de Vaugirard.   There, in July, their second
child, a girl, Léopoldine, was born.   The young mother,
who attributed the loss of her little son to the carelessness
of a wet-nurse, insisted on giving her other babies the breast.
Her grand and languid beauty looked well in a flowing
peignoir.   She sat, in her little salon over the carpenter's
shop, like a Madonna with her child.   Léopoldine was the
most beautiful of babies, and from the first hour of her life
she was her father's darling.   If marriage had revealed much
to Victor Hugo, fatherhood disclosed a still deeper wealth
in life.   No man can have had a larger bump of philopro-
genitiveness.   Children, and especially his own children—in
later days his grand-children—were to him not only the
dearest of pets and playmates, the sunshine of life, but also
that mysterious talisman, that secret token which, in our
hours of distress and doubt, revives our faith in an Eternal
Order, and re-establishes our contact with God, with goodness, with that which exists beyond appearances.   All that
a skylark could be to Shelley, a flower to Burns, a fish sport-
ing in the sea to Coleridge, the sight of a little child was
to Victor Hugo : they were the signs and signets vouch-
safed to him by an Invisible Power, his divine confederate.
And at the same time children were the most delightful
things in the world : laughing flowers, loving sunshine,
visible music.   Our Olympian, so grave and majestic—and
at times irritable or jealous—had treasures of patience at
their disposal.   His children had the free run of the study.
They might tear his unfinished MS. ; draw houses and " bons
hommes " on the margins of his illuminated missals ;
shatter his old china.   There was an amnesty ready.   Never
was he happier than when he sat, the four children gathered
on his knees, replying to their hundred questions with two
hundred answers.   If French poets, like English parsons,
hung texts in their studies, Hugo should have chosen

Sinite parvulos venire ad me.

And if sometimes in later years we feel disposed to deny

to Victor Hugo that gift of " an exquisite sensibility," which his father praised in him, we have but to turn to his poems on childhood to feel that the praise was deserved.

In 1825 there was only one baby in the cradle, and her tiny feet were too pink and tender to carry her into mischief. She was named after the General—she was the goddaughter of Countess Hugo, the seal of a complete reconciliation. Over her cradle met the two grandfathers and renewed their youthful friendship ; Madame Foucher, already brushed by the wing of Death, forgot her sufferings to smile at the little girl. A touching page discovered in Madame Victor Hugo's papers and published for the first time about 1906 in M. Gustave Simon's *Roman de Sainte-Beuve*, describes these early days.

Victor Hugo, when Léopoldine was born, felt paternity in all its force, and gave his newborn child all the love which he multiplied in the coming years for his other children. The dear baby, whom its mother nourished with her milk, slept in the same room as her parents, and, at daybreak, she would climb from her cradle into their bed and try with her tiny fingers to open her mother's eyelids, and make her understand it was time to wake. The mother would resist the tenacity of her baby, but Léopoldine always carried the day, and then what delight, what laughter for all three !

The young couple took with them in all their walks and outings their swaddled darling, who, carried by her nurse, went first, her face turned towards the happy parents following. But the sight of her was not enough for the father. He would take her in his arms and talk to her ; and she would smile and twitter ; before she was a year old she began to talk.

After Léopoldine came Charles. And now the father would celebrate his paternal pride in verse that I scarcely dare attempt to render—and how clumsily !—as listening to the nightingale one mimics inharmoniously the notes of its music, hoping that this absurd imitation may yet give some sense of the movement and rhythm of its song.

When June casts a green shade, or when November's gloom
Lights a great fire with dancing shadows in our room,
    Where we draw round and talk—
With what delight we watch our youngest-born appear !
We laugh, call out his name ; the mother, half in fear,
    Applauds his tottering walk !

There's nothing in our world as innocent and gay !
The sweet adventurous voice that still would say its say,
  Though the words come amiss ;
The roving, wondering glance that ever roams and shifts.
He gives his soul to Life as simply as he lifts
  A fresh mouth for a kiss.

Hearken, O Lord, my vow, and grant my prayer for those
I love, for brothers, friends—ay, even for my foes
  The most unreconciled.
Preserve us from a June no crimson roses throng,
A hive without a swarm, a cage without a song,
  A home without a child.[1]

The young couple were soon the centre of a knot of chosen friends. The *Conservateur Littéraire* had by this time gone the way of all flesh and most periodicals, but Victor Hugo, Alfred de Vigny, Soumet, and a few others regrouped themselves round the *Muse Française*, which flourished between July 1823 and July 1824, under the editorship of the two brothers, Émile and Antony Deschamps. The *Muse Française* was to the Romantic school all that the *Germ* was to the Pre-Raphaelite Brotherhood : a forcing-house that hastened its flowering. 1823 was the halcyon summer of the Restoration. The recent victories of the war in Spain had salved the pride of the nation, and Chateaubriand, who had urged it on and called it *his* war, exulted. The triumph of the Ultras seemed to inaugurate for France a

---

[1] Soit que Juin ait verdi mon seuil, ou que Novembre
Fasse autour d'un grand feu vacillant dans la chambre
  Les chaises se toucher,
Quand l'enfant vient, la joie arrive et nous éclaire,
On rit, on se récrie, on l'appelle, et la mère
  Tremble à le voir marcher.

 . . . .

Il est si beau, l'enfant, avec son doux sourire,
Sa douce bonne foi, sa voix qui veut tout dire,
  Ses pleurs vite apaisés,
Laissant errer sa vue étonnée et ravie,
Offrant de toutes parts sa jeune âme à la vie
  Et sa bouche aux baisers.

Seigneur ! Préservez-moi, préservez ceux que j'aime,
Frères, parents, amis, et mes ennemis même
  Dans le mal triomphants,
De jamais voir, Seigneur ! l'été sans fleurs vermeilles,
La cage sans oiseaux, la ruche sans abeilles,
  La maison sans enfants !

future of chivalry and honour which should bring into the region of practical politics the ideal of poets. What more natural than that, in this dazzling noon—so soon to be overclouded—a little band of chosen spirits, a Happy Few, should build themselves, on the summit of a peak, a hermitage and a watch-tower ?

Les plus jeunes vantaient Byron et Lamartine
Et frémissaient d'amour à leur muse divine.
A. DESCHAMPS.

An enthusiastic review of *Les Méditations* soon brought Lamartine himself into their sphere. Chateaubriand was an immense and friendly luminary just beyond their orbit ; but the chief glories of the *Muse Française* were Victor Hugo and Alfred de Vigny. A dozen young men, all of them gentlepeople, Royalists by birth or conviction, Catholics by good breeding and vague religiosity, chiefly serious in respect of art, elaborated in their young Review an attention to details of style and technique that the poets of the Empire had never dreamed of. They were ardent archaeologists, admirers of Gothic art and early poetry, readers of Walter Scott. Alfred de Vigny was at that time a young officer in the Guards, in garrison at Courbevoie or Vincennes. He was twenty-five years old, Victor Hugo twenty-two. Among these intimates of the *Muse* the custom was to call each other by the Christian name—Alfred, Victor, Antony, Jules—and the ladies of the little circle were generally invested with some pastoral name—Aglaë or Clelia—unless their own was particularly pretty. One day a member of the band asked Victor Hugo if his wife also might drop the formal Madame, and be known to the initiates as Adèle. But the grave young poet refused. He was as dignified as a Spanish hidalgo and as jealous. All his life Victor Hugo possessed in the highest degree two qualities which appear incompatible : he was solemn and he was fascinating. Yes, he was solemn and dazzling as a starry night, and with the night's fantastic, elfish charm. He took himself, and indeed everything, very seriously ; and yet he was refreshing, illuminating, entrancing in his gentle brilliance. When he was nearly

eighty people still praised his " grâce éblouissante," his
" nobles façons." Judge what he must have been at twenty-
two. But he allowed no liberties, and his wife, even to his
intimates, remained Madame Hugo.

Victor had another friend, Alphonse Rabbe. No
Royalist he, no man of fashion, but a critic, a man of parts
and erudition. He was, I think, Victor Hugo's first intimate on the Liberal side. Rabbe was an eloquent, a brilliant
companion, and yet condemned to dwell aloof, cut off from
his kind by a painful and hideous ulcer that gnawed the
flesh of his face. Victor, always inclined to assume that
physical deformities are compensated by some invisible
excellence, attached himself closely to this unfortunate
friend, and tried to draw him within the warm circle of
his own fireside. Rabbe resisted and refrained, and one
day, when Victor remonstrated, assured his would - be
host that this abstention was wise and necessary : until
the Hugo baby should be born the expectant mother
ought not to look upon that monstrous face. The young
poet was moved almost to tears. He dedicated " à mon
ami R——" the most touching of his Odes, in which he
deplores the cruel fate that isolates a being dowered with
a warm heart and with glorious gifts, but assures him
that what is sown in suffering shall be reaped in the immortal harvest of genius. The Ode appeared in print.
Rabbe was furious at his friend's blundering generosity.
A tactless hand had snatched away his decent bandages
and made his hidden sore an object for public pity. Victor,
full of remorse and surprise, was obliged to protest that the
Ode had never been intended for Rabbe. It was inspired,
he said, by quite another person—an old school friend—
yes ! long ago in Spain—no, Rabbe had never met him !—
a certain Ramon, Duke of Benavente. Rabbe grimly insisted that, in volume form, the dedication should appear in
full ; and perhaps the young grandee, if he existed, may
have learned with astonishment how great was his genius
and how solitary his fate. Rabbe, for his part, did not
fill the full measure of the one or the other. An overdose
of a narcotic put an end to his life on the first day of the
year 1830.

As time went on, Victor Hugo, less engrossed by the *Muse Française*, made the acquaintance of other Liberals in literature.

About the time when the split between Chateaubriand and Villèle first began to disintegrate the solid block of the Ultras, a certain newspaper editor, a philosopher in his way, Monsieur Dubois, the editor of the *Globe*, called upon Victor Hugo. The *Globe* was a journal founded in 1824 as a Liberal and intellectual organ ; M. Dubois hoped to reconcile the young lions of the Romantic movement, now that Chateaubriand had set them in motion towards the Left, with his staff of brilliant young critics fresh from the University. Victor Hugo was more or less the Laureate of the Court ; when Charles X. had been crowned at Reims in 1825, with all the pomp and ceremony of mediaeval tradition, Victor Hugo and Lamartine were the two poets chosen by the King to attend the coronation and celebrate it in their Odes. "There are but two poets for me!" the king would say, "Baron Victor Hugo and M. Désaugiers." Despite this royal favour, the affairs of Greece, the drastic laws muzzling the Press, the censure, were detaching the young poet from the party of the Court. Monsieur Dubois felt it—divined in the air the dawn of a literary revival, and determined to secure, for his great organ of the Opposition, the most gifted young author of his time.

He has left a charming account of his call on Victor Hugo.

I visited Hugo in his modest and charming sanctum of the rue de Vaugirard. There, in the *entresol* over a carpenter's shop, I saw, in a tiny drawing-room, a young father and a young mother swinging to and fro a child a few months old, and stopping now and then to join its little hands in prayer before some Madonna and Child after Raphael ; they had some quite good copies. Although perhaps a trifle theatrical, the little scene was none the less spontaneous and charming, for at every moment the impulse of the heart kept breaking through, especially in the case of the young mother, and I was touched and charmed.[1]

M. Dubois was right in suspecting that the Romantics

[1] Lair, *Un maître de Sainte-Beuve*.

were ripe for a change. Now that the King had come to his own again, the result disappointed their expectations.

Order, orthodoxy, etiquette, ruled society and distributed influence according to certain fixed conventions and settled forms, in which there appeared no place for enthusiasm, passion, or liberty. The traditions of Louis Quatorze, carefully exhumed from long-unvisited hiding-places, gave to the Court of Charles X. an indescribable atmosphere of mustiness, fustiness, dustiness, as though the *poudre à la Maréchale*, shaken out of the toupees of the *Émigrés*, had fallen lightly over everything, equalising all surfaces, obliterating all colour, all accent, everything that differentiates individuals. What was there in common between the priest-ridden and prejudiced coterie that now ruled France and the young Romantic School, just coming into flower, with its lyric poets, its flamboyant colourists, its orators and journalists ? Where, in this neatly pigeon-holed Paradise of the Faubourg-Saint-Germain, was there room for a young genius of humble provincial nobility, such as Alphonse de Lamartine or Alfred de Vigny, to say nothing of the mushroom rank of Victor-Marie, Baron Hugo ? Influence, power, importance were for the Polignacs and the La Rochefoucaulds—for the Lords of the Soil.

The France of those early years of Charles X. was prosperous enough. Justice, perhaps, has never been done to the Prime Minister, Villèle, the real ruler of the kingdom, who for seven years carefully controlled its destinies— a long-headed, patient, practical statesman, intensely reactionary, determined to restore the *ancien régime* and efface every trace of the Revolution, yet biding his time, going warily, leading the nation step by step, as a prudent driver guides a shying horse, past every landmark capable of alarming its independence or arousing its revolt. Villèle was an excellent administrator. Agriculture flourished ; industry began to prosper and spread. The country, which in 1815 had accepted the Restoration with an empty treasury and a terrible war-indemnity to pay, in less than ten years had become rich. French *rentes*, which had been a mere scrap of paper in 1815, stood at par in February 1824 and attained five francs premium in May. Villèle hoped to

consolidate the Restoration by a judicious combination of
prosperity and despotism. Five and twenty years later
Louis Napoleon will copy his prescription and France will
accept the dose ; it is an old Roman nostrum : *panem et
circenses.* But Villèle, if he gave the bread with a free hand,
was too niggardly with the circuses. Villèle was a Clerical ;
under him, the " parti-prêtre," the priestly party, ruled the
country ; they were timid and cautious, afraid of all that
could amuse and distract a nation accustomed to excitement, war, splendour, poetry, art. In fact, under Villèle,
France kept a good table, filled its woollen stocking with
savings, but France was bored.

Villèle had come into power in December 1821, but it
was not until 1824 that he broke openly with Chateaubriand.
Their dissensions shook the Ministry and France itself.
Chateaubriand was nothing that Villèle so effectively was,
and pretty nearly everything that Villèle was not. He had
spurred on France to go to war in Spain, in order to restore
a tyrant (that miserable Ferdinand), and now he wanted
France to go to war in Greece, to liberate the nation of
Leonidas—in fact, he would have had France fight any-
where, for any cause, so that again her banners might stream
victorious, and hide out of sight the disgrace of 1814, the
dismay of 1815, the degradation and inferiority that no
mere riches can efface from a vanquished people. Chateaubriand was a poet in prose ; his *Atala,* his *René* had inaugur-
ated the Romantic movement. As the author of the
Génie du Christianisme, of *Les Martyrs,* he looked upon
himself as the eldest son of the Church, but he was emphatic-
ally not of the " priestly party," no friend of the Jesuits
nor of the Congregation. Far more in the hour of his
disgrace than in the hour of his triumph Chateaubriand
was the idol of the young Romantics. Little by little as
they followed him they detached themselves from the
Government and became accessible to the influence of
Liberal ideas. . . .

For Victor Hugo, personally, another and more intimate
inspiration hastened the process. General Hugo had been
right when he remarked to General Lucotte : " The lad
thinks like his mother, the man will think like me." As

soon as they remade acquaintance on Victor's marriage,
the tenderest affection united them, and the good-natured,
debonair, free-thinking old soldier acquired an extraordinary
authority over his genius of a son. We remember the tender
remorse of Marius in *Les Misérables* when, too late, he visits
the little house at Blois of the " Brigand de la Loire "
and discovers that the formidable bandit, the bugbear of
his childhood, had been a very gentle old officer, devoted
to flowers, unselfish, cherishing the image of his absent son.
More fortunate than Marius, Victor Hugo had known his
father in time to enjoy, during some half-dozen years, his
constant companionship. The General came oftener and
oftener to Paris, and would sit by his son's hearthstone,
" comme un chevalier antique," while Victor would listen
spellbound to his stories of Spain, of Fra Diavolo, of Thionville, and of Napoleon. Little by little he caught the old
soldier's enthusiasm for the Emperor and shared his dis-
abused yet generous view of life and things, so different
from that which prevailed in the *Cénacle* :

> Mon père, ce héros au sourire si doux.

There is in one of Hugo's last books of poetry a picture
of General Hugo which very tenderly portrays the middle-
aged man, obliged to retire from active life in the full force
of his faculties (General Hugo was barely forty-three when,
for the second time, he was forced to surrender Thionville
in 1815), regarding the world he had left with a serene and
on the whole an optimistic detachment :

> Mon père était un sage pur,
> Un de ces penseurs vrais qui, dans le monde obscur,
> Montrent un front serein même à l'épreuve austère,
> Qui cherchent le côté rassurant du mystère,
> Et se font expliquer l'énigme du destin
> Par le splendide chant des oiseaux du matin.
> Il était souriant toujours, jamais sceptique,
> Aucune bible, aucune illusion d'optique,
> Ne troublait son regard fixé sur le réel,
> Il était confiant dans la beauté du ciel.[1]

Victor Hugo had the immense pleasure of proving himself as useful as he was devoted to this amiable optimist.

[1] *Toute la Lyre*, " La Pensée," xxiv.

He helped him to find a publisher for his *Memoirs*; he read
the paternal poems, and we smile at his honest efforts to
find " ingénieux " or " joli " the General's excursions into
verse.   By Victor's influence, the King removed the ban
which exiled Léopold Hugo from the capital, and appointed
him a lieutenant-general of division in the Royal armies, in
full possession of his rights, titles, and emoluments.   General
Count Hugo came to live in Paris and settled in the house
in the rue Plumet (nowadays the rue Oudinot), which Victor
has made visible to all the readers of *Les Misérables* : the
house in which Jean Valjean lived with Cosette.   But of
all Victor's kind offices none, I think, touched the father so
closely as his son's conversion to the cultus of Napoleon.

On the 7th of February in 1827 Victor Hugo, economi-
cally glancing at the *Gazette* on the bookseller's stall
under the arcades of the Odéon Theatre, saw the report of
a scandal which had occurred the night before at the
Austrian Embassy, where there had been a gala.   All
Napoleon's marshals who bore Austrian titles had been shorn
of their foreign style.   The Duke of Reggio had been
announced as Duke Oudinot ;   the Duke of Trévise as
Marshal Mortier ;   the Duke of Dalmatia as Marshal Soult ;
the Duke of Tarento by his name of Macdonald.   The
Ambassador had calmly confiscated the souvenir of
Napoleon's victories.   Victor Hugo felt all the soldier's
blood in his veins rise to his face as he read how Napoleon's
Generals, one after the other, had left the ball-room in
solemn silence.   He felt that his own father had been
insulted, and he went home and wrote the first " Ode à la
Colonne," the first impassioned address to that great pillar
on the Place Vendôme which supports the statue of
Napoleon.   Thus the third book of his Odes, composed
between October 1825 and June 1828, which opens in
honour of Louis XVIII., of Charles X., of Lamartine, of
Chateaubriand, idols of the Ultras, concludes with a magnificent outburst in pity and praise of Napoleon.   The poem
appeared in February 1827, arousing a storm of indignation
or enthusiasm, for it marked the secession of Victor Hugo
from the ranks of the Ultras to the Liberal camp.   " In 1827
in your ' Ode à la Colonne ' you deserted, you abjured the

sane tenets of the legitimate monarchy ; the Liberal faction clapped and applauded. I groaned." So wrote Hugo's cousin, the Marquis de C. d'E., in 1846. And General Hugo, with the Liberals, applauded. He had that last joy—he heard his Royalist son acclaim the veterans of the Empire, he saw his Benjamin set his feet in the trace of the paternal footsteps, before he died. A year later an attack of apoplexy struck down the old soldier as suddenly as a ball in the heart. He was not five-and-fifty years of age. Both Hugo's parents, like his two brothers, died comparatively young.

In this volume of 1829 there is a stanza in which we read the promise (more than the promise) of what Victor Hugo will become. It is dated May 1828.

> So, I unseal the abyss where all your thrones were hurled ?
> Yes ; we require a chaos who would frame a world !
> Yes : in the night a voice has spoken to my soul,
> Bidding me rise and lead the people to their goal,
>> And, with the century gone by,
>> Confront our lapsing century.[1]

There was something in Victor Hugo's genius that made him always the Poet-Laureate of a political party. We have seen him the eloquent Pindar of renascent Royalism ; a taste for splendour, for the enormous, the immense, the grandiose, has converted him (under the influence of General Hugo) to the cultus of Napoleon. But in this prophetic stanza for the first time we catch the ringing accents of the future Poet-Laureate of Democracy, and the shibboleth of the People falls grandly from his lips.

[1] Des révolutions j'ouvrais le gouffre immonde ?
C'est qu'il faut un chaos à qui veut faire un monde !
C'est qu'une grande voix dans ma nuit a parlé,
C'est qu'enfin je voulais, menant au but la foule,
 Avec le siècle qui s'écoule
 Confronter le siècle écoulé.

CHAPTER VIII

A PRINCE OF POETS

THE *Muse Française* was even less long-lived than the *Conservateur Littéraire,* but the young writers who had composed its staff survived and grouped themselves anew round Victor Hugo. They were the gifted court of a Prince of Poets. One of them, Gabriel de Saint-Valry, described the impression produced on his acolytes by the young master :

We were seduced, fascinated, by his gentle ascendancy—so much purity, grace, and imagination united to so bold and vigorous a genius ! All who came within his sphere of influence were touched by a feeling of friendship and enthusiasm as lively and as passionate, almost, as love itself. Genius was imprinted on his spacious brow, and something strong, puissant, inspired, rang in his lightest accent.

This little circle, or *Cénacle,* as one of its members baptized it, was not composed only of poets. There was a sculptor, David d'Angers ; there were several painters, Louis Boulanger, Devéria, Delacroix ; an architect, Robelin ; most of them lived in the outskirts of the place de Vaugirard, and often of an evening they would assemble in Madame Hugo's narrow drawing-room. Beautiful, silent, sensible, she listened over her sewing, putting in now and then a lively or appropriate remark, while her guests discussed and studied Gothic architecture or mediaeval poetry, bringing to the debate some picturesque engraving of an ancient tower, some quaint or biblical page from an old romance or chronicle. Victor Hugo, that modern Manichee, would seize the pretext of a particularly contorted gargoyle or vigorous epithet to assure his listeners that the principle of art was essentially *double,* and that the beautiful could not

become manifest in its full completeness without the necessary foil of the chaotic, the horrible, the monstrous, or the
grotesque. And these young poets emerged from the
Elysian Fields of Classicism and discovered a world of
infinite ecstasy and rapture on the one hand, and on the
other of outer darkness and gnashing of teeth : the world
of the Middle Ages.

They talked, they listened, feeling confusedly that some
great renewal of Art and Letters was impending of which
they were to be the heroes, the martyrs, or the witnesses.
Then, if the evening was fine, Madame Hugo would put on
her cashmere shawl and her gauze veil and say : Let us
go and get a breath of air under the plane-trees ! But a
bench on the boulevard was too dull for their young activity.
They would walk on and on across the plain, to see the sun
set behind the dome of the Invalides, pushing sometimes as
far as Notre-Dame. They would scale the towers and catch
the bright splashes and pools of crimson light in the river,
the exquisite reflections of the eastern sky, the frail thin
grey line of the houses, which looked as though they had but
one dimension—Victor taking notes of every variation of
colour and relief " as if he were a painter," said his wife.
The ardent glory of the solar rays had a singularly stimulat-
ing effect on his imagination ; those sunsets of 1827 and
1828 fed his mind as fully as the wild seas of the Channel
will do a quarter of a century later. Even his ideas seemed
to come to him through the medium of light and colour, so
that one evening while he was gazing at the sunset, the
fancy slid into his mind that he would write a book of
songs and ballads about the brilliant, burning East. Victor
Hugo had never been in the East. His childish memories
of Spain and Naples were the nearest he could get to that
dream of splendour. But, in those years, all Europe was
occupied with a possible expedition to liberate Greece, with
the heroism of Canaris, with Byron, and the tragedy of
Missolonghi. Firmly held back by Villèle and the King,
France, like a hound on the leash, was straining every nerve
in her effort to join the New Crusade—was just breaking
loose ! The great Romantic painters were painting the
massacres of Chio. The Eastern question was the fashion

and the passion of the hour. There would have been nothing strange in the fact that Victor Hugo also should care to try his hand at a " Turquerie." But it is interesting and very characteristic to observe that his conception sprang from no emotional or intellectual origin but came to him " in a way I cannot explain — d'une façon assez ridicule, l'été passé en allant voir coucher le soleil." [1]

When these poems appeared—the ballads which conclude the third volume of *Odes* (1826) and the lyrics called *Les Orientales* (December 1828)—their audacity, brilliance, music, rapidity, and unparalleled virtuosity produced an impression which the English reader may perhaps liken to the profane outburst of Swinburne's *Poems and Ballads*. Not that there was anything morally shocking in Victor Hugo's volumes. But there was a general impression : " C'est magnifique, mais ce n'est pas la guerre ! " Under the Empire, under the Revolution, and in fact since the death of Voltaire, poetry had been dull. Parny was not dull, but at least he was neat, small, and finicking in his licentious grace ; and readers had a vague idea that poetry might be pretty but must be dull. The poems of André Chénier (though written under the Revolution which, as we remember, cut off the poet's head) were not published until 1819, a year or so at most before the appearance of Lamartine's *Méditations*, and were, with these, the factors and sponsors of the first Romantic movement. Certainly, they were not dull ; but neither were they, in their serene Hellenic beauty, aggressively, bewilderingly, exhilaratingly clever ; they had not the picturesque splendour, the startling perfection and acrobatic accuracy of rhythm, rhyme, and strophe ; the winged imagination, the dramatic emphasis of this new poetry, which seemed, instead of interpreting the world like the lyrists of yesterday, to create for itself a sphere outside Reality and to exist with no relation to Life and no importance save that of Art for Art.

This phase of Victor Hugo's genius is not that which I prefer—who could prefer it ? Yet even to-day it is impossible to read without a smile, an involuntary " Bravo ! Bravo ! "—as if we saw an acrobat juggling with his score

[1] Préface aux *Orientales*.

of golden balls that rise and fall in the air like a fountain,
or heard some *prima donna assoluta* trilling her cadences
more liquid than a nightingale's. There is no soul in this
sort of Art, but what good fun it is! Open the *Odes et
Ballades*:

> Mon page, emplis mon escarcelle,
> Selle
> Mon cheval de Calatrava ;
> Va !
>
> Piqueur, va convier le Comte,
> Conte
> Que ma meute aboie en mes cours,
> Cours !
>
> .   .   .   .   .
>
> En chasse ! Le maître en personne
> Sonne.
> Fuyez ! Voici les paladins,
> Daims !
>
> Il n'est pour vous Comte d'Empire
> Pire
> Que le vieux burgrave Alexis
> Six !

or the *Pas d'Armes du roi Jean*:

> Cette ville,
> Aux longs cris,
> Qui profile
> Son front gris,
> Des toits frêles,
> Cent tourelles,
> Clochers grêles :
> C'est Paris !

Now turn to the exquisite *Rêverie* of the *Orientales*.

> Oh ! Laissez-moi ! C'est l'heure où l'horizon qui fume
> Cache un front inégal sous un cercle de brume,
> L'heure où l'astre géant rougit et disparaît.
> Le grand bois jaunissant dore seul la colline,
> On dirait qu'en ces jours où l'automne décline
> Le soleil et la pluie ont rouillé la forêt.
>
> Oh, qui fera surgir soudain, qui fera naître,
> Là-bas—tandis que seul je rêve à la fenêtre
> Et que l'ombre s'amasse au fond du corridor—
> Quelque ville mauresque, éclatante, inouïe,

Qui, comme la fusée en gerbe épanouie,
Déchire ce brouillard avec ses flèches d'or !

The third and last volume of *Odes et Ballades* was published in the end of 1826.　On the 2nd and on the 9th of
January 1827 there appeared in the *Globe* two long reviews,
unsigned, whose critical and capable judgement was informed by a sentiment of lively sympathy.　They were not
only good reviews but remarkable meditations.　Victor
Hugo went to the office of the newspaper to learn the
name of this weighty critic, and heard from M. Dubois
(who had been professor in a Parisian Lycée before he took
to editing the *Globe*) that the writer was one of his old
pupils, in whom he took a special interest, a medical student
by profession, but of so delicate an instinct and so deep an
erudition as regards literature that it was probable he would
leave the hospitals and make himself heard as a reviewer :
his name was Charles Augustin Sainte-Beuve and he lived
in the rue de Vaugirard, at No. 94.

"And I live in the rue de Vaugirard at No. 90 ! " exclaimed Victor Hugo, and went straight forth to call on his
critic, but found him out and left a card.　The next morning
about twelve o'clock Victor Hugo and his wife were sitting
at breakfast when the bell rang, the door opened (for there
was no close time for visitors in that household ; at breakfast or at dinner the poet received any caller), and there
entered a small, frail, pale young man—not only plain but
ugly (" pas laid, vilain," said Madame Hugo)—with a large
nose, no complexion, a scanty handful of harsh yellowish hair,
small eyes—therewithal obsequious and awkward in manner
—one of those shy youths who seem all boots ; but with so
admirable a glance of penetrating intelligence that the final
impression was one of delicacy, sensitiveness, and charm.
" Un jeune homme pâle, blond, frêle, sensible jusqu'à la
maladie, poète jusqu'aux larmes," wrote the sentimental
Lamartine, more charitable than Adèle.　This was the critic,
Sainte-Beuve.　In 1827 he was twenty-three years old, two
years younger than Victor Hugo, one year younger than
Adèle.　They were all quite young people.

The talk turned naturally enough on Sainte-Beuve's
review.　After a while, Madame Victor Hugo, who had sat

listening as was her wont, broke in to ask who had written a
criticism, which she thought much too severe, on the novel,
Cinq-Mars, which their friend, Alfred de Vigny, had published recently. Sainte-Beuve was obliged to own that he
was the culprit. And then he turned again from the wife
to the husband. At this first interview he seems to have
had a very vague impression of Madame Hugo—indeed, he
admitted later that for six months he barely noticed her,
being completely carried away, dazzled, rapt in the contemplation of Victor Hugo. The beauty, the sweet benevolent address, the genius, the simple friendliness of the
poet, went to his head and intoxicated him with the magic
philtre of a first great friendship. He barely remarked the
beautiful Adèle. He owned in later days that her loveliness

" . . . ne m'avait pas parlé tout d'abord "—"indeed," he goes
on, " for more than half a year I had no particular feeling about
her ; my sentiments were in a state of suspense which was not
indifference but rather a refinement of respect. When she was
present I bowed to, but rarely addressed a word to, my hostess,
answering her, when she spoke, without turning my head, and
seeing her, as it were, without looking."[1]

He knew she was beautiful, "fort belle," but, he adds,
" with one of those rare and foreign kinds of beauty to
which it is necessary to accustom our taste." . . . Alphonse
Karr also, we remember, noted her " beauté étrange et un
peu sauvage."

And now began a daily intimacy which was to last,
without a break in its enthusiasm, for more than three
years. Sainte-Beuve was soon a regular morning visitor.
In the spring of 1827 the Hugos and their two children
left the rue de Vaugirard for a pretty cottage in a sort
of lane situated behind No. 11 rue Notre-Dame des
Champs. A long alley, once a rural path between border-
ing trees, led to the modest home hidden away from the
street. The long, low structure, since divided and numbered
27 and 29, still exists at the end of its green and grassy
avenue, which in those days was continued by a little
garden planted with laburnums and a rustic bridge. The
proprietor, an old lady, kept the ground floor for herself,

[1] *Volupté*, p. 104.

but let the upper story to Victor Hugo. Of all his many homes it was the happiest ; for he still possessed the fullness of love ; and fame came to him there, when he wrote *Hernani* and *Marion de Lórme*. While he was busy writing, the babies rolled on the grass-plot under the windows and played with the blossoms that fell from the laburnum branches. Every afternoon Madame Hugo minded the children while her husband's friends—Louis Boulanger, Robelin, or Sainte-Beuve—would drop in for a little talk or to leave a message. As for Sainte-Beuve, the faithful disciple, he had followed his friends to the rue Notre-Dame des Champs. The Hugos lived at No. 11, he and his old mother at No. 19.

Madame Hugo was a charming lady, but Victor was a world ! Carried away in his orbit, Sainte-Beuve became the prophet of the Romantics :

I soon seized the importance of these new ideas, which I then heard for the first time, and which suddenly, immediately, opened before my eyes new views on style and the technique of verse. As I was already occupied with an old sixteenth-century poet, I was prepared to find examples, and make applications, illustrating Victor Hugo's theories. From that day I was devoted to that branch of the Romantic School of which he was the chief. . . . An enthusiastic period opened in my life, 1827–30. The volume which I have called *Les Consolations* is entirely consecrated to that deep devotion, that interior worship ; it is the pure and ardent sanctuary in which lie embalmed the happiest years of my youth.[1]

To Victor Hugo this new friendship was not less precious than to Sainte-Beuve. He was happy in his marriage, very happy, devoted to his beautiful wife, who was the one woman in the world to him—*la Reine* ! But, occupied with her home, her health, her babies, and the difficult problem of making both ends meet, she had not the time, even had she possessed the mind, to be his intellectual companion. Sainte-Beuve was that. In September 1828 the critic made a short sojourn at Tubney Lodge near Oxford, and Victor Hugo writes to him :

---

[1] Sainte - Beuve, *Postscriptum aux Portraits contemporains*, vol. i. Victor Hugo.

What a good habit we had of seeing each other constantly, of exchanging our ideas. I was accustomed to seeing you, to dreaming over the harmony of your verses. Your absence leaves a great blank. And in my eyes the rue Notre-Dame des Champs appears depopulated ! Your letters, kind and charming as they are, cannot replace your high and varied talk, and all the poetry of your heart and mind.

I cannot tell you with what an eager curiosity I follow you on your journey ; every detail of your letters is precious. I see the play of light and shade in the bas-reliefs, and the gleam of the stained glass in the Gothic windows of those fine old churches that you have visited, happy fellow that you are !

And while you pass on from sensation to sensation, our days are all alike. You know our daily round ; only of late Nature has weaned us from our sunsets. In this mid-September the sun sets just at our dinner hour. I am sorry ! It's the first theft of winter !

.   .   .   .

We are expecting Lamartine. Paul Foucher, Boulanger, the Devérias, David, embrace you and thank you.

Thus two young men, in the early summer of life, brilliantly gifted, each in his separate line capable of opening new horizons and discovering a new world—the one as noble in his moral nature as superb in his genius ; the other a being of the rarest and most exquisite delicacy of taste and fibre—met and made friends, each of them gaining infinitely by contact with the other. The world affords few more touching or exhilarating spectacles than such a comradeship. We think of Racine and Boileau, of Goethe and Schiller, for the intimacy of Wordsworth and Coleridge, of Byron and Shelley, was more purely intellectual, less close, less absolute, less vivifying.

In either life these three years of their daily friendship will count as something more than an event — will rank as that which the ancients named an epoch, from a Greek word meaning a halt—because it is a pause in the course of our days, towards which our actions seem to tend, from which they seem to flow. Victor Hugo has more than one such watershed in his existence. None was more important to his happiness or his development than his acquaintance with Sainte-Beuve.

CHAPTER IX

ONE of the earliest letters that Victor Hugo wrote to his new friend was to invite him to a first reading of a drama in verse, *Cromwell*, in which the poet had embodied his dramatic theories. On the 12th of February 1827 Hugo read *Cromwell* to a public of poets in Madame Foucher's large drawing-room at the Hôtel des Conseils de Guerre. The first line of the drama raised a long roar of applause from all the young lions of Romance, for it was a challenge to the Classicists, who did not admit in serious poetry the mention of anything so precise and particular as a date ; this first line was an outrage on the typical and the Universal, for it ran :

> Demain, vingt-cinq juin mil six cent cinquante sept.

I imagine that the Romantics did not listen to much else of the interminable and incoherent drama, but that they kept murmuring in their shaggy beards the fortunate line :

> Demain, vingt-cinq juin mil six cent cinquante sept,

occasionally convulsed in a storm of clapping and wild shouts of praise as the full flavour pervaded them. But Sainte-Beuve listened ; and, since he was a man of exquisite taste and an admirable literary conscience, he admitted that, despite great qualities of picturesqueness and vigour, the play was much too long, imperfectly vitalized, and bore less clearly the stamp of genius that he had admired in the lyrics. Victor Hugo accepted with much patience his suggestions and corrections, and promised that he would bear these details well in mind on another occasion ; but he said nothing about correcting *Cromwell*, for, ever eager to cover all the ground he saw in front of him, our poet was impatient of retracing his steps.   Victor Hugo was no rewriter.

Cromwell had not been written for the stage : the play- ing of it would take about six hours ; and, in fact, *Cromwell* was much less a piece than a manifesto, as was clear when the poet published it at the end of the year with the famous Preface which was the programme of the Romantic theory. Victor Hugo began by asserting that the great Founder of the Romantic movement was Jesus Christ ; for does not Christianity affirm that man is double, soul and body : the one miserable, constantly humiliated, grotesque ; the other, immortal and sublime ?   " De ce jour le drame a été créé ! " For the drama, with its struggles and its contrasts, is Christian and Romantic, even as Tragedy, in its solemn serenity and unity, is Pagan and antique.

" The poet of the modern world," said Hugo, " is not Racine, but Shakespeare or Molière ; for the object of modern Art is not Beauty but Life ; and that which gives us the keenest sense of Life is not the lovely but the characteristic, even though that be ugly, odious, or deformed.   A multitude of figures, a quantity of details, a sense of the scene, an impression of time and place startling in their exactness, a realization of all that is individual, peculiar to a moment and a person ; in fact, an insistence on local colour, on every exactest detail of Nature and Truth, are not only permissible in drama, but necessary, though Tragedy, reserved for the Type and the Abstract, hold them beneath her notice."   In fact, he concluded (I continue to resume his argu- ment in a few bold strokes), "the conventionality of the eighteenth century may attempt to oppose the impulse of a young genera- tion.   It will be in vain !   These young men who have seen Napoleon—' nous, jeunes hommes sévères, qui avons vu Buona- parte '—we refuse to be the train-bearers of an outworn super- stition trailing in a world that has no place for its encumbering chlamyde."

In that Preface (published in October 1827) Hugo dis- claims any intention of writing for the stage under the conditions of censure and political interference then pre- vailing :

Until a happier season the author will continue to remain absent from the scene ; and the day will always dawn too soon which shall at last decide him to quit, for the agitations of an untried world, his chaste and dear retreat. God grant that he may never repent of having exposed the virgin obscurity of his name and person to the shoals and squalls and tempests, to the miserable intrigues and persecutions of the dramatic life !

In this last phrase we seem to hear an echo of the counsels of Sainte-Beuve. For in truth our ambitious Victor was not averse to those storms and chances. He had quaffed the draught of Love and now he was all athirst for the cup of Glory. But Sainte-Beuve, though so large a mind, was none the less essentially the man of a coterie. He would have had Victor continue in his " chère et chaste retraite," and bade him never quit the laburnum-shaded lawn of his quiet *rus in urbe*, leaving great verse unto a little clan, discreetly admired by the Happy Few in his modest youth, and after his death immortal and illustrious for all time. Steadily and persistently he attempted to influence Victor in this sense. But, besides the poet's own genius, there were other factors that pushed him towards the stage. The fame of *Cromwell* had reached the theatrical world ; managers and actors were constantly approaching Victor Hugo. And then there was the material side to be considered : the question of daily bread, of the fowl to put in the pot, of the future of three children (in 1828 there came a third), of the responsibilities of the head of a family.

Cromwell had been dedicated to General Hugo, who had lived to enjoy this success, and the daily visits of his celebrated son to the house close by, in the rue Plumet (now renamed the rue Oudinot), before that attack of apoplexy which carried him off in February 1828. His sudden death was a blow to Victor Hugo :

I have lost the man who loved me more than any one in the world. A good and noble being, who looked on me with some pride and a great deal of love, a father whose eyes were never off me. And I am young to lose that support and comfort.[1]

Victor felt like the great Reformer who exclaimed, on returning from his father's funeral : " Nun bin ich der alte Doktor Luther." At six-and-twenty Victor was " le

[1] Lettre à Victor Pavie, 29 fév. 1828. Correspondance.

père Hugo." So long as his father lived he had had a background and a resource. He was isolated now and felt poor and solitary, for what had seemed a considerable fortune had suddenly crumbled into dust. The Countess Hugo claimed for her share the property at Blois, the only part of the inheritance that was liquid and undisputed, and though Victor and his brothers felt this to be unjust, rather than go to law with their father's widow they left her the house and land. For more than two years the estate in Sologne found no purchaser. The estates in Spain had been sequestered by Ferdinand VII. ; further indemnities due to the dead man for land in San Domingo were retained by another hand ; the pensions, of course, died with the General : " par conséquent, rien ou peu de chose à receuillir dans les débris d'une grande fortune, sinon des procès et des chagrins." Not without pride, but not without anxiety, the young father of a growing family looked before and after and saw his cares increase :

Destined to a large fortune under the Empire, the Empire and my fortunes went down in the same gale. I found myself at one-and-twenty a married man, a father, with no income save my daily earnings, living from hand to mouth, like a man of the working-class, while Ferdinand VII. enjoyed my revenues in Spain. . . . Obliged to live and keep my household together on the earnings of my pen, I have never let out that pen for hire. For good or evil, the result of my labour has been Books not book-making. A poor man, I have cultivated Art as disinterestedly as if I had been rich, for Art's sake, with my eyes fixed not on the present but on the future. Obliged to make of the pursuit of Letters both my dream and my business, I have never sacrificed the dream to the business.[1]

All of which is true.

The death of General Hugo, and all the cares that ensued —the increased responsibility with regard to Eugène being one of the heaviest—fell upon a household already saddened by the death of Madame Foucher. That patient lady died of her cancer in the autumn of 1827. She had been no great intellectual light. But she was missed. And the lack of her prudent maternal influence counts for something in the private history of the Hugo household during the ensuing years.

[1] Letter to Armand Carrel, 15 March 1830. Correspondance.

Our young poet, our indefatigable Pegasus in harness, was hard at it noon and night, labouring to maintain his wife and family. Poetry pure and simple would not supply the staff of life—could be but a garland of vine leaves or laurel twined round that staff as a thing of beauty. The novel and the theatre were surer sources of income. In 1829 Victor Hugo, who had found the three editions of *Han d'Islande* remunerative (and not less so a story, dating from his schooldays, rewritten and named *Bug-Jargal*), began to meditate a long mediaeval novel, of which the scene and the veritable heroine should be his beloved Cathedral : *Notre-Dame de Paris*. And during this busy summer, in which he adumbrated Esmaralda and Frollo, he wrote two plays, this time in view of the theatre, two of his best plays, *Marion de Lorme* and *Hernani*, and composed a proportion of the marvellous lyrics which he was to publish two years later under the title, *Feuilles d'automne*.

Nor was this all. I must return again to the imperishable masterpieces of a glorious year ; for the moment I salute them and pass on to a study which also saw the light in 1829—in March, two months after *Les Orientales*—and which concerns us who examine the soul and the life of Victor Hugo less as a marvel to be treasured for its own peculiar beauty than as a sign, the first sign, of that intense humanitarian instinct, that deep fund of social compassion, which more and more, as the years go on, will possess and dominate our poet. This is the *Dernier jour d'un Condamné*.

One day that winter (the winter of 1828–29) Victor Hugo was crossing the place de l'Hôtel-de-Ville, when he remarked a knot of people surrounding the slender red silhouette of the guillotine. It was two o'clock in the afternoon ; there was no execution at that hour, but the headsman was rehearsing his part for the evening or the morrow ; setting up his instrument, tightening here a screw, oiling there a joint or nut. The sliding knife gave him some trouble. At last it worked properly, to his satisfaction. And to see the man so busy, as conscientious and as unconscious as any other mechanic, interested in his tools, talking quietly with the people round, filled our poet with a cold wave of horror more deadly than that he had felt in witnessing the fatal act itself. For he had seen a man beheaded some years before. Further back still, in 1820, he had crossed Louvel on his way to the guillotine. Louvel was the assassin of the Duc de Berry. The young poet, whose Ode on that crime was the first act of his poetic career, and who at that time was inspired by the most chivalrous and even childish ultra-Royalism, had certainly no sympathy for Louvel ; and yet to see the man there, in full health, with years of life before him, on his way to be killed in cold blood, was a shocking experience. Victor had felt his heart traversed by a double pang—pity for the murdered man, and pity for the man who was just going to be murdered. The sight of that cheerful mechanic in the place de l'Hôtel de Ville, oiling his machine in the sunshine as he passed the time of day with his neighbours, brought back in full force that old accumulation of horror—Louvel ; the execution he had seen in 1825 ; and also an old highwayman whom he had noticed one day, his arms tied behind his back, his bald head glistening in the sun, as he was led to his last punishment. Fused in the fire of his imaginative memory, they united to form *Le Dernier Jour d'un condamné*.

All this was pure Art ; it was also grist to the mill, but it was not enough. Victor Hugo had in his mind two subjects suitable to the stage : one of them (to us, reading it ninety years later) seems trite enough ; we have seen it in so many variants (and never more brilliantly than in Alexander Dumas the Younger's *Dame aux Camélias*), but I think Victor Hugo was the first to employ it in his *Marion de Lorme* ; it is the possibility of pure love, real true love, flowering suddenly in the heart of what we conventionally call " a bad woman," and the consequent repentance and reclaiming of that Magdalene. The other subject was, for Victor Hugo, almost a lyric subject, and therefore more natural to his genius. It was the story of a brigand chief— a sort of Spanish and sixteenth-century Robin Hood. This Ishmael, whose hand was against every man, should have a heart pure, deep, romantic, and passionately given to an adored being, a young girl, Doña Sol, the flower of the ancient race of Silva, promised in marriage to her uncle, the sexagenarian Ruy Gomez. Of course Hernani, the

" chef de bande," wins Doña Sol, and of course their tragic
death is one with their nuptial hour.   But these dramatic
episodes are but the shell of *Hernani*; the kernel is a
passion as young, as fervent, and as enraptured as that of
Romeo and Juliet.   For it is the love of Victor Hugo and
Adèle Foucher.   In a lyric from the *Feuilles d'automne*,
dated May 1830 (but we must place scant reliance on our
poet's dates, and the piece is perhaps postdated), he tells us
how one day he opened the casket that held the treasure
of his boyish love-letters, and read them in what a passion
of admiration, pity, almost remorse !   Had he been for her
indeed that demigod ?   Was he once so strong, so pure, so
full of dreams ?

> Oh, que cet âge ardent qui me semblait si sombre,
> A côté du bonheur qui m'abrite à son ombre
> Rayonne maintenant !

and how brightly, seen from the sheltering shadow of his
present happiness, gleams that ardent age which thought
itself wrapt in melancholy.   Now he has felt, he has seen,
he has experienced, he has possessed, all that which we can
possess.   Like Browning, he has known how hard it is to
reconcile

> Infinite passion, and the pain
> Of finite hearts that yearn.

And out of his great love he would make something
that might endure when the heart that conceived it should
be in ashes.   And so Hernani loves Doña Sol.   The *Lettres
à la fiancée* are translated (sometimes almost as literally
as Shakespeare translated the chronicles of Holinshed) into
the music of Hugo's verse.   And Doña Sol herself is the
image of Adèle.   She is simple, confiding, proud ; she is
" calme, innocente, et pure."   She has Adèle's trick of
speech—a dreamy silence broken by sudden gushes and bursts
of swift, hurrying, eager discourse, full of questions, of
interruptions, of exclamations.   Though so simple, she is
not easy to deceive, being straightforward, sensible, and
just ;   she is full of pardon for the " fou furieux," the
" sombre insensé," who adores her and torments her in his
jealous passion ; for Hernani is not a man like other men :

> Tu me crois, peut-être,
> Un homme comme sont tous les autres, un être
> Intelligent, qui court droit au but qu'il rêva ?
> Détrompe-toi ! Je suis une force qui va !

Yes, Hernani is Victor Hugo, " chef de bande." Doña Sol is the lamp of his night, which knows no other illumination save

> La flamme de tes yeux dont l'éclair est ma joie.

And Doña Sol is Adèle, like the Edel of *Han d'Islande*, like the Marie of *Bug-Jargal*, like the Pepita of *Le Dernier Jour d'un condamné* who, even in that sombre prison, revives so unexpectedly the remembrance of the black-eyed little girl who was Victor's playfellow in the garden of the Feuillantines.

Thus, from the Spain of his childhood, and his memory of the village of Hernani, to the love of his full-grown years, the matter out of which the poet was to work a masterpiece lay ready to his hand. And yet it was not his first choice. The other subject appears less intimate. It was called, in its earliest version, *A Duel under Richelieu*, and it contains a sombre and romantic portrait of the great Cardinal, for which modern historians have called Victor Hugo over the coals, as well as much political matter capable of a more recent application. The hero of the piece is the usual Hugoesque young man, grave, independent, dignified, self-righteous, and without the faintest trace of humour ; no less than Hernani, Didier is a good deal like our poet himself. At Blois—the scene of the play is laid at Blois—the noble Didier meets an ideal being, Marie, with whom he is ecstatically in love ; and from the loose talk of a knot of idle men of the world he learns that the lady of his worship is just a woman of the town, a courtezan from Paris—not Marie, but Marion, not Mary, but Moll. And yet there is no sign of that dreadful treason on her sweet face.

> Oui voici, son beau front, son œil noir, son cou blanc—
> Surtout son air candide.

Marion de Lorme is a study of jealousy. Victor Hugo was easily jealous.

He began to write *Marion de Lorme* in June, reserving

Hernani for the autumn.   He would work all morning, save
for the interruptions of callers (Sainte-Beuve dropped in
most days), and would continue right on till two or three
in the afternoon, when he would throw down his pen and
set out for the long solitary walk, the " constitutional "
which his health demanded and during which he cleared up
his ideas and solved the problems raised by the morning's
task.   On his return he would find a friend or two, and
probably Sainte-Beuve (who, at No. 19 in the street, was
almost their next-door neighbour), talking with each other
and with Adèle.   Sainte-Beuve has described, in prose and
verse, these visits, when Victor Hugo would be absent, " sorti
pour rêver," and he would find Madame Hugo seated in the
window, her feet raised on the bar of a second chair, a
tambour frame in her lap, but her embroidery forgotten,
her elbow on her knee, her chin in her raised palm, her
proud, dazzling, and yet gentle profile turned towards the
sky.   He was no longer unaware of her beauty—" cette
beauté, douce, altière, étincelante " ; and these long intimate conversations had become the dearest thing in life.
to the lonely, the sceptical, the sensitive Sainte-Beuve.
Madame Hugo was deeply religious ; to her, his Sister-
Confessor, he confided the scruples, the awakenings of faith
which were beginning to torment the arid certitudes of his
soul.   And she would turn her calm, kind, mother-like glance
upon him,

> Plus fraîche qu'une vigne au bord d'un antre frais,
> Douce comme un parfum et comme une harmonie,[1]

hoping to draw him into the fold of the Catholic Church.
" Délicieux moments, où l'on ne demande rien, où l'on
n'espère rien, où l'on croit ne rien désirer ! "   Moments
which Sainte-Beuve later will attempt to fix in their
tantalizing and exquisite happiness in his novel of *Volupté*.

Adèle Hugo, so often silent, so frequently absent-
minded, nonchalante, almost negligent, whose " distrac-
tions " were proverbial in the household, found no lack of
subjects in talking with Sainte-Beuve.   His religious difficulties interested her ; and his pleasant mischief, his gossip,

[1] Sainte-Beuve, *Les Consolations*.

amused her. I fancy she was sometimes unconsciously
bored by the solemn tension of her husband's talk. But I
think that at this time she was not at all in love with
her penitent. Sainte-Beuve was her confidant, and since
her mother's death she had no confidant in all her little
difficulties with the children. She was used to brothers, to
brothers-in-law—doubtless she thought that Sainte-Beuve
(whom Victor used to call his third brother) had taken the
place left empty by Eugène. He was equally the younger
brother of the genius and of the beauty, and no one of the
three realized as yet the danger of their comradeship.
" Couple heureux et brillant," wrote Sainte-Beuve, hardly
knowing which he loved the best.

When Victor returned from his walk he would be hailed
with glee by Madame Hugo and her companions. They
would beg him to read or recite the fruit of his morning's
work. But sometimes Victor Hugo would turn the tables,
and insist that Sainte-Beuve (who was busy then on his
second volume of verse, *Les Consolations*) should repeat some
of those laborious, involved, yet often touching and sometimes felicitous poems which, to an English ear, recall the art
of Coventry Patmore. Sainte-Beuve was shy. If he saw that
escape was impossible, he would whisper a word in the ears of
little Léopoldine and turbulent Charlot, bidding them make
as much noise as they could during the operation. At last,
all the poems having been communicated, the talk would begin
again, more general now, and last until late in the evening.

But next morning Victor Hugo would return to his play
and to all the business that its production entailed. He
had read *Marion de Lorme* to a circle of literary friends.
The success had been immense, the three first theatres in
Paris disputed it, when, at the critical moment, the Censor
refused his sanction. Blind and obstinate, the censure
under Charles X. was even more drastic, more unenlightened,
more exasperating and futile than the *Anastasie* of our
modern times ; but it is easy to see what in this case the
Censor shied at. I have said that *Marion de Lorme* is a
study of jealousy ; but it is also a political play. There is
a Minister, infinitely more powerful than the King, cold-
blooded, ambitious, autocratic, who leads the irresolute

monarch by the nose, as Tartufe leads Orgon ; there is a King of France, a mere tool in the hands of his Minister, who has many virtues as a man, but none as a monarch, very pious, a mighty hunter in the sight of the Lord. The Minister is Richelieu and the King is Louis XIII. ; but they are uncommonly like M. de Villèle and Charles X. The Censor was not deceived ; he forbade the production of the play.

Victor Hugo had read his drama to Balzac, Musset, Nodier, Vigny, Dumas, Mérimée, Sainte-Beuve, Delacroix— what an assembly ! Crowding the little drawing-room of the rue Notre-Dame des Champs, they had applauded, had declared the piece a masterpiece. Baron Taylor had carried it off for the Théâtre Français, wresting it from Harel, who wanted it for the Odéon, and from the Director of the Porte-Saint-Martin. Glory and profit seemed at hand. When the cup was dashed from his lips, when his wife, nervous and excited, broke into tears ; when his friends cried shame on the Censor ! Victor Hugo remained outwardly calm ; but he wrote to the Minister and demanded an interview. When the Minister refused to remove the interdiction he wrote to the King.

One would like to have assisted at that interview. King Charles X. had been the political idol of Victor Hugo in his salad days, and one of the first to encourage our poet ; it was he who, as Comte d'Artois, had sent Victor the Order of the Lily in 1815. The son of Napoleon's Count had been named by him Baron Hugo. It was he for whom Victor had prayed at Reims :

O Dieu, garde à jamais ce roi qu'un peuple adore !

praising the King, as he lay prone and prostrate before the altar, while the Archbishop stooped to anoint him with the sacred chrism. Alas, the King had remained too prone, too prostrate before the power of the priests ! An old man now, still handsome despite the tired glance, the hanging lip, the look of blurred fatigue, and still most courteous and charming in manner. Adèle Hugo, in her *Victor Hugo raconté* ; the poet himself in *Les Rayons et les Ombres*, have told us what passed at that interview : how the King,

affable and pleasant as ever, smiled at the poet's quarrel
with " mon pauvre aïeul, Louis Treize " ; how the poet left
his play (or rather his fourth act), copied on vellum, in the
hands of His Gracious Majesty.   They parted excellent
friends ; but a few days later Victor Hugo was informed
that the King, to his great regret, could not authorize the
production of *Marion de Lorme.*   As a compensation, he
offered the poet a third pension on the Civil List—a pension
of four thousand francs.

Madame Hugo, in her Memoir, would have us believe
that the poet refused the pension, imperiously, as though
he murmured : *pecunia tua tecum sit !*   But we possess the
letter in Victor Hugo's Correspondence.   It is the letter of
an honest gentleman, whose conscience compels him to
refuse a gift that would prove most handy—more touching,
I think, than a dramatic refusal would have been.   He
could not be very haughty in rejecting the proffered bounty,
while carefully stipulating that he hopes to retain the
pensions awarded him six years before.

This earlier allowance, though modest, will suffice me.   It is
true that nearly all the fortune of my father has been confiscated
by the King of Spain, contrary to the treaty of 1814.   It is true
that I have a wife and three children ; it is true that I help to
support widows and kinsmen who bear my name.   But I have
been fortunate enough to find in my pen the instrument of my
independence, so that this earlier pension of £80 a year suffices ;
indeed, it is chiefly precious in my eyes as a token of His
Majesty's goodwill.

It is also true that, earning my bread by the labour of my
pen, I had counted on the legitimate profits of my drama,
Marion de Lorme.   But since this play, though written in all
the probity of an artist's conscience, seems dangerous in the
eyes of the King, I bow to his decision, while hoping that an
august will may change in this respect.   All that I asked was
that my play should be acted.   And I ask for nothing else.

This letter is dated the 14th of August 1829.   A fortnight
later Victor Hugo was hard at work on *Hernani*, which he
read to the actors of the Théâtre Français on the first of
the following October.

CHAPTER X

On the last day of October the Minister returned the manuscript of *Hernani* to the manager of the Théâtre Français, with the Censor's permission to produce the play. The rehearsals and all the business of the stage came in the very nick of time to distract the thoughts and engage the attention of our poet, who, in these three last months of 1829, was perhaps nearer a nervous breakdown than at any other moment of his career. For years past he had worked with scarcely a month's calm interlude of rest ; the death of his father, the question of a possible lawsuit with his stepmother, the increasing madness of Eugène, the needs of a growing family, the Censor's refusal to pass *Marion de Lorme*, had set him face to face with pressing worries and constant money cares : we know that when *Hernani* was produced the poet had two pounds—fifty francs—left in his pocket ! An inflammation of his eyes added to his anxieties ; for how could he work while kept to a darkened room, unable to read or write ? His letters, dictated at this date, to Sainte-Beuve (absent on an excursion to Strasburg), to Charles Nodier, to Adolphe de Saint-Valry, are full of gloomy forebodings, harping on his pecuniary embarrassments ; on the sequestration of the General's fortune ; on the furious cabal of literary rivals ; on the imagined ambush of his enemies, and the fancied defection of his dearest friends ; on the persecution of the Government ; on the " network of hatred and calumny woven round my steps on every side " (as he complains to Nodier)—on the " brigand's cave of the newspapers and the cut-throat ambush of the green-room," as he puts it to Sainte-Beuve ;

on the sudden and strange extinction of all joy and all
delight. And remembering the history of Eugène, we feel
that *Hernani*, with the praise and prosperity and bright
good fortune that ensued, came like a draught of strong
and perfumed wine, to refresh the weary poet and pater-
familias, to give him strength for the trials and troubles
that 1830 still held in store, and to restore his accustomed
placid serenity.

Adèle Hugo, though no reader of poetry, was a good
judge of a play or a novel. She admired *Hernani*, and was
determined that it should be a huge success : was it not *her*
play ? Was she not Doña Sol ? Although delicate in
health during those winter months of the rehearsals (for she
was beginning another *grossesse*, the fifth in seven years),
Madame Hugo threw herself heart and soul into the task of
organizing victory. The winter of 1829–30 was one of the
severest of the century, and the poet, when he set out for
his rehearsals, used to put list slippers over his boots in
order not to slip on the ice in the streets. His wife, having
wrapped him up in greatcoats and mufflers, sat down in
her drawing-room, no longer quietly bent over her seam or
her socks, but eagerly awaiting the arrival of her confederates. " Je suis chef de bande ! " she said, laughing—
she, too, was a brigand chief like Hernani. What a change
of scene when Sainte-Beuve returned from his little journey
in Alsace ; he was furious ! He had always disliked and
disapproved the stage. And now, what was his beloved
sanctuary of the rue Notre-Dame des Champs but a sort of
superior green-room, an arsenal of theatrical intrigues, over
which his dear idol complacently presided ? Impossible to
resume those intimate and confidential talks which wandered
from subject to subject, grave or gay, tender or vivacious,
through the waning hours of the afternoon and often far
into the evening : " Madame Victor " nowadays was never
alone. The quiet avenue echoed to loud guffaws ; the
staircase shook under the thick boots of art-students and
long-haired poets, tramping up and down in a continual
stream ; and often the disgusted critic would turn back
and not pursue the tenor of his way. If he entered the
drawing-room, he would find " Madame Victor " encamped like

a general in the midst of his staff, a map before her eyes—
a plan of the theatre, rather : she was organizing the *claque* !
She would just look up—" Ah, how do you do, Sainte-
Beuve ?　Great news !　We have Charlet's studio !　You
see we are as busy as we can be."　Who knows ?　Perhaps
she would hand him one of those crimson quires of paper
which she was cutting into little squares (on which her
husband would stamp the Spanish word :　*Hierro*, iron),
that served as theatre tickets to be distributed to the
leaders of his tribes.　Théophile Gautier, splendid, active,
beautiful as a Greek god in the efflorescence of his twentieth
year, was " Madame Victor's " right hand, and he would
lead the talk, combine the arrangements, and manage to be
everywhere at once.　Sainte-Beuve could not get a word in
edgeways ; he would sit down in a corner, bewildered, feeling himself useless and in everybody's way ; he had no
talent for this sort of thing.　Then he would rise up and
steal away, sick at heart, indignant, hostile.　At last he
could stand it no longer.　The thing had gone on for three
months !　In February 1830, on the eve of the production
of the play, he wrote to Victor Hugo, refusing to review
Hernani for the *Revue des Deux Mondes* :

Vous n'en pouvez croire vos yeux, mais cela est bien vrai.
Je suis blasé sur *Hernani* !

and at the end of this long and strange letter there is a
postscript stranger still, which, to a less critical person
than Sainte-Beuve, might have suggested the origin of his
exasperation :

And Madame ?　She whose name should sound upon your
lyre only when your hearers had sank upon their knees ?　She
also is exhibited, the whole day long, to profane eyes, distribut-
ing theatre tickets to more than eighty young men whom,
yesterday, she scarcely knew by sight.　The chaste and charming familiarity, which was the very crown of friendship, is
desecrated for ever by a vulgar tumult !　The name of devotedness prostituted to base utility, nothing valued save material
considerations !

The postscript, crossed on the margin of the letter, by
a feverish and furious hand, shows the unbalanced passion

of the writer.[1] Sainte-Beuve, when he wrote it, was surely
not quite in his right mind.

But the Hugos, husband and wife, were too deeply
absorbed in the forthcoming battle of *Hernani* to pay much
attention. The idea that the Royalists and the Classicists
were preparing a cabal was not a figment of Victor's excited
imagination. Ever since the publication of the *Ode à la
Colonne* the Ultras had looked upon our poet as a renegade.
If Béranger chose to vaunt Liberal ideas and sing the glory
of Napoleon, well, Béranger was by birth and breeding a
bourgeois and a Liberal ; they expected no better. But
that the son of " la respectable Madame Hugo," the young
genius whose Odes had charmed the Royalist salons of 1820,
should abjure the doctrines of the Altar and the Throne,
filled them with a sort of horror. And they meant to protest.

But the Latin Quarter, the studios, the Liberals, backed
Victor Hugo. *Hernani* became a political event (I think
one may say that in Paris most events have a political
lining), and more than the poet's fame and fortune was
implicated in its success or failure. *Hernani* was the rehearsal of a revolution. The ardour and excitement of the
young Romantics was extreme : " It's war to the knife ! "
cried Théophile Gautier, exultant, and on the 25th of
February 1830 the play was produced. The author had
decided that there should be no *claque*, no official
clappers of hands and fabricants of applause, but that the
places given to the *claque* should be added to his share
of tickets ; he would organize the *claque* himself with
the students and his friends : poets, painters, sculptors,
musicians, critics, printers, and especially architects—all
the young architects of Paris seem to have marched like
one man. The stalls, the gallery, the orchestra, were filled
with these devoted warriors. The curtain was to go up at
seven. At one o'clock in the afternoon several hundred
shaggy and magnificent young men ; some in cloaks and
sombreros ; some in striped and high-collared waistcoats
à la Robespierre ; some, like the handsome Théophile, neat,
but not gaudy, in scarlet satin, with the hair combed down
to the eyes and over the shoulders ; some in velvet toques

[1] Published by M. Gustave Simon in *Le Roman de Sainte-Beuve*.

à la Henri II—brief, a motley carnival of youth, art, and
enthusiasm, invaded the astonished corridors of the correct
and classic Théâtre Français.   The fastidious Sainte-Beuve
was among them.   How he must have suffered !   For
these brave barbarians were not less malodorous than magnificent.   With a six hours' wait in prospect, they came
armed with sausage and beer, with garlic and cabbage ;
they feasted, they caroused.   They sang to pass the time.
When the public entered on the stroke of seven the noise
was deafening and the stench considerable.

The curtain went up, and the play began, before two
publics, absolutely hostile ;   the public of the boxes, with
its white shoulders, its diamonds, and its good taste ; the
public of the parterre and the gallery, with its shaggy locks
and its startling incoherences.   The first acts were a battle.
But genius, love's young dream, and the delight of beauty,
are magic powers against which no politics or principles
prevail.   The fourth act finished in a thunder of applause.
The fifth act was a triumph such as the theatre has
seldom witnessed.

Before the poet left the theatre he had in his pocket six
thousand francs from a publisher who wished to bring out
the book of the play ;   he learned that the receipts for the
night were nine thousand francs, a sum at that time un-
precedented in the annals of the Théâtre Français.   Here
was an agreeable supplement to the two pounds which was
all that remained in his table drawer at home.   His cares
were removed.   His cup was full of the heady draught of
glory.   He went back into his box and sat down by his
young wife.   Years after the Duchess of Abrantès, writing
to Madame Victor Hugo, recalled that wonderful evening.

I shall never forget the First Night of *Hernani*.   And you,
so beautiful, so lovely, crowned with white roses and so luminous
in your happiness !   I had never met either of you at that time,
and it was the look in your lovely face, lighting it up so, that
made me feel I must know you both.

The whole theatre looked at the young couple with the
eyes of Madame d'Abrantès, and, turning towards their box
in a spontaneous movement of homage, acclaimed and
applauded the husband and the wife, Hernani and Doña Sol.

CHAPTER XI

1830

FOR five and forty nights the battle of *Hernani* disputed with the political situation the attention of Paris. The first triumph was never repeated ; the combat grew fiercer and fiercer, yet never ended in a reverse. " Were they able to finish the last act ? " Madame Hugo would ask her husband every night on his return. And *Hernani* managed regularly to gain that port. The public, often hostile, was always numerous ; and when in the middle of April a prior engagement of the principal actress brought the stormy campaign to a close, the Romantics could consider that the victory was theirs.

Hernani, I have said, was the rehearsal of a revolution. The spring of 1830 multiplied the signs of the times. The King and Paris were almost at daggers drawn. Tired of concessions, Charles X. had determined by main force to restore the *ancien régime,* counting on some great military success to gild the pill. First the King and his Ministers had hoped, by a private arrangement with Russia, to get back for France the left bank of the Rhine, but early in January 1830 they had to renounce that dream, which the new preponderance of Prussia rendered manifestly impossible. They fell back on a scheme for capturing Algiers. But Algiers was not, like the Rhine, a word to conjure with.

On the 18th of March 221 Deputies, or Members of Parliament, sent to the Throne an address bidding the King beware of the incompatibility between the policy of his Ministers and the temper of the nation. The next day Charles prorogued the Chamber. Parliament was dissolved on the 18th of May. " You and M. de Polignac (the French Premier) are the two best-hated men in France ! " said a journalist to Victor Hugo.

Hugo and M. de Polignac were heads of opposing factions. The Minister was a feudalist and a mystic : a man of the Middle Ages. When the King expressed a doubt as to the wisdom of an extreme measure, he answered that the Blessed Virgin, appearing to him in a vision, had assured him that all was well ; and the King was comforted. Meanwhile, Victor Hugo was writing in his *Journal of a Revolutionary of 1830* :

My old convictions, my Royalist and Catholic ideas of 1820, have fallen to pieces, fragment after fragment, during the last ten years under the repeated shocks of age and experience. Something of them still is left in my mind ; they are there like religious and poetic ruins. Sometimes I go out of my way to salute them with respect ; but I enter there no longer to say my prayers. . . .

I still admire the heroes of La Vendée ; I love them no longer. I still admire Mirabeau and Napoleon ; I hate them no longer. The feeling of respect that I preserve for the heroic Royalists of La Vendée is now only a play of imagination and a homage to virtue. I am no longer a Vendean at heart—though something still lingers in my soul.[1]

While the French were landing in Algeria—while France was preparing for the General Elections—Victor Hugo was busy with his private affairs as well as much occupied with public events. He was relieved of his money anxieties : between the book and the play the royalties of *Hernani* had brought him in more than eight hundred pounds in the course of the spring ; but he was intensely occupied. The publisher of *Le Dernier Jour d'un condamné*, a certain M. Gosselin, furious at finding that the poet had sold *Hernani* to another firm, reminded Victor Hugo that, in 1828, he had contracted to give this M. Gosselin, in April 1829, the manuscript of a novel to be called *Notre-Dame de Paris* ; the date was now more than a year overdue and not a line of the story was written ! The Shylock of a publisher insisted on his rights ; now was the moment to bring out

[1] *Littérature et philosophie mêlées*, i.

a book, while Paris was ringing with the fame of *Hernani*.
At last, thanks to the kind offices of the editor of the
Débats, author and publisher came to an arrangement :
Victor Hugo was to send in the manuscript not later than
the 1st of December, and pay M. Gosselin a thousand francs
for every week's subsequent delay. Unfortunate poet ! He
had travelled far from the mediaeval romantic frame of mind
in which he had conceived *Notre-Dame* ; his brain was no
longer busy with Gothic cathedrals, with the dualism of
the beautiful and the grotesque, with the Paris of the
fifteenth century ; but all alive with the fortunes of his
plays, and with the form that the future of France was
taking on day by day before his eager eyes. To turn
from objects so absorbing and considered with such rapt
attention to tell a story and pay an old debt was no welcome
task, and he could not accomplish that task in peace and
quiet. On the 15th of April, Quarter-day in Paris, his
landlady gave him notice to quit. The tumult and turmoil
of the invading Hernanists had been too much for the good
lady's nerves ; she liked them no better than did Sainte-
Beuve, and remarked that when she settled in the rue
Notre-Dame des Champs it was because she had considered
it a quiet situation. Well, the flat would have been small
after the advent of the expected baby. Hearing of a roomy
apartment to be let, among trees and market-gardens, in
the still almost countrified quarter of the Champs Élysées,
between the river and the avenue, Victor Hugo decided to
emigrate to that remote unpopulated part—" cette ville
déserte de François-Premier," as he calls it in one of his
letters—and established his household at No. 9 rue Jean
Goujon in the beginning of May.

But what was this upheaval, what the avidity of publishers, what even the anxiety attendant on Adèle's expected
confinement, to the troubles that 1830 still held in store ?
Sainte-Beuve had received the news of the Hugos' removal
in a sort of stupor of despair. *Hernani* had been a loathed
interruption to their peaceful intimacy ; this was worse
than an interruption—this was, terrible word ! a removal!
It was useless to remind him that the rue Jean Goujon is
perhaps three miles distant from the rue Notre-Dame des

Champs—just a pleasant walk. What comfort is that to a man who has been more than a next-door neighbour, almost an inmate of the same dear accustomed house ? " A thunderbolt has fallen ! " cried Sainte-Beuve. " Le tonnerre est tombé sur moi "—" I have been struck by lightning ! " And in the accompanying flash he read, in terror, the state of his own heart.

Gradually the centre of his interest had shifted from Victor Hugo to Victor Hugo's wife. Genius dwells in a world of its own, and it is only because it does so dwell that it can bring us the gifts that it creates ; but genius, enwrapped in its glorious cloud, is apt to seem a little distant, unresponsive, even dull, to the mere mortals who are its humble companions. Sainte-Beuve, on those afternoon calls, had encountered a lonely young woman, very willing to listen to his theories of education, his recommendations of a gentle strictness, an " austère douceur," in dealing, especially, with Léopoldine ; it was delightful to have a friend who noticed the difference of her moods, affectionately teasing her on the contrast between the " Madame Victor " of yesterday, languid as a thirsty flower, silent, absent-minded, and still undressed at dinnertime—and to-day's Madame Victor, bright and active, bubbling with fresh talk and laughter, enthusiastic, almost garrulous. She recognized herself in the poems Sainte-Beuve made about her ; in Victor's she was just an Angel. But there were some of her friend's poems that she did not see.

> N'avoir qu'un seul désir, n'aimer qu'un être au monde,
> L'aimer d'amour, ardente, idéale et profonde ;
> Voir presque tous les jours, et souvent sans témoins,
> Cette beauté, l'objet de mes uniques soins ;
> Lui parler longuement des doux secrets de l'âme,
> De l'une et l'autre vie ; et, sitôt que la flamme
> Qui sort de son regard s'est trop mêlée au mien,
> Ralentir tout à coup le rapide entretien. . . .
> Vivre ainsi, se gêner, mentir à ce qu'on aime,
> Enchaîner cet aveu qui vole de lui-même,
> Mordre sa lèvre en sang, pétrifier ses yeux
> En pâlir, en mourir . . . et sentir que c'est mieux !
> *Suite à Joseph Delorme.*

When Sainte-Beuve wrote these touching verses, for

him, at all events, the murder was out.   He knew that he was passionately in love with his friend's wife.

Let us do him justice ; he tried to get free.   Even before the Hugos left his neighbourhood he had aroused their astonishment by his irregular, capricious ways, by his infrequent visits, his crossness and sulkiness when present : the most assiduous of their friends had suddenly become the least to be relied on.   A short while before their removal, in order not to see them go, Sainte-Beuve had gone on a long visit to their common friend, Ulric Guttinguer, at Rouen.   Victor Hugo evidently had no suspicion at that moment of the reason of his friend's withdrawal, for we find him writing on the 16th May :

If you knew how much we miss you ! What a dull void your absence leaves even in the midst of our family circle, even among the children, and how we regretted to move without you into this deserted city of Francis the First.   If you knew how at every moment we want your advice, your attention, your conversation of an evening, and your friendship all the time ! There's an end of it !   And the habit of it is rooted in our hearts. But you will not do it again, I hope ?   This is the last time you will leave us to our fate ?   In that case the experiment will have its good result, inasmuch as you will not repeat it, and Normandy will have saved us from Greece.

In June Sainte-Beuve returned to Paris ; and it is, I think, at this date that we must place the confession that he made to Victor Hugo of his passion for Adèle.   We have not the date of this incident, but we know it existed ; and a change in the tone of the Correspondence warrants us, I think, in placing it here.   Victor Hugo appears at first to have taken the confession lightly, as evidence of the unbalanced and imaginative state of his friend ; no suspicion of his wife seems to have crossed his mind.   It is with the tenderness of an elder brother that he seeks to reason away that which he took for a fantastic scruple : the husband and wife join in asking Sainte-Beuve to stand sponsor to their expected child.   But Sainte-Beuve appears rather irritated than calmed by so much magnanimity, and writes to his friend :

Oh, do not blame me !   Keep of me, you at least, a memory

unique, entire, alive, imperishable! Even in my melancholy I count on that. I have dreadful, wicked thoughts! Hatred, jealousy, misanthropy. And I have no more tears. I analyse everything with perfidy and a secret bitterness. And since so it is, it is wiser to hide oneself, to try to regain one's calm, to let one's bitter draught settle without disturbing the dregs of it, and to accuse oneself to one's own conscience, or to such a friend as you.

Do not answer, my friend! Do not invite me to go and see you. I could not! Only ask Madame Hugo to be sorry for me and to remember me in her prayers. Farewell—for ever.

SAINTE-BEUVE.

This letter is dated the 6th of July. A rush of public events came just then to interrupt our three high-minded young people in their new version of the *Nouvelle Héloïse*. The Revolution of July burst out in its brief and irresistible violence and in three days changed the face of things in France.

Perhaps the smallest of its upheavals was the wreck of Sainte-Beuve's project of going to Athens as secretary to the Embassy. When the storm broke out he was not even on the way to Athens, but in Rouen, absent from Paris, in terrible anxiety about his friends, losing, as he afterwards deplored, his one heroic chance of curing all his ills with a ball in the head on some Parisian barricade. Meanwhile the Hugos were in the thick of things; their little girl, Adèle, was born on the 25th of July, and on the 26th, when the first rifle-shots were shattering the slates on their roof, Madame Hugo was very ill. She recovered, but for more than a year after that tragic confinement she was but the shadow of herself, pale, thin, often kept for days at a time in her room with backache and languor, a weary invalid.

Victor was prodigiously interested in the Revolution. The old order had sunk, as it were, down through a trap-door, giving place to the new. On the 5th of July the French armies had occupied Algiers: the beautiful old Pirates' nest, which for centuries had tyrannized the Mediterranean, was henceforth the fairest of the French possessions. Elated by this happy feat-of-arms, King Charles had decided to accomplish his long meditated *coup d'État*. On the 25th of July he had signed Four Edicts or Ordonnances, of which the first abolished the liberty of the Press, the second dissolved the newly elected Parliament (in which the Liberals had gained fifty votes), the third limited the suffrage to holders of landed property, and the fourth appointed the date of a fresh General Election. On the 26th the Ordonnances appeared in the official gazette. And on the 27th, 28th, and 29th the " Trois glorieuses "—the three glorious days of the Revolution of July—sent the Bourbons spinning out of France. A few days later, on the 9th of August, the Liberal Duke of Orleans, appointed by the Chamber, took his oath under the title of Louis-Philippe the First, and received from the hands of the four Marshals, the crown, the sceptre, the sword, and the mace. Thus the nation and the army united in establishing the Monarchy of July. Victor Hugo accepted the new order with acquiescence but without enthusiasm. The conduct of the people during the brief revolution had filled him with admiration, and in the first days of August we find him writing to Nodier, and again to Sainte-Beuve : " La population de Paris s'est admirablement conduite pendant le combat et après la victoire." From that moment he was at heart a Republican, accepting the government of Louis-Philippe as a sort of corridor leading from one room to another. As a guide through this corridor he would have preferred the Duke of Reichstadt, Napoleon's banished son. Still, the important thing was to arrive, without excess, at that Promised Land of a Republic. We find him writing in his *Journal of a Revolutionary of 1830* :

Some people mean by a Republic the war of all those who own neither a halfpenny, a virtue, or an idea against all who possess any one of the three.

My idea of a Republic (for which we are not ripe as yet, but which all Europe will acclaim a hundred years hence) is Society sovereign of society ; its own protectress, in the shape of a national militia ; its own judge, as a jury ; its own administrator, as a Commune, and governing itself by means of an electoral college.

These great events and foreshadowings ; Adèle's illness and the birth of their little girl (" Je suis bien content de ma petite fille ! Voilà enfin un de mes ouvrages qui promet

de vivre," he writes to Nodier), the organization of their
new home, and his strenuous and unflinching labour on
Notre-Dame de Paris (for the allotted time was running out
and those fatal forty pounds a week were beginning to loom
on the horizon),—all these occupations and occurrences had
doubtless diverted the poet's mind from Sainte-Beuve and
his scruples ; but that trouble was not yet at an end.　Far
from it !　When, in September, Sainte-Beuve arrived to
stand godfather to the little girl he was gloomier than ever,
and he complains in a letter to his friend Victor Pavie :

I am not loved as I would fain be loved, I dreamed of love
and I have not obtained it.

After the baptismal ceremony Sainte-Beuve again disappeared from the Hugos' horizon ; in the beginning of
November his newspaper, the *Globe*, published his Preface
to a new edition of his first book of poems, *Joseph Delorme*.
Even now it is, I think, impossible to read that Preface
without a profound compassion for the miserable, misguided,
self-tormented young man—and that compassion sprang a
hundred times quicker and fresher in the hearts of Victor
Hugo and his wife.　The poet, up to his eyes in *Notre-
Dame de Paris*, has left scarcely any letters for the autumn
of 1830, but he shoved aside his daily task to write, out of
the fulness of his friendship, to Sainte-Beuve :

4th November.

Think of your friends—especially of one, of him who writes
to you now !　You know all you mean to him, you know what
trust he has in you, both for the past and in the future.　You
know that if your happiness were poisoned, it would poison his
for ever, because he needs to know you happy.　Do not give
way !　Do not disdain all that makes you great, your genius,
your life, your virtue !　Think that you belong to us, and that
there are two hearts here of which you are ever the dearest, the
constant theme.—The friend who loves you best,

V. H.

In one of his novels Balzac has remarked that in feeble
natures discouragement, dejection, easily turn to envy, to
hatred of those who succeed, who possess what they desire.
It was so in the case of Sainte-Beuve.　He wrote to his

friend on the 7th of December a letter more romantic, I
think, than any of Saint-Preux's to Julie or to Wolmar :

MY FRIEND—I can endure this no longer. If you knew how
my days and nights go by, in what a contradiction of passions,
you would pity the man who has injured you, and you would
wish me dead, and not blame me, but keep an eternal silence.
Already I repent of what I am doing at this very moment ; the
idea of writing to you seems to me as mad as all the rest ! But
whichever way I turn, it is to dash myself against impossibilities,
and since I have begun, I may as well go on. If you knew,
alas ! my feelings when I hear your name—when one of our
friends mentions any circumstance concerning you or Madame
Hugo—how all the past starts back into life, the smallest details,
our walks on the plain, our visits to the Feuillantines, and all
the peaceful blessed life I hoped always to lead in your society.
If you knew what memory unchains in the bottom of my heart
during my wakeful nights—how the torments of the damned
rend me from three or four o'clock in the dark until the daylight !
Then my heart closes, and a thin ice forms on the surface, and
nothing is visible until, next night, the abyss opens again.
Oh, I am full of despair, of rage ; sometimes I have a real longing
to kill you, yes, to assassinate you ! Forgive me these horrible
impulses. . . . But think, you whose life is filled with so many
thoughts—realize what a void is left in mine by the loss of such
an affection : *What ? Lost for ever ?* I cannot go to see you.
I'll never cross your threshold again ; it is impossible ! But
never think it is out of indifference. Ah, do not pronounce that
word. Beg Madame Hugo never to pronounce that word :
Inconstancy, which I hear now on all sides. Inconstant ? I,
with you ? Can you say it ? Have you forgotten already ?
Is it because I loved too little that our friendship has come to
an end ? Is it not rather an excess of feeling that has killed
it ? . . .

But now, what place could I take by your fireside now that
I have deserved your mistrust, now that a suspicion has slunk
between us, now that your anxious vigilance is always awake,
now that Madame Hugo cannot meet my glance without having
first consulted yours ? There is nothing for it but to draw
back, and it is a sort of religion to abstain. You were good
enough to tell me to come as I used to do, but it was merely
compassion and indulgence on your part, . . . and what for you
is merely awkward is torture to me. . . . No ! I bury our friendship in my heart, as I ask you to bury it in yours, and ask
(Ah, be generous !) Madame Hugo to bury it in hers. . . .

And, perhaps, some day, my friend, when I shall be alone in

the world, with no old mother to nurse, no possible wife to hope for, no new system or theory to adopt, when I shall have grown old—when Madame Hugo herself shall be old—who knows! if I return to the paths of piety, of chaste and austere religion, to the practice of virtue, perhaps, then, my friend, after some act of expiation that you will find for me, you will let me come back and finish my days under your roof ; you will again have confidence in your friend, and sometimes you will leave me alone with her who is worthy only of you, and whose worth I never misunderstood—no, I swear it !—whose price I always appreciated !

Victor Hugo read this immense letter—I have not quoted all of it—and generously showed it to his wife.

I have my wound (he wrote to Sainte-Beuve), and you have yours.   Let us be indulgent to each other.   The painful shock will subside.   Time will heal the sore.   And in the days to come our present sufferings will be another reason for our friendship.

It was Christmas-tide—the time for reconciliations.   The godpapa sent a box of presents to the little Hugos.

Bonjour, Sainte-Beuve (writes Léopoldine).   Je te remerci bien de ta belle poupé.   Nous tambrasseron bien quan tu vindra voir Papa et Maman.

And Victor Hugo adds :

Come and dine with us the day after to-morrow.   1830 is a thing of the past.

CHAPTER XII

" NOTRE-DAME DE PARIS "

1830 was ended ! But not so *Notre-Dame de Paris*. During the bombardment in July Victor Hugo had removed his precious manuscripts from his house in the exposed suburb, as it then was, of the Champs-Élysées, to the Fouchers' solid mansion in the rue de Cherche-Midi. And a note-book full of material for his work had been lost. This had thrown back the hard-pressed author ; but the publisher, more reasonable now that he saw his client hard at it, had let himself be propitiated, and had allowed him eight more weeks in which to complete the task.

In the middle of January 1831 the last word was penned ; in the middle of April the book appeared. The Press was not favourable. People were no longer concerned with the question of Art for Art, with the Middle Ages, with the Romantic movement. A new spirit was abroad and the newspapers were filled with a fresh shibboleth ; on every page appeared the words : Progress, Order, Asphalt, Steam, Garde-Nationale, Democracy, Legality ; for we are now in the reign of Louis-Philippe, the Bourgeois King. The journalists, therefore, and even such a critic as Sainte-Beuve, had but half-hearted praise for *Notre-Dame de Paris*. But, fortunately, there remained a good million or so of Parisians, proud of their Cathedral, interested in the history of their city ; proud also of Victor Hugo, interested in him. They snatched the editions from the printing press, and *Notre-Dame de Paris* had an immense popular success.

Notre-Dame de Paris is unlike any other novel of Victor Hugo's. It has an extraordinary grace, and, if I dare say so of our Titan and his works, a prettiness, a delicacy of

its own.   It is without the fluidity and the sublime tenderness of *Les Misérables* or *Les Travailleurs*, or *Quatrevingt-
treize* ; and it possesses so much more beauty than his
earlier books that we cannot compare them, or we might
find a certain resemblance to *Han d'Islande*, romantic and
fantastic as it is.   But it is Victor Hugo's drawings that
best compare with the complex and innumerable outlines,
the play of light and shade, the picturesqueness, the mediaeval quality of *Notre-Dame*.   The story attempts to por-
tray the life of the fifteenth century in Paris in all its heights
and depths, its fairness and foulness, from the thieves' den
to the Cathedral belfry, from the laughing young women of
the world in the noble's palace to the torture-chamber in the
crypt.   (Never once, in the course of the year that I was a
nurse during the war, did I attend an operation without
remembering that torture-chamber in *Notre-Dame de Paris* !)
And every detail is original and finished with the same loving
exquisiteness—just as the trefoils and gargoyles far out of
sight on the towers of the Cathedral are no less carefully
chiselled than the faces of the saints in the Portals ; every
symbol is elaborated with an ardour of feeling that masks a
hidden irony.   And, in fact, if we strip the story of all
this wealth of detail, often so beautiful that we lose sight
of the plan beneath, the fable of *Notre-Dame de Paris* is
sad—sad, and as simple, and as epic as a story from the
Légende des Siècles.   It is the tale of a young girl who flits
through the multitudinous and complicated ways of life, as
extraneous to its regulations, as natural, as pure, and as
capricious as a wind-sown wild flower.   This is Esmeralda,
the foundling gipsy, with her goat.   And they symbolize
Caprice, Imagination, Beauty, the Eternal Feminine (as
Goethe would say), drawing all hearts, acknowledging no
law.   Four men love Esmeralda, follow her, attempt to
win her : there is Frollo, the cleric, who is Science and
Passion ; there is Gringoire, the poet, a friendly creature, of
all the most akin to the young girl, being himself irresponsible, harmless, seeing in the world nothing but Beauty ;
there is Quasimodo, the dwarf, the man of the people, with
his great heart and his dog-like devotion ; and there is
Phébus de Châteaupers, a gallant young officer with nothing

particular inside his handsome pate. And of course Esmeralda chooses him—just as Life chooses him. For, with the
exception of Gringoire, every other character in the book
comes to a tragic end—who can forget Esmeralda hanging
from the gibbet like a broken flower, or the anguish of the
hermit mother, the dizzy fall of Frollo from the height of
his tower, or Quasimodo, in the vault with the dead girl,
enjoying his death in the darkness ? It is true that Hugo
tells us that Phébus also " fit une fin tragique "—his tragic
end, however, was merely matrimony :

> S'il me plaît de cacher l'amour et la douleur
> Dans le coin d'un roman ironique et railleur,

writes the poet in his *Feuilles d'automne.* For if he has
nothing but irony and raillery for human beings, those
trivial puppets of destiny, if for them he has neither love
nor hope nor faith, nor any gospel save the word ΑΝΑΓΚΗ
—Necessity—yet his heart is dilated with all the theological
virtues when he turns from them to that which will outlast
them—the beauty of the Cathedral. "There is," says
Sainte-Beuve in his not very interesting criticism of the
book, "something architectural in Victor Hugo's imagination—something picturesque, angular, *vertical*, and fantastic."
This, at any rate, was a remark worth making ; and never,
not even in *Les Orientales*, was Hugo more completely the
pure artist, " l'homme qui ne voit dans le monde que l'art,
et voit le monde dans l'art," than in this archaeological,
rather than historical, romance.

The real heroine of *Notre-Dame* is the Cathedral, which
Victor Hugo knew inch small, which he had visited perhaps
a thousand times in his eight-and-twenty years, which he
loved and, above all, in which he recognized the expression
of his own genius. Victor Hugo was of the same race as
the mediaeval masons who had transposed into stone the
immense variety of Nature. Here was an example to show
that Beauty can exist outside the limits of Measure, Unity,
Order ; that there can be a grace and a grandeur independent of the laws of classic perfection ; a Beauty that
draws its elements from the abundance and the complexity
of the elements that it associates, in a harmony as elastic

as that of the trees in a forest or the leaves on a bough. Everything in Gothic art is calculated, but nothing is exact, no angle true, no line straight, and it is this supple and, as it were, spontaneous asymmetry, these almost imperceptible curves and irregularities, which give their look of growth and life to these immense Cathedrals. Whether we see them from without, with the contrast of their vast plain stretches of masonry, their portals full of piled-up figures and shadows, and their towers soaring high in the air and sprouting into innumerable pinnacles and gargoyles that break the line and soften every contour ; or if we go inside and pass from the tower into the cave-like twilight of their vast naves, with their sheaves of pillars, no two alike, and some bright rose-window, pure red and pure blue, flowering high in the wall like a glorious blossom of light, a Gothic cathedral has the same living beauty as a natural object, and expresses, not a plan elaborated in the mind of a man, but the huge and innumerable beauty of the Universe. Which is what Victor Hugo will attempt to express by much the same means. And his genius, like the genius of Gothic art, is full of the sense of contrast ; half the beauty of a twelfth-century church is its opposition of light and shade ; its divergence of directions, if I may use such an unwieldy phrase to suggest the force of the buttresses clinging to the earth—clutching the soil—and the push upwards of towers and spires and ogives rising, urging aloft ; its moral variety also, its assembly of angels and monsters, of doves and wolves, nothing is common or unclean ; the cabbage leaf or the carrot may ornament a chancel column no less than the lily or the hawthorn flower ; the scold, her hand raised for a blow (as in the Portal of Amiens) neighbours the saint ; the unclean beast has his place no less than the Lamb of God. I think Victor Hugo must have discovered his theories in examining a Gothic cathedral. Contrast was the very law of his art. He saw the moral world as we see objects in strong sunshine, each cut out in sharp relief and doubled by the depth of its shadow. He could not imagine Beauty without evoking the image of Deformity, nor dream of ambition without the sense of a possible collapse, nor enjoy Love without remembering Death, nor turn to Faith without feeling on his shoulder the cold touch of Doubt. But also, and more and more as time went on, he could not look on a fallen woman without seeing in her a possible angel, nor see deformity and not believe it to conceal a beautiful soul, nor suffer defeat but his heart would beat high for the coming triumph, nor endure bereavement without the dim instinctive sense of a life beyond. And this turn of his mind perhaps explains how as Time and Chance accumulate their trials and troubles in the track of our once happy Prince of Poets, he will become more obstinately idealist and optimist, until in his later phase he cannot contemplate the strong material outlines of the earth—which he visualizes with such extra-ordinary plastic relief—without a suggestion of the mysteri-ous invisible Other-world. Like his Gilliatt, like his Titan, our poet will tear a rent in the tissue of the Universe and find himself face to face with that Something divine and unutterable which waits on the farther side of the veil.

CHAPTER XIII

AUTUMN AND TWILIGHT

Soon after that New Year's meeting of 1831 a' decisive interview took place between Victor Hugo and Sainte-Beuve. What passed between them it is difficult to say, although we possess a very full brief of the case : the letters of Victor Hugo, printed in the Correspondence ; the letters of Sainte-Beuve to his friend, more recently published by M. Gustave Simon in his *Roman de Sainte-Beuve* ; with other writings of his to Madame Hugo, or about Madame Hugo, given by M. Louis Barthou in his *Amours d'un poète*. Still, much remains obscure, unproven ; all the more difficult to understand that our modern world has moved so far from the standpoint of the Romantics of 1830. . . .

First of all, in those days there was no divorce. Yet, in the eyes of the Romantics there was no duty, no right, no law comparable to that divine unwritten law which binds the lover to the beloved. They would say with Faust : " Gefühl ist alles ! " (And sad havoc they made of their lives in attempting to guide them by the sole beacon of an erring heart !) Feeling, and especially Passion, were, to them, the sacred manifestations of the Force that moves the sun and all the stars, and to attempt to constrain and govern these by any social contract or religious bond was almost a sacrilege.

And of these Romantics, Victor Hugo was one of the shining lights. He would try, therefore, to behave as such : magnanimously, disinterestedly, not priding himself on his marital privileges, not exacting his pound of flesh according to contract, but submitting the law to the dictates of the heart and the letter to the spirit.

There are fashions in sentiment no less than in all other human modes of expression. While Society exacted an

indissoluble marriage-tie, the Romantics believed in what
I suppose they would not have called Free Love, but to us
it seems very much like it. They also placed great faith in
the virtue of mutual confession ; in explaining, pointing-
pole in hand, all the secret complications of a guilty love,
especially to the person likely to be injured by it. They
adored their lady, but not without accusing themselves to
her husband. They murmur, with Sainte-Beuve :

> Et je plains l'offensé, noble entre les grands cœurs.

It is not easy to put ourselves back into their state of
mind, to understand this luxury of woe, to appreciate their
interminable explanations, which seem to us indelicate and
shocking, and which certainly, after every fresh admiring
yet recriminative outburst, left the three young people with
whom I am here concerned sunk still deeper, still more hopelessly, in the Slough of Despond.

What did Victor Hugo propose to Sainte-Beuve in that
mid-January of 1831 ? What was it to which Victor Hugo
refers in his letter of the 18th March, that even chance,
known only to his friend and himself, which he offered with
the firm resolution, for his part, of abiding by the result ?
From all we can divine in the light of subsequent events,
it was some such choice as Ibsen's Doctor hero offers to the
Lady from the Sea : Adèle was to decide which she would
favour of the two men who loved her, and the other was
to completely disappear. And the result was naturally much
the same as in the case of the Lady from the Sea. Victor
Hugo doubtless felt himself unutterably generous. But
Sainte-Beuve was indignant. He thought his friend was
playing with loaded dice. For Adèle Hugo was above all
things a mother ; no consideration would induce her to
deprive her little ones of either of their parents. Hugo
must have known her inevitable answer. The least subtle
of men, and one of the least sensitive, Hugo was fond of
thinking that he could manage lesser mortals for their good,
and in this mood would invent complicated and yet candid
machinations worthy of a barbarian chief. No feature in
his character was so calculated to exasperate the more
subtle of his friends—Sainte-Beuve, Vigny, Baudelaire, even

Balzac—each and all in turn revolted from these clumsy comedies which it was an insult to their intelligence to suppose they could not pierce at a glance. In the rôle of Artful Dodger, Victor Hugo was beneath contempt. He spread the net in front of the bird and weighted it with fair white stones. Sainte-Beuve in his anger called his friend (in a review of his poems) a " crafty Frank." Well, there was a strain of that in the son of Lorraine.

Sainte-Beuve appears to have refused the ordeal and yet to have accepted the penalty. He would retire, not only from his friends' surroundings but from Paris, from France. Early in April he was in Brussels ; he had already secured the promise of an appointment as Professor of French Literature at the University of Liège, and he proposed to naturalize himself a Belgian subject. Sainte-Beuve was a man of the North ; his mother English, or half-English ; his father a Picard ; he was a native of the town of Boulogne. Belgium was for him no desperate exile. He had little private fortune ; he lived by his pen. His chair at Liège was not without its advantages. Victor Hugo, at all events, jubilated and felt all his old friendship for Sainte-Beuve revive.

And Sainte-Beuve from Brussels writes in the kindest strain :

Je suis à vous autant que jamais—à vous, homme loyal et fort, à vous caractère constant et inébranlable.

His love for Madame Hugo seems to have passed into a phase of fraternal anxiety about her health.

Try and send her into the country, or to take the waters. Her health is not irremediably injured ; it is a nervous gastritis, a form of indigestion, which would yield to treatment, to change of air and scene, to a change of thoughts also—drives, walks.

The Sainte-Beuve of the rue de Vaugirard reappears for a moment—the timid yet shrewd and kindly medical student. Sainte-Beuve is staying in Brussels in the house of the Saint-Simonians. He also has felt the need of a change of scene and thought. He is striving to put Humanity in the place left vacant by Adèle—he is trying a change of idols, apparently with satisfactory results.

In this more spiritual and almost disinterested frame of
mind he returns to Paris in May, in order to make his
final arrangements before taking up his abode at Liège.
And in the Hugo household his ancient place awaits him.
Can they see too much of a friend from whom they are so
soon to part ?   Madame Hugo is distressed by her penitent's
Saint-Simonism ; she feels herself responsible for his soul.
It is doubtless through the Hugos that Sainte-Beuve makes
the acquaintance of the Abbé de la Mennais at Juilly in
June.   And " Monsieur Féli " is soon the confidant of our
Saint-Simonian.   A scene in *Volupté* reveals how, while
forbidding a carnal passion, the Man of God permits a
distant Beatrice, leading the soul from purgatory to a tryst
in an Eternal Hereafter. . . . The feelings of the lovers have
soared to a higher plane, they seem to have found peace
in that " sentiment supérieur à tous les autres " which
Balzac so beautifully describes in his *Madame de la Chan-
terie* : " amour d'âme à âme, sentiment immense, infini, né
de la charité catholique." Why, then, is Victor Hugo so
changed ?   That recurrent eye-trouble which was never
permanently to impair his sight, but so often deprives him
of vision in moments of overstrain and nervous stress, has
again reduced him to a darkened room and the absence of
books.   One day he finds his wife in tears, and it is the
occasion for some heart-rending verses.   The rehearsals of
Marion de Lorme (which appeared on the stage that summer)
cannot divert his thoughts.   How should they ?   The subject of the play is jealousy.   These lines, written in July or
August for the remodelling of the last act, are not merely
the eloquence of a dramatist : Didier has forgiven Marion,
but refuses to escape from prison.   How could he live
knowing her unfaithful ?

> Mais vivre près de toi, vivre, l'âme ulcérée !
> O ciel ! moi qui n'aurais jamais aimé que toi ! . . .
> Tous les jours—peux-tu bien y songer sans effroi ?
> Je te ferais pleurer !   J'aurais mille pensées,
> Que je ne dirais pas, sur les choses passées.
> J'aurais l'air d'épier, de douter, de souffrir,
> Tu serais malheureuse.

Victor Hugo is no less suspicious, restive, violent, irritable than Didier. He is (as Sainte-Beuve observed) another Didier, more passionate than sensitive, deep-hearted, constant, true, but not attentive or delicate, who says to his idol : " I love you ardently," and not " I love you tenderly."

In June the Hugos, husband, wife, and little ones, went to spend the heat of the summer in the valley of the Bièvre, near Versailles, with their friends the Bertins : M. Bertin (whose portrait by Ingres is familiar to all lovers of the Louvre) was that editor of the *Débats* who had patched up matters the year before between Victor Hugo and his publisher. The Hugos have bade their adieux to Sainte-Beuve ; they will probably not see him again. That chapter is closed. Victor Hugo, in his ungenerous joy (for so far can jealousy change a temper naturally grand and large), cannot refrain from an insolent cockcrow of triumph. He writes to Sainte-Beuve on the 1st of July.

Our hosts are charming, and so kind that I do not know when we shall tear ourselves away. My wife is enraptured, cheerful, enchanted, happy, and quite well. One could not be in pleasanter quarters. That is the luncheon bell ! Well—do not forget to write to us from Liège.

It was unwise to turn the knife so cruelly in the wound : " Ravie, gaie, émerveillée, heureuse, bien portante ? " Perhaps it was not only the air of Bièvre that so completely had restored Madame Hugo's health ? Perhaps she suspected already a piece of news which Hugo's letter may have helped to fix and determine ? The poet received an answer which flung him into the depths of despondency. In obedience to the advice of his best friends, Sainte-Beuve had decided to throw up his professorship at Liège ; he remained in Paris.

In his ill-concealed tortures of the spring, in his triumph at Bièvre, Victor Hugo had run off the rails which he had laid down for his conduct—had shown himself just the jealous husband, not the sublime, magnanimous soul, compassionate to all human weakness. In his answer to Sainte-Beuve he continues to appear, although very touching, very human, none the less inexorably decided to assert his rights and protect his one ewe lamb whether she would or no. In fact, as so often happens in the great trials of character, he appears a being wholly different from his own image of himself ; not the calm, serene Olympian, but a man absolute, proud, jealous, with the most violent sense of proprietorship, yet sincere, faithful, broken-hearted, and, as it were, in mourning for both his friend and his wife ; like Quasimodo when, from the tower of Notre-Dame, he looks on the ruined bodies of Frollo and Esmeralda—sighing : " O tout ce que j'ai aimé ! "

On the 6th of July, regretful but resolute, he forbids Sainte-Beuve all access to his house. Sainte-Beuve receives the blow standing, and riposts the next day with a correct and sensible answer. But a nearer, a dearer hand had avenged the affront. Madame Hugo, worn out by her long illness and distressed by constant scenes of jealousy, considered (or so she said) that her family of four children was sufficient to occupy all her capacities, and doubted that her husband's fortunes could provide for more ; she decided to remain under his roof only as his dearest friend, merely as his Egeria, his household divinity, the mother of Didine and Dédé, Charlot and Toto, those idolized little beings, unbreakable links between their parents.[1] This was the cruellest cut of all. On the 7th of July Hugo answers Sainte-Beuve's letter received in the morning :

. . . You are right, my friend, you are right from first to last. . . . Your behaviour has been loyal and perfect. You have done nothing to wound any one—it is all my delusion, my unfortunate head. I love you more than ever—would give my life for you if that were any use. It would not be giving much. For, listen, Sainte-Beuve—I tell you this as a secret,: I am not happy. I am no longer happy ! I have acquired the certainty that the being who possesses all my heart has ceased to care for me. I have learned that perhaps with you it was a very near thing ! I repeat to myself all that you say, but the bitter drop is enough to poison all my life. Ah yes, pity me ! I am most miserable. I do not know on what footing I stand with the two persons I love best in all the world. You are one of the two ! Pity me—love me—write to me !

The Hugos returned to Paris despite the kindness of the Bertins and the heat of summer ; Madame Hugo was con-

[1] Gustave Simon, *La Vie d'une femme*, p. 200.

fined to her room. It is probable that the state of her
health required this measure ; but in Romantic circles
Sainte-Beuve confidentially spread the rumour that Hugo,
mad with pride and jealousy, kept his wife under lock and
key ! If Adèle and Sainte-Beuve were to meet, " il faudrait
du sang, des coups d'épée." [1] Hugo was a being " whose
soul, made of granite and iron, had no communication with
other souls." We recognize the *charabia* of Sainte-Beuve.
And, in fact, Sainte-Beuve, always subtle and various, could
never accustom himself to the violence of Hugo's reactions.
This is the moment, I imagine, when he composed the
extraordinary, the indecent poem of the *Livre d'amour*, in
which he compares Adèle, " tendre agneau," struggling in
the iron grasp of her jealous consort, to a lamb carried off
into his den by a lion. He seems to have been seriously
alarmed. He knew the poet's excessive imagination.
Already, on the 8th of July, he had written to him :

> Are you sure that you do not bring, to your relations with
> that person—so dear and so delicate as she is—something
> excessive which frightens her and freezes her ? Your suspicions,
> your fatal imagination reduce her to a state which seems to
> justify that suspicion and renders it more harsh and burning.
> You are so strong, my friend, so accentuated, so out of scale
> with our ordinary dimensions and our imperceptible fine shades,
> and, especially in your impassioned hours, you descry, in the
> objects you look upon, the colour of your own glances and the
> reflection of your own phantoms. Try, then, my friend, to be
> calm. Let the limpid brook flow peacefully at your feet without
> troubling the waters, and soon your image will reappear again.

The advice was good, and Hugo was not above taking
it. But he did not invite his friend within his doors.
Madame Hugo's health obliged her to keep at home. For
more than a year at least, if not for several years, there
was neither meeting nor correspondence between that lady
and Sainte-Beuve, except such messages as may have been
conveyed through their common friend, Ulric Guttinguer.
Meanwhile Victor Hugo recovered his peace of mind, his
sane outlook on things, and from time to time would cross

[1] Cf. Fontanez, *Journal romantique*, Oct. 31, 1831 ; quoted by Simon,
Roman de Sainte-Beuve, 156.

the bridges on to the left bank and look up his old friend—
especially (as the ironical critic was not slow to remark)
when he had a book of poems ready to fall from the press,
expectant of a review.

Feuilles d'automne was published in December 1831—
autumn leaves already ? Withered relics of all that had
been so fresh, so full of hope. Victor Hugo was twenty-
nine when he felt his soul shiver in the chill October of the
years. His next volume (which, though it appeared four
years later, was largely composed in these earliest thirties)
will be entitled *Songs of Twilight* : *Chants du crépuscule.*
In 1831 our poet could not dream that he was destined to
endure another half-century. His life was to have more
than one cycle in it ; he will know a renewal. The storms of
March and the splendours of August will come round for
him again. But these first autumn leaves, this twilit
music—this sense of the fall, the drift, the hopeless end of
things, corresponds to the close of his youth, to the extinction of his faith, to the disenchantment of his early
love. He will feel another love ; he will discover a vaster,
an infinite Divinity ; he will know a vigour of middle life
compared to which his spring will appear as an exquisite
but puny adolescence, but these things are not yet.

Already in *Feuilles d'automne*, if Victor Hugo has not
attained the full stretch of his wings or the full sweep of
his lyre, he is more than a poet, he is a great poet. Victor
Hugo is never more grandly himself than when in a mood
of retrospect, or in a vision of the future. When he is
flatly face to face with actual things, when he addresses the
woman he loves, or even the tyrant he hates, when he
speaks in the present indicative tense, sometimes he is
blunt or heavy or fatuous or even absurd in his exaggera-
tions and antitheses. When he says : *it was !* he touches
things too deep for tears. When he prophesies : *it shall
be !* he is often sublime.

Feuilles d'automne is written in a mood of retrospect,
full not only of melancholy but of maturity. The poet is
no longer the young lover who tuned his lyre so confidently
in praise of the King and his lady. In the shadow of that
thirtieth year, which is the last of youth, we see him seated

by his hearth, with his books and his children about him,
full of interests but also of cares ; the woman who loved
him yesterday passes, hiding her tears ; no prayer is on his
lips, but a mysterious shudder—" l'effarement de l'Infini,"—
has filled his soul with the chill prevision of what may lie
on the further side of life ; his genius is riper, fuller, more
generous than it ever was, but a certain fantastic grace is
there no longer.

So enthroned in his glory and his lassitude, he looks
back on the past and sees that it was good—sees himself
a little child with his father and his mother, caught up in
the whirlwind that devastated, and fertilized, all Europe,
swept from France to Italy, from Italy to Spain in the track
of Napoléon ; sees his father banished to that white house
by the Loire ; sees his mother dead ; sees the fall of the
Emperor ; sees the new King on his shrunken throne, and
the tottering of that throne ; turns his eyes from the
Bourbon, still beloved but incorrigible, to the son of Bonaparte exiled in Austria ; sees dynasty after dynasty over-
thrown, creeds outworn, philosophies inadequate, theories
imperfect.   And he asks himself :

> Which is the path ?   Denial, Faith or Doubt ?
> O black cross-roads, whose paths go branching out !
> The wise man halts beneath the wayside bough
> Murmuring : " Lord, I go ; but guide me, Thou ! "
> And hopes, and hears, beyond his waiting-place,
> The oncoming footfall of the human race.[1]

This halt by the roadside, " nel mezzo del cammin di nostra
vita," has one deep and never-cloying delight : the grace of
the little children who play about the poet's feet, until, tired
out, but still laughing and still babbling, they come home
for their supper of milk and nuts.   But before they sleep,
let him join their hands in prayer.   He bids them pray for

---

[1] Que faire et que penser ?   Nier, douter ou croire ?
Carrefour ténébreux ! triple route ! nuit noire !
Le plus sage s'assied sous l'arbre du chemin
Disant tout bas : j'irai, Seigneur, où tu m'envoies.
Il espère, et, de loin, dans les trois sombres voies,
Il écoute, pensif, marcher le genre humain.
                                                 À mes amis, L. B. et S.-B.

all, for the quick and the dead, and, first of all, for their
father and mother.

> Va, donc, prier pour moi !   J'en ai plus besoin qu'elle.
> Elle est, ainsi que toi, bonne, simple et fidèle.
> Elle a le cœur limpide et le front satisfait.
> Beaucoup ont sa pitié, nul ne lui fait envie ;
> Sage et douce, elle prend patiemment la vie,
> Elle souffre le mal sans savoir qui le fait.
>
> *La Prière pour tous.*

Innocent as her own children, this dove-like creature no
longer fills all the imagination of our poet.   The love of
woman also is a fading, falling leaf !   These things alone
remain eternally fresh 'and green : Country and Liberty,
Nature, Humanity.

> J'oublie alors l'amour, la famille, l'enfance,
> Et les molles chansons, et le loisir serein—
> Et j'ajoute à ma lyre une corde d'airain.

In his next volume, *Les Chants du crépuscule*, this brazen
cord vibrates more plangent and more piercing than we
have heard it yet.   Here are the poems written on the
Revolution of July ; the second, the veritable, Ode à la
Colonne ; the magnificent Ode on the Death of Napoléon's
son, the Duc de Reichstadt, whose not impossible accession
to the throne of France had been, since 1830, Victor Hugo's
dream in politics.   Here, too, are these stanzas—these
" méchantes strophes," as the poet calls them—thrown off
at a moment's notice for the public funeral service for the
revolutionaries fallen on the barricades, stanzas which now
rank, next to the " Marseillaise," among the national hymns
of France :

> Those whose devoted death redeems their native land
> Merit that round their tomb, praying, the people stand ;
> Among our glorious names their name is first of all !
>   Their fame all other earthly fame transcends ;
>   The nation, like a mother, bends
> To lull their sleep beneath the funeral pall.
>
>   France, that endures from age to age !
>   France, our eternal heritage !
>   Praise to thy martyred sons, our pride !
>   Praise be to them that on their trace

Follow and throng to take their place,
Willing to die as these have died ! [1]

After these, after other political poems, in which the
great Liberal Reformer already appears, there are the customary poems to Adèle—not one volume, since the first in
1822, had seen the light without this homage.   It is in
danger, at last, of becoming stereotyped.   There is an excess,
perhaps, of white lilies, of sweet grave eyes, of babies clinging to her skirts, of little orphans rescued, of prayers for
the dead ; she still presides the assembled songs—virginal,
maternal, almost divine.

Oh, qui que vous soyez, bénissez-la.   C'est elle !
La sœur, visible aux yeux, de mon âme immortelle !
Mon orgueil, mon espoir, mon abri, mon recours !
Toit de mes jeunes ans qu'espèrent mes vieux jours.
La femme dont ma joie est le bonheur suprême ;
Qui, si nous chancelons, ses enfants ou moi-même,
Sans parole sévère et sans regard moqueur
Les soutient de la main, et me soutient du cœur ;
Celle qui, lorsqu'au mal, pensif, je m'abandonne
Seule peut me punir, et seule me pardonne.

The homage is so magnificent that we dimly wonder :
Was it quite sincere ?   After all, in 1830, had his wife
shown herself so impeccable ?

Ève qu'aucun fruit ne tente

sings the poet, bestowing on his injured spouse a certificate
of immaculacy.   For evidently this child-like angelic being
was an injured wife.   Opposed to three or four lilied lyrics
dedicated to her there are a dozen others fragrant with the
roses and raptures of unlawful love, full of passionate adora-

---

[1] Ceux qui pieusement sont morts pour la patrie
Ont droit qu'à leur cerceuil le peuple vienne et prie.
Entre les plus beaux noms leur nom est le plus beau.
Toute gloire près d'eux tombe et passe éphémère ;
    Et, comme ferait une mère
La voix d'un peuple entier les berce en leur tombeau.

Gloire à notre France éternelle !
Gloire à ceux qui sont morts pour elle !
Aux martyrs, aux vaillants, aux forts !
A ceux qu'enflamme leur exemple,
Qui veulent place dans le temple
Et qui mourront comme ils sont morts !

tion, and remorse, addressed to another woman—a woman
who has sinned and suffered, a woman in whose mind,
matured by many sorrows, the poet can hear the long
reverberation of his own melancholy thoughts, who shares
his love for Nature and that sense of beauty which the *bourgeoise*
Adèle has never understood ; a woman " au cœur charmant,
sombre comme la nuit " ; a woman, still young, no doubt,
but no longer very young, disenchanted, humiliated, embittered, superior to her fate, a woman to help and save.
Who is the original of this second image on the altar ? The
veil thrown across her features only served to excite the
malicious curiosity of Paris. Sainte-Beuve, furious, indignant (and quaintly decked in the pride of conscious virtue),
seizes on his pen to avenge Adèle by a scathing review of
the *Chants du crépuscule*. The political poems are all very
well, though the poet was perhaps not wise to add that
brazen cord to his lyre—he was already too much given to
the sounding brass and tinkling cymbal, *tanquam aes tinniens !*
In Sainte-Beuve's eyes, Hugo is no longer the reformer
of French poetry, but " an energetic and subtle Frank," a
barbarian who has hastily assimilated the culture of Byzance,
and whose decadent art is an exquisite danger to letters.
But it is when he turns from the political to the personal
poems that Sainte-Beuve becomes really virulent. He
accuses Hugo of throwing " a handful of white lilies in the
eyes of the public " ; he reveals the various inspirations of
the lyrics. He shows the poet seated by the seashore with
his mistress, planning out a love-poem with the careful
exactness of a Euclid. He blames something emphatic,
exterior, and hollow as Hugo's inspiration : " Depuis que
M. Hugo s'occupe du théâtre, on dirait que le théâtral a
gagné." At this point, accustomed to read between the
lines of our Sainte-Beuve, we remark to ourselves :

" Evidently there is another lady, and she is an actress ! "

CHAPTER XIV

THE PRINCESS NEGRONI

In October 1832, Hugo found time to settle himself and his family in that handsome corner house of the place des Vosges, where they remained until after the revolution of 1848, and which we may say that he continues to occupy to-day, since the city of Paris has bought the house and made of it the Musée Victor-Hugo. The place des Vosges is the place Royale which Henri Quatre constructed on the ruins of the royal palace of Les Tournelles. Though now plunged in the dullness of an industrial and popular quarter, it is still one of the architectural glories of Paris. There has been no change in these stately old mansions since their completion in 1630. A cloister runs all round the square, supporting on its low and rather squat arcades the noble façades of red brick, edged with a light freestone, which, with the steep roofs of leaded blue slate, time has paled to a faded tricolour. The arcades are low and heavy ; the first stories immensely high, with tall windows opening from floor to ceiling ; the pitch of the roof is agreeably broken by dormer windows in the style of the Renaissance. In the middle of the square there is a garden with a fountain. Hugo, despite his cares and trials, was a proud man when he brought his beautiful wife and his four children to live in the *piano nobile* of the house at the south-eastern corner —the apartment which, two hundred years before, had been brilliantly occupied by Marion de Lorme.

It was a home for a poet, for a prince of poets, and therein Hugo held his court. He filled the great rooms with ancient tapestries, with jars of Oriental china, with carved oak, and—suddenly displaying the talent of his

grandfather, the master-cabinetmaker of Nancy—he himself devised and constructed beautiful pieces of furniture,
which we may still admire there to-day. Here in the evening he received his friends, his flatterers, in crowds, and
grew accustomed to that circle of attendant spirits, that
atmosphere of adulation, which will henceforth be to him
as necessary as bread or water, and which will slowly disintegrate his moral nature. For, when Love went out at
the door, the need of Flattery flew in at the window. " Le
poète a besoin d'une vie accompagnée," wrote Hugo in one
of his last speeches. He at least could not live without
love, applause, enthusiasm, admiration.

We get several glimpses of him in his glory and find
him less amiable than of old in the rue de Vaugirard. " A
middle-sized man with a fat and puffy face," wrote Count
Rudolph Apponyi in 1834. He had grown stout. " The
world and his waistcoat are not wide enough to contain
the glory of Victor Hugo—or his corpulence," jested Théophile Gautier. " Hugo is worse than an egoist, he is
a Hugoist," sneered Heine, and in fact, as we know,
our poet's device was *Ego Hugo*. An Englishman, John
Forster, travelling with Charles Dickens in 1846, has left a
pleasanter picture, admiring the sober grace and self-posses-
sion of his host.

Rather under the middle size, of compact, close buttoned-up
figure, with ample, dark (?) hair falling loosely over his close-shaven
face. I never saw upon any features so keenly intellectual, such
a soft and sweet geniality, and certainly never heard the French
language spoken with the picturesque distinction given it by
Victor Hugo.

Charles Dickens noted Madame Hugo, " a little, sallow
lady, with dark flashing eyes." " Her strange, almost wild
beauty (wrote Alphonse Karr) was embalmed in an apparent
serenity which sprang from a wandering fancy, a frequent
absent-mindedness." Under her painted ceiling, among her
Venetian mirrors, old gilded furniture, and Persian carpets,
she too was a picturesque figure in the Hugo collection.
And, so far as her husband went, she was not much more.
For Madame Hugo was not a manager, had no sort of

genius for housekeeping, and, since their explanation after 1830, she had lived like a sister in the poet's house.

Hugo certainly suffered both physically and morally more than she could imagine from this situation. His was a powerful and a sensual nature, a prodigious temperament. His barber complained that Hugo's beard took the edge off any razor. At forty he cracked the kernels of peaches with his teeth ; even in his old age, according to that agreeable trifler, Lockroy, he ate his oranges with the peel on and his lobsters in their shell, " because he found them more digestible." His appetite (which was hungry, not greedy) alarmed the good Théo. " You should see the fabulous medley he makes on his plate of all sorts and conditions of viands : cutlets, a salad of white beans, stewed beef and tomato sauce, and watch him devour them, very fast, and during a long time."

" Hugo is one of the Forces of Nature ! " cried Flaubert, " and there circulates in his veins the sap of trees."

This was the man who was condemned to live like a widower in the house of the ailing, beautiful woman he adored. I think it was not only love for Sainte-Beuve that kept Madame Hugo from her husband ; I have sometimes wondered whether her prudent father, M. Foucher, put his spoke in the wheel. Father and daughter were great cronies now ; he was a widower with a little girl of twelve or fourteen whom the elder sister mothered. And the old gentleman was alarmed by the fragility of Adèle (whose mother had died young), and feared for the future of four little children whose father was a poet with no solid fortune behind him. Hugo's grandfather had had twelve children—his great-grandfather eight. Doubtless that poor Countess Hugo had escaped, thanks to the separation on her return from Spain. At least, so I imagine M. Foucher holding forth. Meanwhile Hugo was writing.

> Si jamais vous n'avez, à l'heure où tout sommeille,
> Tandis qu'elle dormait, oublieuse et vermeille,
> Pleuré comme un enfant à force de souffrir,
> Crié cent fois son nom du soir jusqu'à l'aurore,
> Et cru qu'elle viendrait en l'appelant encore,
> Et maudit votre mère, et désiré mourir.
>
> *Feuilles d'automne.*

So long as Adèle had loved him—so long as he could say of her as one day he wrote of their daughter : " Rien qu'en m'aimant, elle m'aidait "—he had been blind to her deficiencies. He had not remarked how her mind wandered as she listened to his vibrating discourse ; how she forgot her housewifely duties in these long absent-minded reveries, when she would sit, like a drugged thing, gazing at nothingness ; he did not complain of her poor housekeeping, at the fire unlit in his study, at the linen unmended on his shelf. He thought such things natural in a delicate woman. Adèle Hugo was one of those Southern natures who pass from a state of dreamiest detachment to an impassioned enthusiasm—habitually calm, almost lethargic, but suddenly animated by a fierce exclusive fanaticism for some object, a sick child, a lover, a religious devotion, the staging of a play. There is something in them at once animal, absolute, and severe. Victor Hugo did not see his wife as this instinctive Creole creature, but as an angel, rather a conventional sort of angel, with her children on her knees, and a host of little orphans sheltering under her white wings. Charitable she was, and a good mother, and sincerely religious. I fancy that Hugo naïvely tried to stuff some part of the void in his life with a platonic friendship for Mademoiselle Louise Bertin, the pleasant, clever, spinster daughter of the editor of the *Débats*. The Hugos, during several summers, spent their holidays in the Bertins' hospitable country house at Bièvres. Mademoiselle Louise was almost as good as Victor himself at telling stories to the little ones ; together they cut out and gummed and painted wonderful paper coaches and toys ; together they concocted an opera, *La Esmeralda*, taken from *Notre-Dame de Paris*. It was all very pleasant and delightful, but it was not love. And Victor Hugo's poetry depended on his passions ; passionate love was the stimulant that released his genius. Love was the magic word, the sesame, that opened his treasure-house. He has said so, in prose and in verse, in his letters and his poems, many a time ; and in so saying he simply told the truth. During those eighteen months in which he lived in abstinence, while Adèle cherished her grievance against him, his poetic faculty appears at once complicated and impoverished. *Le Roi s'amuse* is a most ingenious piece of mechanical invention, as nicely calculated as a problem in Euclid, but it leaves us cold ; *La Esmeralda* is a pleasant pastime for a country house ; *Lucrezia Borgia* is far-fetched, forced, and ultra-Romantic—above all, it is in prose !

He felt the lack of the divine spark, and, turning from poetry to politics, sought a different inspiration. But in that region, also, nothing grand, nothing glorious aroused his spirit. The Revolution of July had only served to inaugurate a change of despotisms. The whole nati n was in a state of unrest. There were constant riots an cruel repressions. Those were the days when Casimir Périer, Guizot, and the Conservative *bourgeoisie* were painfully creating a party, and indeed a government, which were in the end to prove the most judicious and the most table that the nineteenth century had so far produced in Fr nce ; but in the beginning its moderate policy pleased no one, and, as a newspaper remarked : " Everybody was dissatisfied with everybody all round." No one was more dissatisfied than Victor Hugo. He had not abandoned the Bourbons in order to further the triumph of shopkeepers.

In June 1832 the cholera was raging in Paris. It had carried off Casimir Périer in May ; in June it carried off General Lamarque, the Liberal orator. t his funeral there broke out a riot of the Republican party, the most serious since 1830. For twenty-four hours the future of the monarchy was in peril. Victor Hugo was not as yet a Republican, but he was daily more disgusted with the methods of Louis-Philippe, Guizot, Thiers—all the idols of the *bourgeoisie*. On the 9th of June we find him writing to Sainte-Beuve :

One day we shall have a Republic, and we shall see that it is good. Let us know how to wait. The Republic that France shall proclaim in all Europe will be the crown of our grey hairs.

Meanwhile—" Sachons attendre ! " Victor Hugo had his system. For the last twelve months he had been, if not conspiring, at least corresponding, with King Joseph

Bonaparte, his father's old patron, at this date an exile in London, to whom he had written in September 1831 :

I believe in the future of your nephew (the Duke of Reichstadt, the ex-King of Rome), he must arrive in the natural course of events. But it is good sometimes that the hand of man should help on the natural course of events. . . . If he gives us guarantees for the furtherance of our ideas of emancipation, progress, and liberty, I dare to stand warrant that all the generous youth of France will rally to his cause—and with that generous youth of France, obscure though I be, I have some influence.

But on the 22nd of July 1832 the Duke of Reichstadt died in Vienna. The hope of the Bonapartists had perished. There was nothing now between the monarchy, which dissatisfied everybody, and the republic, for which France was not yet ripe.

The death of his young Prince was not Hugo's only disappointment of that autumn. On the 22nd of November the play, *Le Roi s'amuse,* had been hooted from the stage of the Théâtre Français on its first night, and on the morrow a Ministerial Order had forbidden any further representation. Victor Hugo was furious. Irritable and nervous as he appeared during this period, the arbitrary action of the Government lashed him almost to fury. Louis-Philippe, on his accession, had sworn never to re-establish the Censure. And what was such an interdiction but a Censure ? The poet summoned the Minister before the Tribunal of Commerce. In a letter to the newspaper, *Le Constitutionnel,* which created some hilarity among his opponents (it is, I think, the first appearance of Victor Hugo in that comic part of Don Pomposo, which, alas ! he will more than once, in all good faith, repeat), the poet implored " la généreuse jeunesse des écoles et des ateliers " not to rise up in revolution to avenge him, nor provoke on his account " l'émeute que le Gouvernement cherche à se procurer " ! Evidently, in Hugo's eyes, *Hernani* had caused the fall of the Bourbons, and *Le Roi s'amuse* might very well occasion the ruin of the monarchy of July. Like Marcus Curtius, he threw himself into the gulf ! Hugo sometimes took himself and his works very seriously.

Meanwhile, three thousand copies of the censured play
sold in a few weeks. If happiness had flown out of the
window, prosperity had come in at the door. Hugo had
been enriched by the frequent editions of his books, above
all by the success of his dramas. Between 1830 and 1833
the Hospital-tax levied on plays in France brought in
forty - seven thousand francs for *Hernani* and *Marion*
alone.

There were no longer quite so many friends round his
table (for, of course, Sainte-Beuve never came; there was a
coolness with Alfred de Vigny, and our poet's quarrel with
the powers that be had alarmed the conservative Bertins),
nor were there quite so many theatrical managers tumbling
over each other in their zeal as there had been in the shabby
little drawing-room of the rue Notre-Dame des Champs.
The failure of *Le Roi s'amuse* had had a refrigerating effect.
But in December 1832 the manager of the Porte-Saint-
Martin called on Victor Hugo and asked him for the play
which he still had in manuscript : *Lucrezia Borgia*, a melodrama in prose. This manager of the Porte-Saint-Martin
was a certain M. Harel—the same who had tried to wrest
Hernani from the Théâtre Français. He saw his way, he
said, to make an immense success of *Lucrezia Borgia*, which
was to be a marvellous spectacle, with gorgeous Renaissance
costumes and furniture, and slow music playing in the
moving parts. Both Meyerbeer and Berlioz offered to write
the music, but the wise M. Harel would none of them : he
said they would distract the audience's attention from the
piece.

And the actresses were to be as splendid as the stage.
The leading lady, of course, would be Mademoiselle Georges,
a great beauty still, if an old beauty (she had been Napoléon's
mistress twenty years before she had condescended to M.
Harel), whose charms were still admirable by limelight.
The other feminine rôle, that of the Princess Negroni, was
given to a certain young Mademoiselle Juliette, the mistress
of a Russian millionaire, Prince Demidoff, whose brilliance
and wit made her a part of the sparkle of Paris.

Victor Hugo had seen this lady at an artists' ball in the
preceding May, and had been dazzled :

Ses cheveux pétillaient de mille diamants,
Tout en elle était feu qui brille, ardeur qui rit.
Blanche avec des yeux noirs, jeune, grande, éclatante,
Elle allait et passait comme un oiseau de flamme.

And the poet, fascinated, contemplated the brilliant bird of paradise, and dared not approach—

Car le baril de poudre a peur de l'étincelle.
Les Voix intérieures, XII.

Nor had he sought again to encounter this radiant apparition. Austere and highly moral, Victor Hugo had a certain contempt for the beauties of the stage. His attitude towards them was always respectful, prudent, and aloof. His brother-in-law, M. Paul Chenay, among others, has noted his distant manner towards the interpreters of his genius:

For Victor Hugo no woman existed save his Adèle. He went regularly to the theatre, directed the rehearsals, took great pains with the staging, but occupied himself with the actors and actresses exclusively from the professional point of view. He ignored all the rest. None of their provocations or enchantments had any effect on him.[1]

And he was proud of his unspotted reputation. In his Preface to *Le Roi s'amuse* he wrote of the author, that is to say, of himself:

Si son talent peut être contesté de tous, son caractère ne l'est de personne. C'est un honnête homme avéré, prouvé et constaté, chose rare et vénérable en ce temps-ci.

In a letter to Mademoiselle Louise Bertin, written about the same time, he refers to himself as " l'homme tranquille et sérieux." He had never had a mistress, and when he saw a possible temptation in his path, his instinct was to pass on the other side of the way. As one of his disciples said: Victor Hugo is an archangel in a church window.

But everything conspired to bring about his fall: his domestic unhappiness, the dissatisfaction and emptiness of his life, and perhaps especially—after the demi-success of *Marion* and the headlong fall of *Le Roi s'amuse*—the triumph of *Lucrèce*. The play is not a good play, but it

[1] Paul Chenay, *Victor Hugo à Guernesey.*

must be a magnificent, an absorbing spectacle. Never has Victor Hugo revelled in more violent contrasts. The banquet in the halls of the Princess Negroni—the gaiety of an orgy suddenly interrupted by the chant of monks—the Latin plainsong alternating with the drinking-chorus—the apparition, among these splendid youths crowned with roses, of the Brothers of the Misericordia, their faces lost in their black hoods, bearing the five coffins that shortly are to receive the revellers' murdered bodies—and Lucrezia Borgia, inexorable as Fate, suddenly confronted with her more inexorable son.

But perhaps no moment of the play struck the fancy of the audience more violently than the apparition of the Princess Negroni ; Théophile Gautier has recorded its extraordinary brilliance, its unforeseen importance—for the Princess Negroni has really nothing to do except receive the doomed guests, and little to say ; she is " une femme charmante, et de belle humeur, qui aime les vers et la musique." When Juliette Drouet appeared in her sixteenth-century Italian robe of rose-coloured damask, brocaded in cloth of silver, her head and neck wreathed with ropes of pearls beneath a panache of frothing ostrich plumes—when this radiant creature crossed the stage with that airy tread, as of a nymph walking on clouds, which all her admirers have conspired to praise, and stood in front of the banquetters, there was a sort of hush of admiration—" Friendship does not fill the whole heart ! " says Don Maffio Orsini. " Ah—what is it that fills the whole heart ? " sighs the Princess Negroni, turning her wonderful eyes on the author in his box. " Mon Dieu ! Qu'est-ce qui remplit tout le cœur ? "

What could the author do, when the whole house was echoing with a thunder of applause—what could he do but pass behind the scenes to express his gratitude, his devotion to Lucrezia Borgia—and to the Princess Negroni ? We see him then (as Juliette was comically to remind him a few years later when she had reformed his taste in dress), awkward, stiff, unfashionable, lost in his bushy locks like an owl in an ivy bush, his dress-coat some four or five years behind the taste of the day, but admirably eloquent

and courtly in his manners. The Princess Negroni stood
before him smiling, her eyes sweet and sad, her smile gracious
and propitiating—" perfide," says Théophile Gautier—but
full of enchantment. She might have been the Muse—his
own poetry come to life. Actress and author looked at
each other, while the clap and thunder of applause continued from the front. Each owed that moment's draught
of triumph to the other ; it was a philtre that they drank
whose effect was to last for fifty years. It was the night
of the 2nd of February 1833.

Little more than a fortnight later, Juliette Drouet was
Victor Hugo's mistress.

CHAPTER XV

ELIDUC

MADEMOISELLE JULIETTE was no great actress and morally not much superior to a woman on the town. She was (as Mademoiselle Georges hastened to inform Victor Hugo) an extravagant minx, as vain as a peacock, wanton, and not to be trusted. She was the heroine of numerous adventures ; behind that Russian prince, we see the figures of Charles Séchan, the scene-painter of the Opera ; of Alphonse Karr, the novelist ; of Pradier, the sculptor, who was the father of her little girl. At the time when she made the acquaintance of Victor Hugo she seemed inclined to specialize in wealthy foreigners, for, doubtless feeling Demidoff no certain support, she had just written to Count Rodolph Apponyi, a handsome Austrian attaché, offering herself to him. The count in his *Journal* for the year 1833 tells us of her letter, flattering, eloquent, " très bien écrite mais trop longue "—just such epistles as she will send to our poet—inviting him to call on her at her flat in the Boulevard Saint-Martin,—a charming little flat, furnished with great taste and knowledge, where the door was opened by a charming little page in livery. There he met the fair lady, more gracious, more lovely, more sweetly smiling than on the stage of the Porte-Saint-Martin, who forthwith scolded him, flattered him, flirted with him, dazzled him and generally threw herself at his head. But Count Rodolph having no use for Mademoiselle Juliette at that moment, easily succeeded in passing her on to one of his compatriots, newly arrived in Paris.

Victor Hugo, of course, thought her an angel, but no one else appears to have shared that opinion. A light woman, indulging a caprice for a candid poet : such was the general verdict. Let Hugo enjoy his little hour of sunny bliss ! It would not last long. Even Madame Hugo appears to have accepted this view of the situation, and we find her father writing to a friend : " Mille remercîments de vos détails sur la Princesse Negroni. Je suis bien aise qu'Adèle soit tranquille."

Father and daughter might have been less easy in their minds had they realized that, behind the last ten years of Parisian adventure, sixteen honest, honourable years had combined to form a being dangerously attractive. The beautiful Juliette was the daughter of a tailor at Fougères in Brittany ; her real name was Julienne Gauvain, but, left an orphan in her babyhood, she had been adopted by a bachelor uncle, Lieutenant Drouet, who, having fought half the battles of the Empire, had been given the command of a coast-guard station. He took the little two-year-old home with him, and she ran wild to her heart's delight on moor and shore. There was a school in the village—but there was also a pond and a wood. Julienne as a rule preferred the water-lilies and the dragon-flies to the glory of good marks ; and something wild and delicious remained with her from these truant years. She was able to share with Victor Hugo what hitherto, in all his affections, he had never found any one to fully comprehend—the most enchanted, attentive, reverent delight in Nature and natural objects. It was a great bond. Over and over again in his poems he refers to this faculty of Juliette's :

> celle
> Qui sait tous les secrets que mon âme recèle. . . .
> Car elle a dans le cœur cette fleur large et pure,
> L'amour mystérieux de l'antique Nature.[1]

When Juliette was ten years old, the uncle who spoiled and adored her (just as Jean Valjean adored Cosette) awoke to the sense of his responsibilities in regard to the child's education. M. Drouet had a sister and a cousin who were choir sisters in the Convent of the rue du Petit Picpus at Paris, belonging to the Benedictine Order of Perpetual Adoration of the Holy Sacrament. Here the little girl

---

[1] À Virgile, *Les Voix intérieures*, VII.

received an education which exalted and exasperated a vein of mystical sensibility inherent in her Breton heart. She, like the nuns, was to be vowed, one distant day, to a service of Perpetual Adoration, only the object of her cult was not the same. Meanwhile, she learned to paint in water-colours, to sing, to recite, and the art of good manners. Mademoiselle Juliette, sometimes as slangy as a street Arab, could also receive in the manner of the noble Faubourg. She was at once more " peuple " and more highly-bred than Adèle Foucher.

At sixteen years of age, in 1822, Juliette left the convent. What became of her then it is impossible to say : her trace is lost. In 1825 we come across her again :—Pradier's model, Pradier's mistress, and the mother of his little girl. It was Pradier who more or less pushed her on to the stage, where she made her way by dint of her radiant beauty, her aerial carriage, and her ambition—rather than by her talent ; she seems to have had no special gift for the theatre. But she learned by heart the rôles of all Victor Hugo's heroines, and could discuss them with him in a mood of passionate interest and vibrating admiration.

If Madame Hugo had been aware of all this, she would perhaps have trembled. But at first she did not greatly fear the stage princess, knowing the austerity and the jealous temper of Victor Hugo. Paris rang with the scandal, but the blacker her friends painted Juliette, the less redoubtable she must have appeared :

> Puisqu'un si noble époux par Phryné t'est ravi

rhymed Sainte-Beuve, and the fires lit by Phryné are flames fed by straw.

It is true that Victor was evidently changed—more absent-minded now than Adèle herself—constantly away from home ; but his quarrels and his jealousies were appeased, at any rate in the sphere of the Place Royale, though rumours came of terrible scenes with his new divinity. In the end of 1833, in the beginning of 1834, more than once the discordant lovers strove to break their bonds ; on one occasion Juliette Drouet attempted suicide. At every turn she exasperated two of Victor Hugo's most sensitive fibres : the jealous horror of unfaithfulness in woman, and his

exact and methodical sense of order.   When he thought of
the past—when he brushed against Séchan in the wings of
his theatre, or ran up against Alphonse Karr at a newspaper office—he hated his idol.   And her manner of life
filled him with stupor.   Juliette had broken with Prince
Demidoff, but she had altered none of her princely habits.
Harel gave her twenty pounds a month.   When that
engagement came to an end, when Victor Hugo imposed
her on the Théâtre Français, during the three years of his
engagement, she was paid at the rate of a hundred and
twenty pounds a year.   Meanwhile the bills came pouring in.
Juliette, who adored her poet, had not the courage to make
a clean breast of them, but went, hat in hand, and all in
vain, the round of her discarded lovers.   Nothing could
have been more galling to the dignity of Victor Hugo, but
judge of his dolorous astonishment when at last confronted
with the copious bundle—twelve thousand francs due to
the goldsmith ; a thousand to the glover ; six hundred to
the washerwoman ; four hundred for rouge, let alone the
dressmaker, the vendor of Cashmere shawls, and the up-
holsterer !   In November Juliette had created the rôle of
Jane in Victor Hugo's new play of *Marie Tudor*, and had been
hissed from the stage—the part had to be given the very
next night to an understudy.   Her future as an actress
looked very dark.   She was just a pretty woman with a
poet for her surety and no Russian millionaire nowadays in
the background.   All the hounds of debt closed in upon her
traces.   Victor Hugo was horrified, not only at the expense
to be met but at the habits which these debts revealed.
Meanwhile Juliette's landlord threatened to turn her out
of doors ; there was a man in possession, and (as she
sorrowfully remarks in one of her letters) her chemises were
sold by auction on the Place du Châtelet, except those which
were already safe in pawn at the Mont-de-Piété.

After one scene, stormier than the others, Juliette fled
to Brest, where she had a sister married.   But if the lovers
could not dwell together in amity, they found it still more
impossible to live apart.   Victor Hugo took the diligence
for Brest.   It is somewhat disconcerting, I must admit, to
find him, while on this excursion, sending to his wife, who

was staying at Bièvres with the Bertins, letters that can only be described as love-letters ; writing : " Je t'aime ! Tu es la joie et l'honneur de ma vie ! " ; writing that what is never weary, never tired of remembering is " the heart of your poor old husband, who was the friend of your childhood, though he has grown old, and you in heart, soul, and face have kept your youth." But such is man ! Victor Hugo, at any rate, was like that Crusader in a mediaeval poem (the *Eliduc* of Marie de France), who loved with equal love the Christian wife whom he respected and the Pagan wife whom he converted to the true faith.

That he continued to love Adèle is certain. Not only are his poems full of her, but also his correspondence. On the 25th of July 1833 he writes to his friend Victor Pavie, in Anjou :

I have by my side a kind and dear friend in my wife—an angel, as you know, you, who revere her : an angel whose heart is full of love and forgiveness. To love—and to forgive : that passes the knowledge of man ! Only God or a woman can compass it.

This habit of deceit, this double life—and especially the prodigious adulation of his Juliette, which fostered in her poet a fatuity, a self-complacency that caricatures the serene sweetness of his earlier years—were certainly detrimental to the moral integrity of Victor Hugo. From this date forward we remark a debasement of the value he sets on love. Juliette will not long remain his only mistress. But especially her influence was evil, because of that unstinted flattery which bathed her hero in a light that never was on sea or land. Although, no doubt, the last relic of the habits of a courtezan, her coaxing ways, her smooth and fawning compliments, were in the main sincere ; for in Juliette's eyes her " Toto " was a god—or at least a demi-god (for she thought him stingy, fussy, fastidious and jealous, which qualities are not divine)—who had saved her alive from the abyss of iniquity and set her straight with her fellow-mortals.

So it was. In the eyes of Victor Hugo she was Marion de Lorme—the courtezan to be purified by a great love and a great repentance. In 1834 he decided to assume the burden of her redemption. Little by little he would pay all her

debts, setting so much aside every month for this purpose.
According to the flesh he was no longer his wife's husband; he
would be Juliette's husband and she must consecrate herself
utterly to him, and by prayer, solitude, voluntary poverty
and work drive out her seven devils.   He hired for her a
small and humble flat of three rooms in which she must be
her own servant, with perhaps some little help for the
roughest toil.   She must live there *in pace*, receiving no one,
never crossing the threshold save on her poet's arm.   In
the secret album of their love he wrote one day :

Never forget, my Angel, the mysterious hour that changed
the course of all your life.   That Carnival night, that 17th of
February 1833, you left without, on the further side the door,
all glitter and display, all tumult and rumour, and the excitement of crowds ; that night you entered into mystery and
solitude and love.

So Juliette lived for years, immured and dedicated to her
earthly idol, no less than the holy ladies of Picpus to their
Lord.   The splendid trappings of her life of sin were sold.
Victor Hugo bought in just sufficient to furnish a tiny flat
hired, at a rent of £16 a year, in the rue du Paradis ; two
rooms and a kitchen.   There Juliette set up house.   Victor
Hugo allowed her some thirty pounds a month, which he
increased by one-third after 1838, of which a part was to be
saved to pay off her creditors, and he strictly inspected her
accounts every week.

My poverty, my cheap shoes, my soiled window curtains,
my iron spoons, the absence of all luxury and all pleasure save
our love alone, prove every hour and every minute that I love
you with all the loves a heart can hold.

So writes, and more than once, the poor Princess Negroni,
once so brilliant, once so gay.   But the hardest sacrifice of
all was that of her liberty.   As a little child, as a woman,
she had been free as air—free and fantastic as a fairy ; and
what were the restrictions of her girlhood compared to those
she now endured ?   In the convent she had enjoyed a
great garden and the society of cheerful companions.   Here,
in her narrow cell, she was immured, buried alive.   She
might neither go out nor receive.   One or two humble

women friends, at most, are allowed to call on her. Her
marketings, her visits to her old uncle (now a pensioner at
the Invalides), or to her little girl at school, even her
appointments with the dentist or the dressmaker, had to
await the leisure of her severe protector. For he was
implacable. A devotee of the natural holiness of woman,
he had no faith in her virtue, her power of resistance. She
was an angel who must be kept out of harm's way! Poor
Juliette suffered in her health, in her beauty as well as in
her spirits—felt herself growing fat, flabby, losing her
elastic tread and her brilliant repartee. The time drags on
her hands. In winter, from lack of fuel and occupation,
she is sometimes driven to spend her day, miserably dozing,
in her bed. She breaks out in accents of bitter revolt:

What am I but a dog in his yard? A plate of soup, a kennel,
and a chain, such is my lot! But there are dogs whose masters
come to take them out a walk. Happy fellows, I envy them!
My chain is riveted too firmly for you to have any idea of un-
loosing it.

And again, with what an accent of wounded dignity:

Believe me, my Victor, this sedentary life, this life of isolation,
is really killing me. I wear out my soul in waiting for you. I
wear out my life in pacing a chamber twelve foot by twelve.
What I long for, is not the world and its stupid pleasures—but
freedom, freedom to gang my gait, freedom to occupy my time
and strength in the useful business of my house and home;
what I want, is to suffer less, for I suffer a thousand deaths a
minute; what I ask is: to live—to live, *like you, like everybody else.*

Gradually, as the bonds that held Juliette to her past
perished in her solitude, the strictness of her sequestration
was relaxed, but not in any notable degree until she had
passed her fortieth year: from 1833 till 1846 the patient
woman lived the life of a recluse. She occupied her terrible
leisure by employing herself as Victor Hugo's secretary,
copying all his manuscripts, filing his letters, helping to
correct his proofs, and he was so abundant a writer that he
gave her plenty to do; still buoyed up by the hope of a
future on the stage, where, as a great actress, she should
interpret her lover's genius. She learned by heart every
female part in his plays; every day she wrote to him

interminable love-letters which were his joy and pride ; she would mend his linen, darn his clothes, of which the neglected state filled her with a certain proud and bitter satisfaction ; at nightfall she would set aside her pen and her needle, build in her icy grate a comfortable fire, prepare an evening meal less meagre than her earlier repasts, in case her " cher petit homme," her " Toto, le plus beau, le plus séduisant des hommes," should appear, and, as often happened, after a supper full of boyish frolic, work silently by her side far into the night.

Then there were also those blessed times, the holidays :

Il fait fameusement beau (she writes on the 17th of September 1835) ; nous allons recommencer notre vie d'oiseaux—notre vie d'amour en liberté, notre vie dans les bois !

These first three summers she lodged in a peasant's cottage *aux Metz*, a few miles from Bièvre, where the Hugos stayed with the Bertins. In later years she accompanied her poet farther afield. By the seashore, in a forest, she felt herself more equally his mate. Lovers of Victor Hugo's Nature poems owe to Madame Drouet an incalculable debt. They should read in M. Guimbaud's invaluable and most moving book [1] the list of the pages which are inspired by her. *La Tristesse d'Olympio* commemorates a visit which they made together to that cottage of Les Metz where he used to house his unlawful lady. Fifty other poems, among the loveliest of our poet's lyrics, were written for Juliette, her lover's companion in these long tramps by wood or shore in which he delighted.

Adèle was more in her element on a lawn, languidly reclining, watching the children play, an embroidery frame beside her. Juliette, frank and free, with her tomboy slang and her wild delight, was never so happy as when, let out of prison, she climbed the Breton rocks, or the Alpine glaciers, or, in the woods of Les Metz, waited in a hollow chestnut tree, which was their trysting-place, the coming of her poet. Although she wrote no books, she was cleverer than Adèle, more direct, more living, vibrating with a hundred delicate varieties.

[1] Louis Guimbaud, *Victor Hugo et Juliette Drouet*, Paris, Blaizot, 1914.

These two women, either charming, reflected their double image in the poet's mind, and in one of his plays, which is not among the best of his plays but on their account interesting, he has portrayed them both. *Angelo, Tyrant of Padua*, is a melodrama in prose, full of romantic figments, hollow walls in which villains walk, crucifixes that reveal unsuspected relations in the past, sbirros, and secret keys ; we expect to find a strawberry mark on Tisbe's shoulder! Like so much of Victor Hugo's prose work, it is at once absurd and charming—none the less delightful, I think, for that solemn poetic foolery, as of a wise child making believe. A great part of the action takes place in the bed-chamber of Caterina, wife of the Tyrant of Padua, " chambre redoutable où nul homme ne peut pénétrer, car y entrer, en entr'ouvrir la porte seulement, c'est un crime puni de mort ! " But it is astonishing what a quantity of persons do manage to penetrate this secret chamber : Angelo himself, and his mistress the actress ; Angelo's wife and her lover ; a Venetian spy ; any amount of ushers, ladies' maids, watchmen, pages, priests, privy-murderers, headsmen, sbirri, and so on—they come in and out, from secret panels in the wall, as easily and freely as they might cross the Place de la Concorde. But these incongruities do not destroy the charm of the two heroines. Caterina is the Tyrant's wife, as pure, as limpid, and as still as a drop of holy water in a crystal stoop—a sweet creature, dreamy and gentle, confiding as a child, paralysed by danger, a timid, eager woman, bold only in defence of what she loves. Although she has been married five years, there is more of the girl in her than the woman, perhaps more of the child than the girl. She has an innocent intrigue with a Platonic lover, and thereupon has broken with her husband : " elle est resteé fidèle à son amour et à son honneur, à Ridolfo et à son mari." Although the jealous Angelo shuts her in her chamber, he cannot make her forget ; he has no power over the heart of the languid, gentle being, apparently entirely at his mercy. She lives in the past, with no remorse for that past. " Je ne suis pas coupable, pas très coupable vraiment ! J'ai peut-être fait quelque imprudence. Mais c'est que je n'ai plus ma mère ! " In Caterina there is a

Desdemona-like quality, innocent, helpless, touching. Like a certain heroine of Browning's, " She's a woman like a dewdrop, so much purer than the purest." And yet she is impassioned. " Did I love her ? (cries Ridolfo). The purest thing—chaste, sacred—a woman like a shrine ! " In contemplating this portrait of Caterina, in comparing it with those lilied lyrics addressed to Adèle Hugo in the *Chants du crépuscule*—all of them written since the affair with Sainte-Beuve—I have sometimes wondered whether these effusions really represented Hugo's view of his wife's character, or whether they were designed as a sort of vestal veil, shielding the reality from public view and protecting Caesar's wife from suspicion, and Caesar from an absurd dishonour. And I have never quite made up my mind. For Hugo, filled with the sincerest remorse for his own adultery, was as capable of the most candid admiration for his wife, as of a chivalrous comedy got up to deceive the public. In either case the verses are admirable, and that after all is our chief affair.

To return to Caterina—she is saved by the cleverness and the heroism of her rival, Tisbe the courtezan, Tisbe the actress, thrown on the streets at sixteen years of age, familiar with every aspect of life : a generous woman of the people, overflowing with life and talk, poignant and picturesque in her expressions, instinctive, sensual, sometimes a little vulgar, as brave as a lion, as tender-hearted as a child, and sparkling as spring-water, garrulous, quarrelsome, jealous and gay, full of wit and quick invention. In Tisbe we have an admirable portrait of Juliette Drouet.

Juliette learned the rôle by heart, as she learned all the female parts in Hugo's plays, and she longed to act it. But he gave the part to Mademoiselle Mars. Since the fiasco of *Marie Tudor*, he seems to have made no great effort to produce his mistress on the stage. Was it that, like Angelo of Padua, he died of jealousy to see her beauty displayed to any fellow in the stalls ? Was it because he mistrusted her talent, or had gauged her capacity for stage fright ? Despite poor Juliette's begging and praying, he did not unlock her prison door. It was only in 1838 that he consented, or appeared to consent, to his mistress's reappearance before the footlights.

I reserve for another chapter the intricate story of
Victor Hugo's reconciliation with the reigning Royal House,
and especially his attachment to the Duke of Orleans and
his wife, through whose intervention, in 1838, our poet
found himself with a stage at his disposal, more or less
dedicated to his genius. For this theatre, the Renaissance,
he wrote perhaps the best of all his plays, *Ruy Blas*. And
he proposed to his enchanted, half-incredulous Juliette, to
create the part of the heroine, Marie de Neubourg. We
may imagine her delight !

It was short-lived. In every human story there are
passages which it is impossible to make clear—and this, for
me, is one of the obscurest in the story of Victor Hugo. If
ever there was a woman whose dreamy detachment was
redeemed by a spirit of magnanimity, it was Adèle Hugo.
But the human heart is full of surprises. I have said else-
where that Madame Hugo, although no judge of lyric poetry,
was a passionate admirer of the drama, her husband's confidant and adviser in every detail of the production of his
plays. When she learned that Mademoiselle Juliette was
to create the part of the Queen in *Ruy Blas* she did an extraordinary thing. She said nothing to her husband, but she
took up her pen and wrote to the Manager of the Renaissance,
begging him to give the part to another actress :

My husband takes an interest in the lady and it is natural
that he should wish to support her claims ; but I can not admit
that an artist, of whose talent the public holds, rightly or
wrongly, a most unfavourable opinion, should imperil the success
of one of the most beautiful plays in the language.[1]

The poet made no protest and Juliette was sacrificed.
She never again appeared on the stage. " We married so
young," wrote Adèle, " I should never think of binding you
to the old woman I have become." But at least, as she
watched over and protected the children of her poet's body,
so too she would jealously guard from harm or scandal the
children of his brain.

Did she, perhaps, exact the sacrifice of Juliette as a
compensation to her rupture with Sainte-Beuve ? For at

[1] Gustave Simon, *La Vie d'une femme*, pp. 228-30.

this moment there was another, a second or third rupture
with Sainte-Beuve.   For some years after 1831, Victor Hugo
had kept his wife and his friend apart.   Sainte-Beuve was
never invited to the house save on such state occasions as
the reading of a play.   But as Madame Hugo gradually
regained her health and spirits, she could not remain
sequestered.   She had a father and a little sister, married
brothers, a married brother-in-law, uncles and aunts, hosts
of friends living in Paris.   She visited the Bertins, and the
Nodiers at the Arsenal, and several other houses where
Sainte-Beuve was also a visitor.   She went to church ; she
went to the theatre ; she shopped ; she took her little boys
to school ; she dined out with her husband.   Count Rodolph
Apponyi, who did not admire her, notes with some surprise
her success in society in his *Journal* for the year 1836 :

Madame Victor Hugo, a person of a very common appearance, yet undeniably handsome.   She talked a great deal, but
intelligently, with too much seeking after effect.   But the
gentlemen seemed to appreciate her immensely.

It is impossible that, frequenting the same circle, Sainte-
Beuve and Madame Hugo should not have met; indeed, more
than one passage in the poet-critic's *Penseés d'août* indicates
the cemetery of the Père La Chaise as the place where they
held their melancholy and sentimental rendezvous.   When,
in 1835, Madame Hugo went to Angers, with her father and
Léopoldine, to attend the wedding of their friend Victor
Pavie, she mentions, without any beating about the bush,
in her letters to her husband, the presence of Sainte-Beuve,
and his kind attentions to them all.   In fact, we *know* that
she met Sainte-Beuve, from that infamous journal in verse
of their love affair which he called the *Livre d'amour* : it
was finished about this date, 1837.   And just about that
time a violent scene, which still remains obscure and un-
explained, expelled Sainte-Beuve anew from the poet's circle,
and on this occasion it appears that Madame Hugo took the
part of her husband.   It has been affirmed, and it may
be true—so surprising is human nature—that the cause of
that angry outburst was a pang of wounded vanity—a bad
review.   Victor Hugo was always absurdly sensitive to

criticism—capable of being flattered by the praise of the *Progrès de Carcassonne* and stung to a contemptuous rage by the blame of the *Libéral de Landerneau*; infinitely greater was the value that he set on the opinion of Sainte-Beuve, who, whether disciple, friend, or foe, was always the first of French reviewers. But may not Hugo have suspected the writing of the *Livre d'amour*? In any case, the poet violently broke with the man who had so grievously wronged him ; and Adèle Hugo sided with her husband. The breach was complete. Its first result was to inspire Sainte-Beuve with some really beautiful lyrics—poems whose deep, restrained emotion and contained sensibility foretell Sully-Prudhomme and, perhaps, Baudelaire :

> Oh laissez moi sans trève écouter ma blessure,
>   Aimer mon mal et ne vouloir que lui,
> Celle en qui je croyais, celle qui m'était sûre. . . .
>   Laissez-moi ! Tout a fui !

But, having expressed his feelings in verse that at last satisfied his fastidious taste, the critic did not persist too obstinately in a passion which it appeared impossible to satisfy. The most intelligent of men, he was not by nature romantic. The charm of the absent Adèle ceased to operate, and he turned his thoughts from love and religion to literature and history. I think that he never forgave his lady's dereliction, and the burning rancour with which he recalled his wrongs helped to cauterize his passion. Those first lyrics, full of wounded love, are none the less penetrating and sincere that they soon ceased to correspond to the poet's mood. In 1840 they appeared, with a few others discreetly culled from the most indiscreet and secret *Livre d'amour*, in an appendix to an edition of Sainte-Beuve's *Poésies complètes*. Madame Hugo read them. Her anger had long since melted—was she ever angry long ?—and she was proud of the poems that she had inspired. She came rushing back, asking forgiveness, or so Sainte-Beuve would fain have us believe. In a letter addressed to the critic a few years later, Madame Hortense Allard de Méritens exclaims :

No wonder that such accents brought a woman back from the end of the world ! And she will call again at your door, and again you will receive her and forgive. And you will do well. One ought to have treasures of pardon reserved for such natures, in part so admirable, and who, themselves, are only conscious of those finer parts.

Against this passage of Madame Allard's letter Sainte-Beuve has scrawled, on the margin of the letter, " Madame V. Hugo," while at the bottom of the page he has written a long footnote :

And so I do forgive her, but that is all ! Come now, admit that a spice of intelligence, a hint of grace, a little sensibility are desirable accompaniments even to a grand and sublime passion—these charming little ingredients are especially useful in the intervals, and they have always been lacking in my superb, stern and violent Adèle.

Their meetings more and more often ended in partings. In 1872 the Hugos' second boy was attacked with lung trouble and dangerously ill. Adèle Hugo in her despair beseeched Sainte-Beuve to call at the house and see the apparently dying " Toto." What happened then ? I know not ; in some way it was the occasion of another rupture ; perhaps thereby Adèle sought to placate indignant Heaven. At any rate, by 1843 Sainte-Beuve must have felt there would be no further sonnets to add to his immortal poem, for then he began the secret printing of the *Livre d'amour*, which was, according to his intention, only to see the light after the death of the three persons primarily interested.

Victor Hugo knew nothing of the printing of that libel (long after the death of Madame Hugo, of Sainte-Beuve, after his return from exile in 1870, he learned of its existence), but he already guessed enough to make him loathe the man who had once been his familiar friend. What is the plot of *Ruy Blas*, the play which he composed in the summer of 1838 ? An infamous snare, laid out of spite and vengeance, by a vile intriguer to entangle the feet of an imprudent lady.

Œil pour œil, dent pour dent, c'est bon, hommes contre hommes ;
Mais doucement détruire une femme, et creuser
Sous ses pieds une trappe et, contre elle, abuser
Qui sait ? de son humeur peut-être hasardeuse,

Prendre ce pauvre oiseau dans quelque glu hideux,
. . . J'aimerais mieux, plutôt qu'être à ce point infâme,
Vil, odieux, pervers, misérable et flétri,
Qu'un chien rongeât mes os au pied du pilori.[1]

All the chivalry of Victor Hugo rose up in wrath to avenge the injured lady on the treacherous squire. But he no longer says : *Date lilia !* The Angel in the House has become a poor limed bird, perhaps imprudent in its flights and flutterings ; an object to be regarded with that mingling of pity, tenderness, and profound disenchantment which is often the ultimate residue of a romantic passion.

Adèle disappears from his poems. Or, if her phantom revisits them, it is as the mother of his children, or else in such ironic stanzas as those called *1822* in the second volume of *Toute la lyre* : . . . Ah, you think it will last for ever, this youthful passion ? You imagine each other perfect ? Alas ! . . . Youth is very young ! Youth is blind !

The woman who henceforth in his life will occupy a place apart, though on no pedestal ; the woman on whom he relies ; of whose faithful tenderness he is sure ; the woman whom he considers as the immortal companion of his life beyond the grave—his *dimidium animae*, is not his wife, Adèle, but her whom he saved from perdition, Juliette.

And Sainte-Beuve, on the brink of old age, reviewing the past, remembering all that his passion for his friend's wife had brought him, and all that it had lost him and cost him, will write against her name this sentence of rancour : " Je la hais ! "

She had been wiser to have remained the Lady of the Lilies.

[1] *Ruy Blas.*

CHAPTER XVI

VICTOR HUGO AS RUY BLAS

WHILE Victor Hugo's heart was divided between his wife and his mistress, his imagination was invaded by the apparition of a Royal Lady, not beautiful, but gentle, candid, courageous, intelligent, and good, for whom he felt something of the love of the moth for the star. She had won his deep devotion by quoting his own poetry to him, at length, in her charming foreign accent : on hearing his name, she had exclaimed that she knew him already ; she had read all his books ! When he had first met her in February 1837, at a fête given at Versailles in honour of her wedding, she had seemed to him a sweet and simple " schöne Seele," impatient of the formal trivialities of courts, to whom he might communicate his humanitarian zeal. She was Helena of Mecklenburg-Schwerin, the bride of the Duke of Orleans, heir to the throne, who had married her in default of the Austrian Archduchess whom Metternich refused. Victor Hugo thought her " une femme rare, d'un grand esprit et d'un grand sens," and considered her insufficiently appreciated in the sphere of the Tuileries. But the King was old. One day Hélène d'Orléans would be Queen of France. The poet went home and dreamed of Ruy Blas, the lowly-born Minister of a Royal Lady to whom he is devoted heart and soul.

Through his friendship with the Duchess of Orleans he approached the awkward, charming Duke, and met from both the royal couple the same flattering sympathy. They attracted him to that court circle which he had viewed with little sympathy after 1830, and from which the disgrace of *Le Roi s'amuse* had still further estranged him. The Duke

exerted himself to procure an audience for our poet, exiled
from the Théâtre Français, " voué aux morts," and from the
Porte-Saint-Martin, " voué aux bêtes," and contrived to place
at his disposal the Théâtre de la Renaissance. Drawn into
the orbit of the Tuileries, Hugo found his prejudice against
the King evaporate before the charm of a singularly gifted
though marvellously obstinate old man, and one day was to
draw for us (in *Les Misérables*) perhaps the most striking
portrait we possess of Louis-Philippe. Meanwhile his new
dream occupied his brain. He had written *Ruy Blas* in
five weeks in the summer of 1838 ; it is one of the most
brilliant of his plays, a masterpiece of versification and of
style. When it had left the stage after more than fifty
representations, the theme continued to absorb him : the
conception of a poet turned statesman, saviour of society,
voice of the people, a great heart, interpreting to the rich
the misery of the poor, like Gwynplaine in *L'Homme qui
rit*. Ultimately, it is what he will become. But, at this
moment of his life, too much personal ambition mingled with
his aims. He was not as yet Gwynplaine ; he was merely
Ruy Blas.

If Victor Hugo had ceased to exist at any moment
between 1843 and 1852, the world would have reckoned
him an eminent public man in whom a great poet had died
young. Literature for him had become a form of politics.
After the brilliant success of *Ruy Blas* in 1838 he wrote
nothing for several years, but in 1842 the Rhine had become
a political question. Roughly speaking, the Government
was all for peace, an English alliance, and leaving things as
they were ; the Radicals were all for war, for repudiating
the treaties of 1815 and claiming the left bank of the Rhine.
Victor Hugo was undecided where to take his stand ; he was
the most moderate of Liberals, the most liberal of Conserva-
tives. And he went to the Rhine to clear up his ideas,
bringing back the material for an agreeable book of travels,
with, at the end, certain prophetic flashes which reveal a
real political insight. Still, it was not that epoch-making
book which he had meant to write. He brought back also
the idea for a play, *Les Burgraves*, a medley of extraordinary
beauty and fantastic absurdity, which fell from the Paris

stage with a crash that I can only compare to the fall of
the statue of the Commendatore down Don Juan's attic
stairs in the Florentine farce of *Don Giovanni con Stenterello* :
" Heavens ! he has broken all to pieces ! He was only a
plaster cast ! "

The other day, in reading Balzac's *Letters to Madame
Hanska*, I came across an account of the first night of
Les Burgraves, which shows what a great critic the great
novelist might have been :

> There is splendid poetry in it (says Balzac), but Victor Hugo
> has never got further than being an *enfant sublime*, and that is
> all he ever will be. Always the same childish folly of prisons
> and coffins and a thousand ridiculous absurdities. The story
> simply does not exist, the invention is beneath contempt. But
> the poetry—ah, the poetry goes to your head ! It's Titian
> painting his fresco on a wall of mud. Yet there is in Victor
> Hugo's plays an absence of *heart*, which was never so con-
> spicuous. Victor Hugo is not *true*.

In 1842 the public chiefly noticed that the wall was only
pisé, not stone ; in 1920 we observe that the painting on it
is by Titian. Among the younger men of letters in France
there is no praise too high for the verse of *Les Burgraves* ;
they read it as a man with a delicate ear may read
Paradise Lost, and yet, perhaps, care little enough how
Milton interpreted the Fall of Man. The plot, the personages
are not considered, but the magical rhythm, the shifting
music of the caesura, the wonder and variety of the sound.
Moreover, for the first time in the *Burgraves*, Victor Hugo
essays the tone of the epic : the *Burgraves* are absurd considered as a play—admirable, if we take them as an over-
ture to the *Légende des siècles*.

Victor Hugo celebrated the Rhine, not only in prose and
verse, but also with brush and pencil. From this visit to
the Rhine he brought back the first of those extraordinary
drawings, which he will repeat and continue in other journeys
in 1840, 1862, 1863, 1864, 1865, 1869—for he never lost his
interest in the Rhine : " Le Rhin est bien plus français que
ne le pensent les Allemands." These drawings, in pencil,
charcoal, sepia, water-colour, sometimes in powdered coal
and coffee-grounds ! heightened by touches of pure gouache,

chalk, gold, even green or red paint, are of an amazing virtuosity. They frequently recall the drawings of Gustave Doré—but sometimes at their best Rembrandt's etchings, so intensely does the poet indicate the depth, relief, and even the height of objects by the play of light. They are nearly always nocturnes, and a critic has called Victor Hugo, " the Turner of the Night." They exhibit nearly all our poet's defects. They are too clever by half and too dramatic, exaggerated, emphatic, over-picturesque, wildly romantic. And they do not exhibit his greatest qualities— that heart-rending simplicity which, without an image or an adjective, can shake the soul with the impression of great poetry, nor his cosmic emotion. The qualities in his drawings are, I think, those which Nature gave him for his poetry ; and the other ones, the grander ones, are those which he achieved by force of feeling and by force of will. For a poet may be born *and* made.

The same remark holds good of the comic element in his plays. Hugo is sometimes unconsciously amusing by his abuse of the melodramatic ; but there are also in his plays passages of real gaiety, drollery, and comic wit. Students of the original manuscripts (and especially MM. Paul et Victor Glachant in their *Essai critique sur le théâtre de Victor Hugo*) have remarked that these passages do not exist in the original drafts of his manuscripts. The comic did not gush as from a spring in the native spirit of Hugo. But some of the most beautiful fountains are supplied from canalized streams. It was a dogma with Victor Hugo that a tragedy needed comic relief. He wrote the tragedy first —and that flowed naturally enough from his pen—and then, as a matter of principle, by force of will, intention, and unrivalled virtuosity, created such brilliant interludes as the tirades of Don César in *Ruy Blas*.

Well, any gardener could tell us that the rose and the vine need grafting, but the danger of poetry so carefully tended is artificiality ; and, since at this moment of his life no great passion tore from Hugo's breast that lyric cry which needs no *fioritura*, no cadenced fall, it was perhaps well that he turned from art to the headier nepenthe of political ambition. There were two possible avenues to public life : the Chamber of Deputies and the House of Peers ; but only householders or landed proprietors could be elected to the Chamber, and our poet owned neither house nor land. The Peers were appointed by the King from various public bodies ; one of these reserves of recruitment was the French Academy. Victor Hugo presented himself for election in 1836 and was refused ; returned to the charge in 1839, was again rejected ; stood a third time in 1840 with no better luck, and finally got his " armchair," his " fauteuil," in 1841. But a purely literary triumph could not satisfy him. The French Academy was but a glorious stepping-stone. In 1845 he was created a Peer of France. Here, too, his candidature had been beset with difficulties, and probably would not have succeeded if he had not had a devoted and royal " canvasser " in the person of the Duchess of Orleans. Her husband's death in 1842 had increased instead of diminishing the importance of this remarkable young woman. Victor Hugo had made her acquaintance eight years previously. Victor Hugo, as we know, went home and imagined *Ruy Blas*. After the tragic death of the Duke his friendship with the Duchess took on a tone of still tenderer respect. And poor Juliette looked on with gloomy eyes—writing to the poet, for instance (on the 20th of August 1842) :

All this fills me with foreboding and despair. For instance, this visit, this morning, to the Duchess of Orleans, though I own it was kind and attentive of you to take me with you in your cab and let me profit by the drive through Paris. Still, it was little less than torture owing to the circumstances—I, half-dressed and scarcely washed, at such a disadvantage compared to that woman, with the prestige of a great misfortune, which in your eyes I know is, after physical beauty, the greatest of all seductions.

Hugo's political ambition had been stimulated rather than crushed by the sudden death of his friend and patron the Duke of Orleans, in July 1842. The young prince had been driving along a lane at Neuilly, when his horses took fright and bolted—he jumped from his carriage and was killed. The Duke's death was almost more than a national misfortune —" a calamity affecting the fate of Europe," said Lord

Palmerston—for he and his Duchess were popular, Liberal,
intellectual, and philanthropic ; the nation loved them, and
they formed a link between the dynastic and authoritative
old king and the turbulent working-class.   Louis-Philippe
was over sixty ; the heir to the throne was four years old ;
a long Regency appeared in the offing, perhaps a revolution ;
all depended on the character of the Regent.   Who should
fill that office ?   The dead Duke had indicated his brother,
Nemours, whose claims were confirmed by the King and the
Government.   But the Liberal Party, and especially the
Intellectuals, led by Lamartine, Alexis de Tocqueville, Odilon
Barrot, and Victor Hugo, proposed the future Regency of
the Duchess of Orleans.   And if that should ensue, which
of them should be the power behind the throne ?   Who
play the part of Mazarin to her Anne of Austria, or that of
Richelieu to her Marie de Médicis ?   No doubt but Victor
Hugo, no less than Lamartine, felt himself ripe and ready
for the rôle.   Mindful of what the future might reserve, but
none the less devoted to the present, Victor Hugo threw
himself into the cause of social reform : the sufferings of the
poor and needy, the question of their housing and their wage,
compulsory and gratuitous education, universal suffrage, the
abolition of capital punishment, the reform of prisons,
arbitrage between nations, perpetual peace.   But especially
he constituted himself the advocate, the special pleader of
that submerged residue swamped in that extreme of poverty
which the French call " la misère."   He was the champion
of the wretched.

It has been said that Victor Hugo lacked political sense,
that his candour, his vanity, and his prolix enthusiasm
fatigued practical men and did not convince them.   Something of this is true.   Too often, instead of the fact, the
date, the precise detail, which should clinch his point, we
find him declaiming, " I said it, so it must be true ! "   And
perhaps it is exact that his intervention in politics was not
immediately successful.   He voted against the death-penalty,
against transportation, and for every law of social reform
that occupied his times ; but he would yield nothing of his
stubborn independence, no party could count on his support :
he soared above them all in the vague inane, and like

Lamartine he might have answered, when asked on which side of the House he meant to sit : " In the ceiling." So his votes enriched consistently neither socialist nor saint, though these alone were sympathetic to his soul. He remained, as he has said himself, " independent in his isolation, nothing more than a meditative mind, solitary and serious " (*Avant l'exil :* séance des cinq associations). But I think that in politics, no less than in science, immediate utility is not the sole criterion. They also serve who only stand and wait, who observe, reflect, foresee. And our present, which was their future, owes even more to the lonely studies of a Pasteur or a Victor Hugo than to the triumphs of the most brilliant industrial chemist or party whip.

When to-day we re-read those ancient debates our sympathies are not with the ironical deputies who hooted the grandiose eloquence of Olympio, and attempted to fluster and confuse him with allusions to his ballads or his plays : " Where's a guitar ? " " Sabine ! Sabine ! Who has seen Doña Sabine ? Is Doña Sabine round here ? " " Bravo for Ruy Blas ! " and so on. We may wish that our poet could have forgotten for a while his metaphors and his antitheses ; we smile when he declares in a burst of grandiloquence, " The people will let your laws attempt to dig their poor little nails into the granite of Universal Suffrage." We had preferred that Olympio were not so constantly Olympian, wrapt in the false serenity of his prophetic mantle ; but we have read the second volume of *L'Homme qui rit*, and we know that, despite his air of pride and detachment, not a pin-prick, not a flicker of the lash of laughter, but went straight to the spot and made a wound. One day some audacious image in his speech awoke the loud hilarity of his audience ; the subject in debate was the grave subject of social reform—Victor Hugo turned to the Clerk of the House, as solemn as if he spoke to the Recording-Angel : " Let it be set down in black and white that these members *laughed* ! " And naturally the laughter redoubled. But we, who see 1848 ready to burst like a thunder-cloud over the frivolous assembly, feel that they were wrong to laugh. Let us pass in review a few paragraphs from our poet's political utterances : they seem less absurd to-day than in

the last years of the 'forties. They will be found in the
first volume of *Actes et paroles* :

The Poet's Mission.—I am to-day the man that I was yesterday, pleading the cause of the great popular family, reminding
you of the sufferings they have too long endured. I am the
Thinker who is the friend of the Toiler. I am the Toiler who is
the friend of the Thinker ; I am the writer who asks for the
working-class no degrading alms, but the honourable fruit of
their honourable labours. I am the man who yesterday, in the
seat of the rich, defended the cause of the people, and who
to-morrow, if needs be, will defend the wealthy in the midst of
the populace. For so I comprehend, with all the meanings it
contains, the word *Fraternity*, which I read, written as if by the
hand of God Himself, above the front of the nations, in the
light of the eternal skies.[1]

Socialism.—I have said : " the Utopia of a certain Socialism ";
but, gentlemen, let me explain. . . . At the root of socialism
there is a part of sad reality, true to-day, true yesterday. There
is the uneasy spirit of our human infirmity which craves for a
happier lot, in a hope of bliss, perpetually deceived, because
such contentment belongs not to our sphere, but to another.
But there is also a distress, keenly acute, cruelly poignant, and
perfectly curable. And we must also reckon with that new
attitude, that firmer carriage, which our French revolutions have
given to the people, placing so high the dignity of man and the
sovereignty of the nation, that the worker of our times, when
he suffers and feels himself oppressed, endures a double, a con-
tradictory pang, wounded both in his actual indigence and in
his potential grandeur.[2]

Destitution.—I am not of those who believe that one day
we shall abolish pain : Suffering is a part of the Divine Law ;
but I am with those who think and affirm that we may hope
to abolish Destitution.

Extreme poverty is a disease of the social body even as leprosy
was a disease ; leprosy has gone, and want shall go. Those
who make laws and govern should strive with all their strength
towards that end ; for until they accomplish it their duty is
unfulfilled. . . .

Gentlemen, all your labour is as nought so long as the suffering
of the mass remains. You have done nothing until you can
remove the despair of the wretchedly poor. You have done
nothing so long as working men, in the prime of their powers,

---

[1] Séance des Cinq Associations, 29th of May 1848.
[2] Débat sur la Misère, 9th of July 1849.

may none the less find themselves without bread to eat ; so long as, after a life of toil, old age sees its last years unsheltered ; so long as usurers batten on our countrysides ; so long as human beings starve to death in our towns ; so long as in their hour of need an honest family, a worthy farm-hand, a good workman, can expect no aid from the State, no helping-hand, no brotherly and Christian law to tide him over a season of distress. You have done nothing so long as the spirit of revolution has for its stimulant the sufferings of the poor. Anarchy opens an abyss, but it is want that digs the pit so deep. Gentlemen, you have made laws against anarchy in vain. Make your laws against destitution.[1]

Universal Suffrage.—The true wisdom of the Revolution of 1848 was that, taking the Gospel for the foundation of its policy, it instituted universal suffrage. Truly a great piece of wisdom, a great act of justice, not only to mingle and dignify in the same sovereignty the upper and the lower class, but actually to go forth and seek in his despondency, in his sad forlornness, his forsakenness, in that degradation which is so unwise a counsellor, the man of despair—and bid him hope !—the man of wrath— and bid him reason ! The beggar, as you say, the vagabond, as you call him, indigent, destitute, unfortunate, and miserable, you consecrate him a citizen. You gave him a vote, and he dropped his rifle ; you gave him political power, and in so doing you stayed him with patience.[2]

The League of Nations.—The day will dawn when your arms will fall from your hands. The day will come when war will seem as absurd and be as impossible between Paris and London, Petersburg and Berlin, Turin and Vienna, as between Rouen and Amiens or Boston and Philadelphia. The day will come when, you France, you Russia, you Italy, you England, you Germany, nations of the Continent, without losing your separate characters and glorious individualities, you will fuse in a superior unity and constitute an European brotherhood, even as Normandy, Brittany, Burgundy, Lorraine, Alsace, join hands in France. A day will come when our battlefields shall be markets, open to all products ; and minds, open to all ideas. A day will come when your bullets and your bombs shall be replaced by votes, by the universal suffrage of the nations, by the venerable arbitration of a great sovereign senate, which shall be to Europe what her Parliament is to England, her Diet to Germany, and our Legislative Assembly to France. A day will come when, in our museums, we shall exhibit a cannon as now we show an

---

[1] Débat sur la Misère.
[2] Le suffrage universel, 20 mai 1850.

instrument of torture, and wonder that men should ever have used such things. A day will come when you shall see two multitudinous and friendly groups facing each other on either side of the Atlantic : the United States of America and the United States of Europe.[1]

In pity for the present, in prophecy for the future, Victor Hugo sought to distract his thoughts from the perpetual contemplation of a grief so great that its chill impact had frozen in his heart the springs of poetry and the sources of romance. This was the death of his daughter Léopoldine. She was the eldest of his surviving children and the most like himself :

> Cette Léopoldine est fille des Césars ;
> Elle attire, elle impose, elle est fière, elle est belle ;
> Mais c'est *Lui*, surtout *Lui*, que sa lèvre rappelle,
> Ce dédain, à demi sous la grâce aiguisé,
> Dit assez l'âpre veine où son sang fut puisé,

wrote Sainte-Beuve in his *Livre d'amour*. And though the same Sainte-Beuve, in a letter to Madame Juste Olivier, has described Léopoldine, in her eighteenth year, as an exquisite girl : " the freshest and the pearliest of all her father's ballads," she was never his favourite, because of that paternal strain which made her so intimately dear to Victor Hugo. She was the closest link between her parents, " l'âme de notre vie et de notre maison," said her father. In February 1843, at the age of nineteen, she made the happiest of marriages with Charles, the still younger brother of Victor Hugo's young and enthusiastic apostle, Auguste Vacquerie. The married children were so glad, so good and so gay that the parents scarcely dared express their sense of loss, though Adèle-Dédé, the little sister, gave voice to her bewildered despair and cried, " O what have I done, mamma ; have I been *very* naughty, to suffer like this ? " As the spring came on, the young couple begged Madame Hugo and the little girl to spend the summer near them, at Hâvre, where they were settled ; they hired a little house, filled the garden with flowers, prepared all as for a festival —and when the eager mother arrived (she writes in her Memoir of Léopoldine), " she would not have changed with

[1] Congrès de la Paix, 21st of Aug. 1849.

Paradise ! " The bride came every day and spent long afternoons seeing and chatting with her mother and sister, while
Madame Hugo painted the flowers out of the garden, or
wrote to her husband, or read aloud his long family letters.
Victor Hugo was in the Pyrenees (with Madame Drouet),
preparing the notes for a book of travel. Before setting
out on his journey he had passed a long day at Hâvre with
his wife and children, and in a letter to Madame Hugo on
the morrow he recalled their enjoyment :

What a happy day we spent together. I was, for my part,
so happy, so perfectly and absolutely happy. I saw you, all
of you, radiant in beauty, joy, life, and health. I felt myself
beloved by this radiant society. And you, my dear, were so
perfectly beautiful, so kind, gentle, charming in your ways to
me. I thank you, Adèle, from the bottom of my heart (18th of
July 1843).

So he writes, the traitor, and sets out on his holiday
with the other woman, little dreaming in what mood he
will meet his family again ! He spends a delightful month at
Biarritz, at Passajes, then fishing villages full of romance and
a wild beauty. He and his companion resume their home-
ward way. They had reached Rochefort, whence they went
a long excursion in the marsh, meaning to catch up the
diligence at a village called Subise, and arriving there half-
blinded with the sun and dust, some time before the coach
was ready to start, they entered a little café, and called for
a glass of beer and the Paris paper. It was the 9th of
September ; the paper was doubtless two or three days
old ; but they had seen no recent news. Suddenly Madame
Drouet beheld the poet turn as pale as death, clap his hand
to his heart as though he would prevent it bursting, rise up
bewildered, turn round, leave his seat, quit the café, the
street, and rush like a madman to the quiet shade of the
ramparts. He had read in the *Siècle* the death of Léopoldine.
It was already six days since she had ceased to exist.
On the 1st of September she had said to her mother that she
and her husband were going to spend a couple of days with
Madame Vacquerie, her mother-in-law, at Villequier, a little
farther up the Seine towards Rouen ; they hoped to be

back on the 3rd or 4th. And on the morning of the 4th Madame Hugo wrote to her truant husband :

Léopoldine and her husband are at Villequier. They left the day before yesterday and will be home this evening. These short separations do not count. I am so happy in the midst of my children that I even welcome any trifling vexation, thinking that these petty annoyances are the small change of misfortune. . . .

That same night she was awoken from her sleep by a peal at the bell ; and Auguste Vacquerie's voice came ringing up the stairs :

" Charles ! Charles is dead ! "

" And my daughter ? "

" Drowned with him ! "

Their boat had overturned in a gust of wind at the mouth of the Seine.

For three days the poet was almost out of his mind. A few days before he had found a letter at Luz from his " Didine chérie—cette lettre était comme toujours pleine de tendresse et de bonheur." And in his mind's eye he saw the fragile creature struggling hopelessly in the cold and angry river :

> Elle était pâle, et pourtant rose,
>   Petite, avec de grands cheveux.
> Elle disait souvent : je n'ose,
>   Et ne disait jamais, je veux.

Years after, ten years afterwards, he was to embalm the memory of Léopoldine in priceless verse. But not at first. The source of poetry seemed seared in his soul. He threw himself wildly, carelessly, into politics ; into schemes for social reform ; into his adventurous love affairs ; into vague, ambitious dreams. We are miles away from the noble and candid young poet of 1830. But the memory of his dead girl was stronger than this superficial agitation. I have seen a spring in Auvergne into which you are bidden to throw a rosebud or a spray of leaves ; they disappear from sight in the water ; but after many days you find them, marvellously changed, transformed into shining crystals, imperishable in their robe of light. So it was with the sorrow which Victor Hugo, in his despair, strove to forget. It sank deeper and deeper into his soul and emerged at last a jewel for all time.

Victor Hugo looks ten years older (Balzac wrote to Madame Hanska in December 1843). It is possible that he takes his daughter's death as a punishment for the four children he has had by Juliette (*sic !*). He hates Sainte-Beuve. . . . Ah, .dear Angel, what a lesson for us in this love-match made at eighteen years of age! Victor Hugo and his wife are a great lesson. Still, even if I were not secured from the follies of Hugo by the force of my passion for you, so serious, so sincere, so unalterable, and that you understand so well, I should none the less be saved by my age and experience and by my ideas as to the importance of the family.

CHAPTER XVII

1848

VICTOR HUGO was in truth the mirror of his age.

Mis au centre de tout comme un écho sonore.

He had reflected, reverberated, the candour, the romance, and the piety of the Restoration, the generous optimism of 1830, the social preoccupations of the early years of Louis-Philippe, and now the demoralized laxity of the later years of the reign. Already in 1840 Balzac had said of him, in writing to Madame Hanska, " The poet shows signs of physical fatigue : *il a considérablement aimé.*" Besides his *liaison* with Juliette Drouet, he was the lover of a Madame Biard for more than seven years ; strangely enough the scandal, which at one moment set half Paris curling its lip and shrugging its shoulder, never reached Juliette in her retirement, until, almost on the eve of the *coup d'État*, she received by the post a packet of letters in her lover's writing, sealed with his ring and with his proud device : *Ego Hugo* ; a line from Madame Biard informed the sequestrated lady that the connection, which had lasted so long, still continued, and that it would be well that Juliette should retire from the scene. Victor Hugo's position was that of Gwynplaine in *L'Homme que rit*, between Dea and the Duchess ; in a way he loved them both. But Juliette naturally would not hear of this arrangement. She agreed that her poet should take several months of calm reflection to resolve which lady he finally preferred, and then bid an eternal farewell to the other one. He decided (and in fact events decided for him) that Juliette, whose wit, intelligence, and character he admired, was, at forty, after all, more indis-

pensable to his happiness than the charming siren who had
youth on her side. For, at bottom, in spite of all, our
poet was still an idealist, and what he really sought in all
the variety of his amours was a kindred soul.

It was not without shame, not without a constant
haunting sense of degradation, that Victor Hugo accepted
his own back-slidings. Not all natures are capable of repentance, of remorse. During twenty years and more the
poems of Hugo record his tragic wonder that an austere
ideal and a lofty soul should not preserve a man from the
hampering snare of the flesh—" la chair ! " ; no mystic has
spoken of it with more revulsion. In the *Chants du crépuscule*,
in an extraordinarily beautiful poem (*A Louis B.*), he compares himself to a bell, which he had seen of old swinging
high in the blue and sunny air, bright with the purity of
its dazzling metal, inscribed with the Holy Name, and which
now he beholds covered with rust and stains, scratched all
over with ignoble superscriptions that obscure the sacred
letters. But, set the bell in motion, and you will hear its
music peal unaltered, undefiled, as glorious as of old. There
is no change in—

> La grande âme d'airain qui là-haut se lamente.

In another piece he goes further still and declares that
the exaltation and flame of sensual love are necessary to
the production of the artist. " God furrows the soul of a
genius with his terrible plough, the passions." And, so late
as the " Quatre Vents de l'Esprit," in his old age, we find
the poet lamenting the tragic attraction of the sexes :

> L'homme est l'énigme étrange et triste de la femme—
> Et la femme est la sphinx de l'homme. Sombre loi ! . . .
> L'homme le plus semblable aux antiques Hercules. . .
> . . . Cet homme, s'il rencontre une femme, veut plaire,
> Tombe à genoux, adore et tremble ; et ce vainqueur
> Du destin est toujours le vaincu de son cœur.[1]

But nowhere, I think, has he expressed so finely the
mingled sense of passion and confidence embittered by the
sense of guilt as in a certain double quatrain of the *Chants*

[1] " Pensées de nuit."

du crépuscule, called " Espoir en Dieu," of which this is the touching close—

> Nos fautes, mon pauvre ange, ont causé nos souffrances—
> Peut-être qu'en restant bien longtemps à genoux,
> Quand il aura béni toutes les innocences
> Et tous les repentirs, Dieu finira par nous.

Repentance, redemption, expiation—such was the circle of ideas in which the genius of Victor Hugo habitually moved, and out of which were to issue his three greatest novels and the immortal *Contemplations*. But who could have supposed it who should have observed merely the outside of his irregular existence ?

Two months had not elapsed since he had taken his seat in the House of Peers, when, one afternoon in July 1845, M. Biard, the artist, accompanied by a Commissary of Police, descended, like the wolf on the fold, on a certain small hotel of the Passage Saint Roch, where he surprised Victor Hugo and Madame Biard. His Peer's medal—rendering him inviolable except to the judgement of his colleagues in the Upper House—just saved our poet from arrest, but the lady was hurried off to the prison of Saint Lazare, and it needed the mild and magnanimous intervention of Madame Hugo to persuade the injured husband to transfer her, for her time of penitence, to a convent. We know how the fair sinner rewarded that kindness : no sooner was she released than she resumed her relations with the poet. But Adèle had no illusions left. She had accepted once for all her situation as the ageing wife of a great poet who had married her in his twenty-first year. She remained his dearest friend. " La seule chose que je ne te pardonnerais pas, ce serait d'être peu heureux."

This adventure of Victor Hugo's had scandalized the Chamber of Peers ; the King and the Duchess of Orleans had brought their influence to bear to make it pass for a freak of genius. But it was, in fact, a symptom of a growing and public laxity of morals.

Two years later a more grievous scandal discredited the Upper House. A Peer of France, ex-Minister of Public Works, a President of the Court of Appeal (the highest judicial court in the kingdom), one M. Teste, was convicted

by the Upper House of having accepted a bribe of about
four thousand pounds for promoting the affairs of a mining
company. The matter was the more serious that the
General-Marquis de Cubières, Secretary of State for War in
two recent Ministries, was also implicated. The month of
July 1847 witnessed a double verdict, sentencing the one to
three years' imprisonment, the other to be drummed out of
the army with loss of all his civic rights. The prestige of
the House of Peers sustained a heavy blow.

Worse was to follow. Exactly one month later, a fourth
Peer of France, the Duke of Praslin-Choiseul, was arrested
for the murder of his wife at the instigation of his mistress.
The victim was the daughter of Marshal Sebastiani, ex-
Minister, ex-Ambassador ; the assassin belonged to one of
the greatest houses in France ; and the crime was a savage
act of fierce barbarity. Victor Hugo (who in his *Choses
vues* has described the trial of M. de Praslin and the
trial of M. Teste) visited the Hôtel de Praslin a few days
after the event, and has left a record of the terrible room
—a duchess's boudoir !—with the bloody imprint of her
desperate hands on the gold fringe of the curtains, on the
silken walls, on the doors, on the embroidered bell-rope, as
she fled from side to side, madly seeking an issue, screaming
for help, till she fell, hacked to death with a knife, and
pierced with the bullets of a pistol. What bully from the
outer Boulevards could do worse ? Within the week, the
son of Napoleon's Marshal Davout, the Prince of Eckmühl,
was arrested as a vagabond for having attempted to murder
his mistress. And the people began to say, " These are our
Peers, Members of our Upper House, specimens of our
governing class : such is their example." The Duchess of
Orleans writes sadly : " Le mal est profond parce qu'il
atteint les populations dans leur moralité ! "

The harvest had failed, and owing to the lack of trans-
ports the risk of famine was imminent. The misery of the
poorer class was great. The influx of workers into Paris
had been enormous owing to the new prosperity of industry—but they were prosperities in which the humbler
mechanics did not share ; their average wage was about
two francs a day ; no provision had been made for their

housing, and the overcrowding of the popular quarters was extreme. The poor in their slums were as angry as they were hungry, and when the King's son, the Duke of Monpensier, in July 1847, spent some eight thousand pounds on a fête to celebrate his marriage with the sister of Queen Isabella of Spain, the crowd followed the carriages of the guests, hooting and cursing, and threw handfuls of mud and filth into the open barouches where the fine ladies sat, frightened, in their brocades and their diamonds.

And Victor Hugo pondered all these things in his heart. His posthumously published volume, *Choses vues*, written at this date, is the most admirable commentary on the Revolution of 1848, and shows incidentally how keenly and vividly our poet could see—when he forgot to be a Seer ! There are no more interesting or descriptive memoirs in modern history. But Victor Hugo could only look on, play the witness. He had lost all political prestige or influence ; he was no longer the leader of the young as in 1830. His tergiversations, though inspired by the most delicate scruples, had perplexed and wearied all his former friends. No one could count on him. In the eyes of the Legitimists he was an arrant renegade, more odious now that he had sworn allegiance to the usurper than when he had compounded with Revolution or conspired with the Bonapartes. The advanced Radicals, and even the Liberals, regarded him with indignant antipathy ; he was their lost leader :

> Just for a handful of silver he left us,
> Just for a ribbon to stick in his coat.

What had they in common with the Peer of Louis-Philippe ? No party was sure of him ; not even the Dynastic Left, with which he thought he voted. Extremely jealous of his independence, and fantastically chivalrous, Victor Hugo bewildered his colleagues of to-day by the flowers which he heaped on the graves of his patrons of yesterday. No sooner had a party fallen from power than it was sure of his praise ; the cause in which he believed no longer was dearer to his heart than the cause for which he fought ; and turn by turn Napoleon at Saint-Helena, or in his grave, King Charles X. at Holyrood, the Church and

Pio Nono at the moment when his party proposed to
banish the Jesuits, form the touching but incongruous
subjects which inspired his poetry and exasperated his
colleagues. The Radicals could not imagine what the man
was driving at ; the Ultras thought the smirched hand of
a traitor touched their altar-cloth ; and all alike resented
his airs of Olympian detachment and serenity, and his
assumption of universal benevolence.

Meanwhile the country hovered on the brink of civil
war. History repeats itself. The monarchy of July was to
perish, even as the legitimate monarchy had perished, owing
to a certain senile ossification of the will in the King and his
chief Minister. The storm was gathering. Louis-Philippe
could no longer bend—it was clear that he must break.
Perhaps no monarch should be allowed to reign after seventy
years of age. The king who fifteen years before had shown
himself so prudent, so wise, so supple, full of concessions to
his political opponents, could no longer brook the faintest
resistance to his purpose. He was more absolute, more
obstinate, than Charles X. For eight years he governed
practically alone, using Guizot as his mouthpiece—" Guizot
est ma bouche," he would say. He was the Czar of France,
without the prestige of legitimacy ; and the people began to
murmur that he had stolen his throne. All means were good
that brought to pass his will ; and Guizot, that personally
incorruptible Huguenot, became a manufacturer of elections
and a wholesale purchaser of votes in the service of a king as
determined to discountenance reform as any other Bourbon.

A curious document was discovered in 1848 among the
private papers of the Duc de Nemours, the King's eldest
surviving son. It is a letter which had been recently sent
him by his brother, the Prince de Joinville : the sailor, the
" enfant terrible " of the numerous Orleans princes, as a
rule so correct and so distinguished :

Excuse me (begins Joinville) for what I have to say about
my father, but we ought to have some quiet talk about him,
and you are the only person I can speak to. We are bound to
look into the future, and it alarms me. The King is inflexible
and will listen to no one ; his will must have its way everywhere : there seems to me a danger in the pressure that he

exercises on every point. . . . Ministers no longer exist ; their responsibility is nil ; all centres in the King. He has arrived at an age when a man no longer accepts criticism. He is accustomed to govern, and he likes to show that he governs. With his immense experience, his courage, all his fine qualities, he knows how to face danger boldly ; but the danger exists ! [1]

This autocratic old gentleman refused to make the least concession, though all the country was rising in meetings and banquets, clamouring for Electoral Reform. And out of one of these banquets the Revolution of 1848 dropped suddenly and as if by surprise. A public dinner had been arranged to take place in a building on the Champs Élysées on Tuesday the 23rd of February. Eighty-seven Members of the Chamber were to attend, practically all the Opposition. The subscribers were to meet at eleven in the forenoon in front of the Madeleine Church, and to march in procession down the rue Royale, across the place de la Concorde, and up the Champs Élysées. No revolution was intended, merely an imposing manifestation. But on the Monday night the Government forbade the banquet. Guizot's veto acted as an immense advertisement. Tuesday the 23rd dawned chill and grey. Towards eleven the rain came down in torrents—a regular February Fill-dyke : the crowd continued to gather in dense and eager masses. Victor Hugo (who has left a vivid account of the Revolution in his *Choses vues*) found the pont de la Concorde occupied by a regiment of infantry, and a brigade of cavalry charging the crowd in the place de la Concorde. He crossed the river to the left bank and the Chamber of Deputies. The Government appeared rather amused than alarmed, the King and Guizot as obdurate as ever, and determined not to grant a single vote, and the Members pettifogging away about questions of legality and the affairs of the Bank at Bordeaux. " Not much use serving a writ on a lion ! " growled the poet and went forth again to see the show. The crowd was still good-humoured—out for a row rather than a revolution ; still, here and there the paving-stones had been torn up, omnibuses and carts overturned, and barricades were being constructed. On the quai de la

[1] Quoted in Émile Bourgeois' *History of Modern France*, i. 286.

Ferraille our poet met one of the Republican Deputies :
" Well, will you get what you want ? " said he. " Does
this mean the Republic ? "

" Oh, not yet ! " exclaimed Antony Thouret. " But we
mean to get Electoral Reform—and perhaps—who knows ?
—Universal Suffrage."

" *A la bonne heure !* " cried Victor Hugo, much relieved
—for his peer's oath of allegiance was beginning to weigh
heavy on his Liberal soul, excited by the tumult and aware
of its justification.

In the middle of the night the tocsin began to toll. A
terrible misunderstanding had changed the face of events.
The crowd, shouting, hooting, but still pacific, was massed
before the Ministry of Foreign Affairs, cheerfully crying,
" To Hell with Guizot " (or the French equivalent), when one
of those waves of pressure which arise mysteriously in such
a throng pushed the whole mass forward, and in the jostling
and confusion a shot rang out from a musket in the crowd,
and the troops, believing they were attacked, fired a volley
into the dense mob in front of them—a feat of rifle-firing
which instantly stretched on the pavement some fourscore
of the rioters, killed or wounded. The bodies of the dead
were laid in carts and barrows, lighted by torches ; and
thousands of Parisians, crying, " Vengeance ! " escorted
them through the streets : before morning Paris was
covered with barricades.

February 24th dawned on a scene of open revolution.
On Tuesday night the crowd had shouted for Electoral
Reform, and their cry was, " Down with Guizot ! " On
Wednesday morning they clamoured, " Vive la République ! " and a roar rang out, " Down with the Bourbons ! "
Before noonday the King abdicated in favour of his grand-
son. When the Revolution broke out, the people demanded
the retirement of Louis-Philippe, the dissolution of the
Chamber, a general amnesty, and the regency of the Duchess
of Orleans ; a very few hours later all this seemed too little.
At two o'clock from the top of a barricade on the place
de la Bastille, Victor Hugo proclaimed that Regency in
front of an armed mob, thirty thousand strong. But his
words awoke no echo in the popular heart.

"We won't be governed by a woman!" cried a voice in the crowd.

"*Governed!* Never!" answered the poet. "Nor by a man! It is because Louis-Philippe would *govern* that his abdication is necessary to-day. But a woman who reigns in the name of a child! That is different. Look at Queen Victoria."

"We are French!" cried the crowd.

And one voice rose, and met no echo: "Vive la République!"

A little after noonday, the Duchess of Orleans, leading by the hand her son the Comte de Paris, had gone to the Chamber of Deputies. On her entrance the Assembly rose to its feet amid cries of "Vive la Duchesse d'Orléans!" "Vive le Comte de Paris," "Vive la Régente." The frail young woman and her child appeared to incarnate Law and Order. Meanwhile the President of the Chamber had proclaimed the Regency. But suddenly a vast mob of armed men, waving flags and rifles, forced the doors of the Chamber, shouting, "Down with the Regency!" "Banishment!" Vainly the Duchess attempted to make herself heard; her friends dragged her away; the Assembly itself dissolved, vanished, submerged by the revolutionary meeting. An hour later the King and the Queen, in a four-wheeled cab, under the names of M. and Madame Lebrun, were rolling their first stage on the road towards England, where the Duchess and her children joined them finally at Claremont, near Esher.

Meanwhile Lamartine, at the Hôtel de Ville, had proclaimed a Provisional Government, in which he himself was Minister for Foreign Affairs, and had issued a manifesto that his Government "*desired the Republic,* subject to the ratification of the people." As with a swoop of wings, Lamartine had risen to the full height of the situation, and now he rode the storm; it was his influence, his genius, which, more than any other factor, saved the honour of France in those ominous days, and controlled the violent passions of a multitude too suddenly victorious. His fascination, his charm, a certain dominating quality in his mind and in his voice, his incomparable eloquence, his moral

courage, made him, in such an emergency, a leader of men.
Alas! he had no staying power. No stronger contrast to
the soaring ascension of Lamartine than Victor Hugo,
bewildered, scrupulous, taken aback by a revolution which
disconcerted all his views. He hesitated and procrastinated.
He was no longer a Monarchist, for there was no longer a
Monarchy; he was not yet a Republican, though he had
always predicted a Republic " as the crown of his grey
hairs." His thick brown locks had not expected that
ultimate adornment so soon. The mingling of philosophy
and poetry, of careful thought and generous impulse, which
enabled Lamartine to organize liberty at home and preserve
peace with foreign powers in front of the most desperate
difficulties, that influx of inspiration which caused him to
improvise from day to day all that was needful and sufficient
for the evil thereof, were qualities which Victor Hugo never
possessed. He was a great poet, a grand dreamer, a prophet;
despite the part he was to play in later life, he was never
in any degree a statesman, though he lived to incarnate the
ideal of a nation when Lamartine had fallen to the state of
a half-forgotten literary hack.

In 1848, as he has said himself, he had not yet taken
his stand on politics. "The vision of Liberty concealed
the Republic." Most of the measures that he voted for in
1848 and 1849 were in fact reactionary: he voted for the
abolition of the national workshops; for the maintenance
of the purchase of substitutes for military service; for the
dissolution of the Constituent Assembly; for the military
expedition to Rome: all of these measures perfectly justi-
fiable and legitimate, but undoubtedly part of the Conservative programme. And it is curious and interesting to
remark that his conversion to the Republic occurred on the
very day—the 13th of June 1849—when he saw that
Republic stricken to death by the coalition of Bonapartists
and Monarchists that was soon to build a throne upon her
grave. As ever, his sympathies went out to the system
that disappeared from power:

It is only in 1849 (he wrote in 1869 to Alphonse Karr) that
I became a Republican. I recognized Liberty when I saw her
vanquished . . . when I saw her in her death-throes I hastened

to her side. I reached the party of the Republic at the eleventh hour—just in time to receive my share of exile.[1]

Meanwhile the Revolution had its repercussion on our poet's private life. His home in the place Royale had been in the thick of the fray ; in these stormy days the faubourg Saint-Antoine was a dangerous neighbour. So the Hugos moved, first to the rue d'Isly, but soon to that apartment of the rue de la Tour d'Auvergne which he arranged with even more fantastic picturesqueness and inexpensive splendour than the house in the place Royale, filling it, as his wife says, with " ses dorures, ses tentures, toute sa fantaisie et ses soins." In the large drawing-room the walls were hung with tapestries which figured the adventures of Telemachus and the Romance of the Rose. The furniture was " Gothic " ; a collection of Oriental China, chiefly cracked on close inspection, but very effective as an element of decorative art, gleamed richly from the tops of the carved oak cabinets. Madame Hugo, in her full-blown forties, reigned magnificently in this artistic home ; her *bourgeois* and simple tastes would have preferred something more ordinary, but doubtless this mediaeval medley suited her style of looks. Her husband was still very proud of her. " Madame V. H. was the handsomest woman present," he says in an account of one of the last fêtes of Louis-Philippe. A young Russian attaché, Count Victor de Balabine, has left a rather intimidating portrait of the lady in 1846 :

Madame Victor Hugo, a large woman, with great flamboyant eyes, black arched eyebrows, and a nose audaciously aquiline, lips of an eloquent fulness, a spherical bust, and prominent hips, with crimped and curly locks of ebony straying in every direction, the whole constituting a sort of beauty which, if I were to meet it on a dark night, would make me take to my heels and fly.

---

[1] *Pendant l'exil.*

CHAPTER XVIII

THE " COUP D'ÉTAT "

THERE were two points as to which Victor Hugo had never changed his opinion : the iniquity of capital punishment and the right of every man to inhabit his native land. Exile was therefore hateful to him under any name : banishment, expulsion, transportation, " interdiction de séjour," or prohibited residence ; from the beginning to the end of his career he never ceased his protest :

> Oh ! n'exilons personne, oh ! l'exil est impie

he had exclaimed in 1832 in his Ode to Napoleon II. (the Duke of Reichstadt) ; it was therefore logical that when, on the morrow of the Revolution, the question came before the Chamber of removing the sentence of exile that still weighed on Louis-Napoleon Bonaparte, Victor Hugo should vote for the return of the prince. He had never seen the son of Queen Hortense. He knew him merely as a rather ridiculous young man who, with a tame eagle in a cage, had tried to conquer a kingdom, and had been ignominiously captured and confined. A dose of the ridiculous in youth is not unlovable and does not at all preclude ability. In his prison at Ham, Louis-Napoleon had matured ; he had published a rather striking work on artillery which had interested the son of General Hugo, and had written a book on the *Extinction of Pauperism* quite in our poet's vein. His air of attentive detachment did not at first displease Olympio, but he thought him singularly unlike the Emperor (whom his cousin Napoleon-Jérome so strikingly resembled), and his foreign accent when he pronounced *compatriot* with almost an initial *g*, and—still worse—Naboleon, was disconcerting. Still, Hugo considered him a man " excellently well intentioned and with a visible quantity of intelligence and aptitude," so that in December 1848 the poet voted for the Prince's election to the Presidency of the Republic, naming to the highest post in the State " un prince révolutionnaire qui, mûri par la prison politique, avait écrit, en faveur des classes pauvres, des livres remarquables."[1]   In fact, Hugo was inclined to favour a candidate who seemed, like himself, partly Monarchist and partly Republican, at once the champion of the democracy and the champion of order. He studied with an interest none the less lively for a haunting mistrust this man who was the nephew of Napoleon, the nephew also of General Hugo's old chief, King Joseph, and the cousin of the Duke of Reichstadt, who had been one of the political visions of Hugo's youth.

But gradually the mistrust increased. What lurked under the surface of this taciturn young man, who seldom spoke in the Assembly and never voted on any question of crucial importance, who seemed indeed, politically, as unattached, as independent, as Hugo himself ?   The surface was agreeable.   " There is a great charm " (wrote Queen Victoria a few years later) " in his quiet, frank manner. Any amiability, any affection shown him has a lasting effect on his temperament, which is curiously inclined to tenderness."   " Distinguished, cold, gentle, intelligent, deferent, and dignified—German in appearance—with dark moustaches—no resemblance to the Emperor," notes Victor Hugo.   But gradually our poet took alarm at the very neutrality of this quiet, rather sentimental and dreamy young man, so anxious not to engage himself to any political party, while his interests were pushed by a coalition of malcontents.   Little by little the President surrounded himself with an almost royal splendour, and when he passed, some voice in the crowd was sure to burst forth with a cry of " Vive l'Empereur ! "   But Louis - Napoleon, aloof and dreamy, seemed still, as the French say, " in the moon," and appeared to do nothing to provoke his own apotheosis.

I have sometimes thought that in this strange and solitary soul of Louis-Napoleon—in the visionary filled with humani-

[1] *Avant l'exil.*

tarian enthusiasm, and yet sequestered in his own insuper-
able egoism; in the fatalist haunted by the word *ananké*;
in the sentimental dreamer hampered by a sensual nature;
in the aloof and ambitious prince; in that mind, not insincere
but incoherent, incongruously filled with great thoughts
ill-assorted; in that enigmatic man of meditation lost in
his interior ideal and suddenly escaping thence by rare
outbursts of dramatic activity, sometimes terrible and
sometimes grotesque—I have thought that Olympio may
have seen a sort of sinister caricature or counterpart of
Olympio—that *döppelganger* whose presence fills us with
horror—who is Ourself with the Soul left out—Ourself as
Satan sees us—of all phantoms the ghastliest and the most
revolting. However it may be, it is certain that from the
close of the year 1850 Victor Hugo, so universally benevolent,
began to look on the Prince-President with a sort of instinctive hate. He saw no longer in him the revolutionary
prince, the apostle of a future democracy: " C'est un
personnage vulgaire, puéril, théâtral, et vain ". " Hybrid of
the Middle Ages with the decadence of Rome "; " sinister
somnambulist "—such are some of the epithets which
Victor Hugo heaps on the Prince-President in his *Napoléon
le petit*.

But that was on the morrow of the *coup d'État*. On
the day before, nothing foreshadowed a military revolution.
Quiet, reserved, and dignified, Louis-Napoleon had calmed
suspicion. On Monday evening the 2nd of December 1851
he held a reception—a sort of levee—as on every Monday
evening, at the Élysée. The last carriage had rolled away,
the city was wrapped in sleep, when, a little before dawn,
the walls of the town were placarded with the Proclamation
of the change of Government. On the stroke of five two
regiments quartered near the Invalides proceeded to occupy
the Palace of the National Assembly, and at the same
moment, from every barracks in Paris, noiselessly and
swiftly, the infantry issued, each regiment to its appointed
place. The cavalry were set in motion an hour later, lest
the ringing sound of the hoofs on the pavement should
arouse the population. Meanwhile, out of the seven hundred and fifty Members of the National Assembly, two

hundred and fifty were arrested in their beds and confined, in company with half a dozen " doubtful " Generals, in the prisons of Paris ; all the printing-presses were occupied by the troops, all the newspapers suppressed.   The worst was the supine indifference with which the people accepted the situation : they considered that the well-to-do middle class had confiscated the social revolution of 1848 to their advantage ; had put all its profits in their pockets, had disinherited the cause of Labour.   No one and nothing was so unpopular with them as the Members of the National Assembly—" Les vingt-cinq francs ! " as the people called them, because they were paid at the rate of a pound a day.   Any new leader who could at one stroke annihilate the hated " vingt-cinq francs " and reinstate Universal Suffrage could secure the favour of the working class.   And on the placards that blossomed on all the walls of Paris the Prince-President promised to do this.   So, as they went to their day's work, the men in blue blouses stopped a minute or so to read Louis-Napoleon's Proclamation, smiled, said : " Ça ne nous regarde pas ! " shrugged their shoulders and went their way.

Victor Hugo was writing in his bed at eight o'clock on that Tuesday morning when his colleague, M. Versigny, entered and told him of the night's events.   If Hugo was not yet arrested his turn was sure to come, and in his desire at once to escape imprisonment and, above all, to arouse the indifferent populace to a swift reaction he dressed quickly and hurried through the streets, which were still silent and as it were aghast, to the house where he was to meet with his fellow-members of the Left—such of them, at least, as were not already under lock and key.   Hugo advised that the hundred and fifty Democratic representatives still at large, draped in their deputies' tricolour scarves, should march in procession through the streets of Paris, shouting, " Vive la République."   It was his first conception, and one that over and over again in the following days he was to implore the representatives of the Republican Left to adopt.   He saw the scene in his mind's eye : the devoted men, draped in their patriotic scarves, issuing two by two in a sacrificial progress, shouting, " Vive la République," and falling before the fire of the tyrant. But this advice was not considered practical. The President had some eighty thousand soldiers massed in the streets. With a flick of a finger he could extinguish their ineffectual resistance.

Their one chance was not to show themselves, but to work, as it were, underground, undermining the popular quarters of Paris. And there, in a house that formed the corner of the rue de Charonne and the faubourg Saint-Antoine, a Committee of Insurrection was elected : Carnot, de Flotte, Jules Favre, Madier de Montjau, Michel (de Bourges), and Victor Hugo. Not one of them was more earnest or more passionately ardent in the defence of freedom, braver, more disregarding of hardship and fatigue, than our poet ; and yet, as we read the account of those fateful days in his *Histoire d'un Crime,* we feel how little fitted he was for the task. The man of long meditations is rarely the chief who can improvise a direct attack upon reality. On his way to the faubourg Saint-Antoine with a fellow-member he had eloquently harangued the mob, and soon they were crying, " Bravo, Victor Hugo ! " " Take care," said a shopkeeper, putting up his shutters. " The soldiers will shoot you ! " " And if they do," cried the poet, " you will carry my dead body through the streets, and my death will be a good thing, if God's justice comes out of it ! " Now all the crowd were crying, " Vive Victor Hugo ! " " Cry, ' Vive la Constitution ! ' " said he. But the fellow-member whispered in his ear, " You will just be the cause of a perfectly useless fusillade. The infantry is round the corner and here are the gun-carriages of the artillery." And then, doubtful, " I hesitated to assume so great a responsibility " (writes Victor Hugo). " If I had seized the moment—it might have been victory, it might have been a massacre. Was I right ? Was I wrong ? " Twenty years afterwards he had not quite made up his mind ; on the spur of the moment— he did nothing.

And so it was over and over again : beginnings of grand actions, commencements of fine speeches, suddenly cut short by the scrupulous fear of doing more harm than good to the men who trusted him.

A little later in the day he was seated in an omnibus, which was full of anonymous citizens of whose opinions our poet was completely ignorant, when the lumbering vehicle was stopped by the passage of a regiment of cuirassiers. There they were, " ces Français devenus des mameloucks," on the other side of a pane of glass. It was more than Victor Hugo could stand. He pulled down the window, put out his head, and cried at the top of his voice : " Down with Louis Bonaparte ! Those who serve traitors are no better than traitors themselves ! " The soldiers paid no attention, but the unfortunate passengers were seized with a fit of panic ; one of them tore open another glass, put his head out alongside of Victor Hugo's, and began to vociferate, " Long live Prince Napoleon. Vive l'Empereur ! " " A bas Louis Bonaparte ! " shouted our poet. " Long live Louis Bonaparte ! " screamed his fellow traveller. " Les soldats écoutaïent dans un silence sombre. La foule regardait avec stupeur. . . ." [1]

Arrived on the northern hill, Victor Hugo meant to regain his house and embrace his wife and daughter, but a friendly neighbour informed him that his house was surrounded by the police ; he consoled himself, therefore, by a visit to Juliette Drouet, whom he had lodged hard by. Seeing the state of excitement that he was in, the courageous woman insisted on accompanying him ; she was as good a Democrat as Hugo himself, but more level-headed. And more than once in the days that followed she saved his life—rising suddenly before him out of the red mist of carnage like a protecting Minerva, calming his frenzied protests, warning him where the police lay in ambush, securing for him a safe asylum—no easy thing to find in days when it was death to harbour a member of the Insurrectionary Committee. A price was on our poet's head. " If you can catch Victor Hugo " (wrote Morny to Maupas), " you may do what you like with him."

On the morning of that second day Victor Hugo was hastening towards the barricade Saint-Antoine. He had a rendezvous there with his colleagues of the Insurrectionary Committee and with Baudin, a young doctor, one of the

[1] *Histoire d'un crime.*

most generous and ardent of the Republican deputies ; but
in the heat of their eloquence on the preceding evening the
hour of their appointment had not been definitely fixed.
Victor Hugo thought it was for nine ; his colleagues expected
him at eight.   And he was later than he had meant, for, as
he was crossing the place de la Bastille—his sole civilian
four-wheeler making a fantastic effect in the midst of that
terror-stricken emptiness hedged round by troops—he passed
before a group of officers on horseback, and the blood rushed
to his head.   He flung down the window of his cab, tore
his deputy's scarf out of his pocket, and waving it wildly,
began to harangue the General :

" You who are there, dressed in the uniform of a General,
it is to you that I speak, sir.   You know who I am ; I am
a representative of the nation ; and I know who you are ;
you are a malefactor !   And now do you wish to know my
name ?   My name is Victor Hugo."

With praiseworthy reticence the General said nothing,
the troops seemed petrified.   The indignant poet felt a
tender, warning, feminine clutch at his arm—a voice in his
ear said, " You will just get yourself shot ! "   Minerva—
in the form of Juliette Drouet, wrapped her votary in a
cloud—or at least bade the four-wheeler to proceed on its
way—and the coachman entered the dangerous defile of the
faubourg Saint-Antoine.   But when Victor Hugo reached
the barricade, that hastily made and insufficient defence—
built of three or four carts and barrows overturned—had
long since been taken by the troops, and Baudin lay dead
amid its ruins—Baudin who, in answer to the jeer of a
woman in the street, had replied, " I will show you how a
man can die for his ' vingt-cinq francs.' "

That day, like Tuesday, was laboriously spent in drawing up decrees that it was not possible to get printed (for
the Prince-President had put all the printing-presses in his
pocket), in trying to raise a revolt that had no firearms at
its disposal (for the Prince-President had confiscated all the
rifles, all the muskets, after the ineffectual rising in June),
in hurrying warily from place to place, hunted from one
refuge to another by the continued approach of the police :
during these four days the devoted Committee changed its

venue no less than twenty-seven times, each time at the
risk of the lives of the members, for they were all marked
men ; and every change was complicated by the necessity
of making known their new address to the leaders on the
barricades and on the other centres. Long afterwards,
recalling those days of danger and discomfort, bereft of
sleep, of all cleanliness or refreshment, almost of food—
when every tramp of a foot on the stair might mean be-
trayal and instant death ; when every street-corner might
mask an ambush ; when, besides Baudin and Dussoubs shot
on their barricades, Doutre got a sabre-cut in the hat,
and both Bourzat and Victor Hugo several bullet-wounds
in their great-coats—our poet wondered at the mingling of
boyish gaiety and professional commonplace which char-
acterized those hours that in the retrospect appeared so
passionate and so tragic. The physical resistance of these
" intellectuals " was extraordinary. " One day Madame
Landrin gave us some clear soup ; and one day Madame
Grévy the remains of a meat-pie ; one evening we dined off
the tablets of chocolate a friendly chemist sent to the
barricade ; often only a bit of bread and a glass of water."
In the chance asylums where the Committee drifted, often
joined by the representatives of the Republican Left, there
were seldom seats enough, and never beds enough, to go
round. The edge of a table, a window-sill, the floor sufficed,
and proceedings would begin as regular, as official, as though
they had been held in one of the committee rooms at the
Assembly. Hardship, danger, had no effect on this handful
of patriots ineffectually opposing their unorganized effort to
a national crime, too skilfully prepared to leave them any
hope in their resistance. Still they resisted.

On the morning of the 4th of December they even
hoped. The popular " faubourg Antoine " had caught the
temper of its representatives. Boulevard Bonne Nouvelle
and rue Montorgueil, a whole system of barricades, had been
organized in the night. The troops were in force, but silent
and patient. Suddenly, at two o'clock in the afternoon, a
burst of musketry fire swept the Boulevard ; without warning and without provocation a group of innocent passers-by,
collected by accident or curiosity at the corner of the

faubourg Poissonnière, were stretched on the ground, killed or wounded ; the cavalry brigades came thundering down the streets ; the infantry followed ; the soldiers had orders to give no quarter and struck sharp and hard — exploring the shops and houses, killing right and left in a general massacre. The number of victims, including the wounded, is generally estimated at twelve hundred. Before Jouvin's glove-shop there was a pile of corpses—an old gentleman with his umbrella, a young man with his eyeglass, among the heaped blue of the workmen's blouses. The Maison Dorée, the Café Anglais, the Café de Paris, ran with blood, for these houses were targets for the firing ; a little boy of thirteen, who fled for shelter into a toyshop, was killed upon a heap of toys ; eight cannon were pointed on Sallandrouze's carpet warehouse ; Dr. Piquet, a man of seventy, was shot as he sat reading in his drawing-room, and the painter Jolivard, as he stood before his easel, fell with a ball in his skull ; Boyer, the chemist, as he sat at his counter, was riddled with the bayonets of the lancers ; a poor little working sempstress as she sat finishing a piece of embroidery in her garret. Before the Theatre of Varieties there were fifty-two corpses, and among them eleven women. Thus, in the twinkling of an eye was Paris transfigured. Victor Hugo saw that scene of slaughter. " J'ai vu cette pluie de la mort aveugle ; j'ai vu tomber autour de moi en foule les massacrés éperdus." Dazed with horror, he lifted his eyes : Juliette stood before him. With a friend no less valiant than herself, she had been seeking him for hours.

By the end of the afternoon the Prince-President had triumphed. There was no heart left in Paris. All the popular force and fury was suddenly extinguished ; it was like the withdrawal of a great tide : nothing now but flat, dull, barren subjection. Nothing on the horizon. On the morning of the 5th of December the members of the Insurrectionary Committee found themselves practically alone ; the representatives of the Left, hunted down by the police, wandered for several days from hiding place to hiding place, and one after the other left Paris in disguise. Exile was their last asylum. Victor Hugo did not know where to lay his head. On the afternoon of the 7th, tired to death, he thought he would try an old cache of his, No. 19 rue de Richelieu ; under the *porte-cochère* a febrile hand grasped his sleeve : " Don't go up ! " It was Juliette Drouet waiting to warn him that there the trap was laid. There was a cab on the stand before the Palais-Royal. They got in. " Where shall we go ? " said Juliette.

" I don't know," said the poet wearily.

" I do," she said with decision, and led him to the house of the Marquis de Montgolfier, a Royalist, a relation of Madame Abel Hugo. No one would look for him there, on account of the political difference. And there Victor Hugo stayed in hiding for nearly a week ; but Juliette left on the 8th for Brussels. She was standing on the platform of the railway station there, in front of the Customs House, on the 14th of December, when the Paris express came in. A workman in the dress of his class leapt out of the train. In another moment he was in her arms. It was Victor Hugo. In the small valise which formed his luggage he had brought a little money, a change of clothes, and a great deal of work—especially the notes and studies for a long, a very important novel on the condition of the poor in Paris, on which he had already been at work for several years, " vaste manuscrit," which his friends urged him to finish, judging it one of his surest claims to immortality, but which the stormy politics of 1848, the manœuvres of the Prince-President, the *coup d'État*, had grievously interrupted. He hoped now to finish it in exile. He called it " Le Livre des Misères." Ten years later he will publish it under the title *Les Misérables*.

For the first months of his exodus Victor Hugo was separated from the members of his household. Madame Hugo remained in Paris. Her two sons, Charles and François-Victor, young men of twenty-five and twenty-three, were both of them in prison for seditious articles in the newspapers, a fortunate confinement which, keeping them out of harm's way during the tragic week of the *coup d'État*, probably preserved their lives. Madame Hugo, accustomed to visit them daily, and to dine with them in their prison every evening, could not leave them to their fate. She was devoted to her two sons, who were, in truth, delightful young men : Charles, handsome, intensely live, buoyant, expressive, his tongue outrunning his thoughts, was extraordinarily like his beautiful mother and yet the living image of his ugly uncle Foucher ; Toto, in mind and person, was more distinguished, less alert, a reflective, studious youth, tactful and gentle. Charles was the more brilliant, and Toto the more charming, just as Léopoldine had more charm than Dédé, who was so much the handsomer.[1]

Madame Hugo was also her husband's agent for the settlement of his affairs. On the 1st of December 1851 Victor Hugo had been almost a rich man. Like many rich men, he did not keep much money in the house ; when the *coup d'État* broke out he found in his strong-box some sixty pounds. He took twenty, left the rest to his wife, and told her to sell their furniture and put his papers in safety before she thought of joining him abroad.

And doubtless it was a queer sort of comfort in Madame Hugo's trouble to reflect that, after all, in Brussels, there was that capable Madame Drouet !

[1] Alphonse Karr, *Le Livre du bord*, t. 3.

CHAPTER XIX

A VOLCANO IN ERUPTION

HUGO remained eight months in Brussels, where, in January 1851, he learned that he was a banished man, " expelled " from France and liable to be transported as a convict to the penal settlement of Cayenne should he attempt to break his bounds. He sought relief in hard work from present distress ; his art alone could assuage the fierce indignation inspired by Louis-Napoleon's successful crime. He was writing his memoirs of the *coup d'État* (*L'Histoire d'un crime*, *Napoléon le petit*), he was meditating *Les Châtiments*. He could not refrain from work, and it was indeed most necessary that he should earn his bread ; although he reduced his own expenses to three francs a day all told, and notwithstanding the strict economy to which he condemned his wife and children in Paris, the little store of money he had in hand could not last long. He writes to his wife from Brussels : " Il faut vivre ici, stoïque et pauvre, et dire à tous : Je n'ai pas besoin d'argent ! " But facts are hard things. With himself and, after February, his son Charles in Brussels ; with a separate establishment for Madame Drouet ; with, in Paris, his wife, Adèle, and François-Victor (who still had several months of prison before him), expenses were inevitable and must be met : three households could not live off air. The poet sighs : " Il faut vendre un manuscrit, et alors je ferai la vie plus large à tous." But the difficulty was to print it. Publishers who had formed a court round the great poet, round the Peer of Louis-Philippe, round the Réprésentant du Peuple of 1848, were shy of the proscript, and calculated the cost of offending the Prince-President, who soon became the Emperor. The Belgian press, in terror of so powerful a neighbour, was no more free than the French. The despotism of the First Empire blossomed anew. "Well, we must hold out and economize," writes Victor Hugo to his absent wife; "Hetzel will go over to London and see if anything can be done there." Meanwhile the Director of the Varieties came to Brussels, with the express permission of the French Prefect of Police, to ask our poet for a non-political play. Maupas and Louis-Napoleon desired nothing better than to divert his energies from politics to literature —by way of an advance the Prince-President remitted the sentence of our exile's second son. But Victor Hugo would not be tempted: "I told him that, after the completion of my book, I would consider the matter, but that I could only break my silence by the sound of a slap in the face of the Prince-President."

Fortunately, those who depended on Victor Hugo were no less courageous than himself. "Bravo for women!" he writes to his wife. "All over the place they are lifting up their valiant heads sooner than the men." His own women were among the staunchest. Juliette, seeing his dire distress for money, offered to leave him and fend for herself—which of course he would not accept. Madame Victor Hugo was no less firm and loyal. He wrote to her on the 22nd of February:

Let me say at once that you are a noble and admirable woman. Your letters bring the tears to my eyes. Nothing is lacking: dignity, force, simplicity, courage, reason, serenity, tenderness—they are all there. When you talk politics, you hit just the right note and all you say rings true. If you speak of our affairs and the family, it is a great and kind heart that finds an utterance. How can you suppose I keep the shadow of a mental reservation? What have I to hide—from you, my Dear, especially? My life, my soul, defy the sunlight! You say that you do not like to write about money matters. I understand. We are poor, and we must traverse with dignity a dolorous pass—which may be quite brief, but which may last a long time. I wear out my old shoes, I wear out my old clothes —no great hardship. And you support all sorts of privations, sometimes suffering, often extreme hardship, which is worse for you, being a woman, and you do it all with contentedness and dignity.

How can you suppose I have no confidence in you? Does

anything belong to me and not to you ?   Do not say " your "
money, say " our " money.   I am the manager, that is all.
When my poor dear boys get to work, and work as hard as I do,
when I find a publisher—in Brussels, in London, in any free
country—when I have sold a MS., I shall say, That's right, and
I shall be more generous for us all.   Meanwhile, we must suffer
a little.   As for me, it is your sufferings I mind—not my own.

All this explains my rigidity in matters of expenditure.   We
are not yet living within our narrowed means—we shall do it,
we have not yet done it.   How can you think that in preaching
economy I show mistrust of you?   My Dear !   If I had all our
fortune there before me I would give it you to keep and only
say, Take care !   I may disappear one of these fine mornings,
and I want to leave behind me, intact, the capital of my earnings.
The dignity of your temper demands it.   You must never be
beholden to anybody.   You must be able to live as you always
have lived without me, just the same as by my side, in your
noble dignity, set above the contact of Governments, men, or
things.   You must need no protection.   That is the future I see
for you and for our children.   Hence my rigid economy.

Victor Hugo, between his marriage and 1845, had earned
some twenty thousand pounds—500,000 francs (as we learn
from a letter to the editor of the *Phare de la Loire*, in his
Correspondance) ; of these he had spent eight thousand and
invested twelve thousand.   But this capital was in 1852
still inaccessible to the exile ; and even when he shortly
afterwards regained possession of it, he would spend nothing
but the income.   In Paris the royalties from his plays had
greatly increased his revenues (as he tells the same correspondent in another letter), which had frequently equalled
and even exceeded three thousand a year (78,000 francs) ;
but his dramas were no longer performed in any theatre in
France.

Not content with economizing—for which she had, in
fact, no share of her husband's gift—Madame Hugo was
anxious to add to the family resources.   It was at this
moment, in view of occupying the dreary days of exile
(which she loathed as perhaps only a Parisian can), while
she earned a little money to boil the pot, that she conceived the idea of writing the story of Victor Hugo's childhood, of his first successes, of his plays up to the production of *Les Burgraves* in 1843—she would go no further

than that, for the poor mother could not face the recital of the death of Léopoldine : the world had come to an end in 1843. It was a scheme which was to develop into the two charming volumes called *Victor Hugo raconté par un témoin de sa vie.*

In August 1852 Victor Hugo left Brussels with his son Charles and joined Madame Victor Hugo and the two younger children in Jersey. They set up house together in Marine Terrace—with Juliette handily lodged just round the corner. Part of every afternoon he spent with her ; she was his Minerva, his companion, but also his secretary, and he kept her well employed. *Napoléon le petit* appeared in 1852, and in 1853 (printed at the poet's expense, for no publisher would take the risk) a volume of poems, *Les Châtiments.* This is a great and epoch-making date in the history of Victor Hugo.

Imagine him in his little house by the seashore, the world outside wet and dark ; the rain and the spray dash their showers against the window-pane ; France is not twenty leagues away, but, in that whirling white-and-grey of waves and mist, of drifting clouds and rain, of driving sails and screaming sea-gulls, Paris seems as distant as it is inaccessible. In summer-time Jersey had seemed a Paradise ; but this wild winter weather suited our poet best for that which he had to do :

I have spent my wrath in writing sombre poems. The book will be called : *Punishment.* You can guess what it is about. You will read it one of these days. Napoleon the Little was written in prose, and so was but half of my appointed task. The wretch was only roasted on one side—I am turning him on the grill.[1]

In his solitude the poet thought of the harder lot of his companions, transported to the feverish marshes of Cayenne ; thought with a still deeper bitterness of those whom the tyrant had bought over, who were grandees of the Empire, academicians, senators like Mérimée, or, like Sainte-Beuve, Professors of the College of France. And he recalled the scenes of the preceding winter—the barricades strewn with

[1] 5th March 1853—à Alphonse Esquiros, Correspondance.

corpses ; that little lad of seven years old whom he had
seen in the rue Tiquetonne, laid dead across the knees of
his old granny—the poet remembered how he had helped
to undress the child and fold him in his winding-sheet ; he
thought of Pauline Roland, most innocent and noblest of
women, sent for her crimes to the African penitentiary of
Lambessa, and dying of hardships too atrocious for her
fragile frame ; he thought of Napoleon the Great, pitifully
dishonoured by the shame and shoddy glory of his nephew ;
and then he thought of Joshua sounding his avenging
trumpet until at last the walls of Jericho did fall. And the
Eternal touched his lips with that red coal which set aflame
the words that fell from the prophetic mouth of Jeremiah.
And he wrote *Les Châtiments*.

Hugo's exile was one of those admirable misfortunes
that unlock the secret treasure of a soul. Indignation,
pity, horror of evil, lifted him above the common round of
feelings ; and the solitary calm of this foreign island
separated him from reality. He lived as in a vision, com-
municating only with things eternal. And in this Upper
Room to which he found himself suddenly lifted he regained possession, and in far ampler measure than of old,
not only of the passion and earnestness of youth, but of
an energy of accent and image, a lyrical abundance, an
invention in rhythm and strophe, a verbal felicity, a
metrical skill, which perhaps no poet save Milton and Pindar
could equal. All that Milton did for blank verse when he
swept his marvellous organ music through the bare and
massive structure of his predecessors, Victor Hugo did for
the French alexandrine when, by a system of time-values
and pauses, of swell and fall irregularly spacing the lines,
of changed stress and shifting cesurae, he made the couplets
come alive and, in his own words, transfigured the shuttle-
cock set round with twelve stiff feathers, sent from racket
to racket in regular rotation, into a singing bird soaring
high in the air :

> Le vers s'envole au ciel tout naturellement,
> Il monte, il est le vers ; je ne sais quoi de frêle
> Et d'éternel, qui chante et plane et bat de l'aile.[1]

---

[1] *Les Quatre Vents de l'esprit*, i. 14.

Besides this great verse, Victor Hugo employs (for the first time, I think, in the *Châtiments*) a scheme of the austerest and soberest simplicity which is no less noble, no less perfect. It is interesting to compare the recital of the murder of the little seven-year-old of the rue Tiquetonne as it appears in prose in the *Histoire d'un crime* and in verse in *Les Châtiments*. The poem is perhaps the more restrained, though either passage is admirable in its grave and sad simplicity : nothing could be plainer, more straightforward than this passage ; the movement is almost the movement of prose, without an inversion, scarcely an epithet, and in its simple tragedy and irony it tugs at our heartstrings as surely as Cordelia's death does in *King Lear*. Nor, in this wonderful book, are music and tragic grandeur, wild prophetic vituperation, rapt elevations of sublime reverie, all our poet has to offer us, for these are interspersed with songs of the sweetest lyric grace, and the most exquisite sense of movement and number. Sometimes, as he wandered along the narrow shores of his island, Hugo felt the soul of his Vendéenne mother swell in his breast—anything ! anything ! to annihilate the reign of iniquity—anything, even a foreign invasion ! And in the far distance he heard the roar, the sinister laugh, of the black lion of Waterloo. When the Crimean War broke out he exulted :

Russia will be as fatal to Napoleon the Little as to Napoleon the Great. Balaclava will be his Berezina. Only our Restoration will be the Revolution.[1]

And he lashed the French Marshal, Saint-Arnaud, who had earned his fine feathers and marshal's rod by his brilliant raid on the Boulevard Montmartre, where he had routed or slaughtered a score of nurses with their perambulators.

But the choicest vials of his wrath were reserved for the Emperor — smiling, successful ; the comrade - at - arms of Queen Victoria, our poet's hostess ; the eldest son of the Church. The Emperor had laughed when one of his courtiers had handed him a copy of *Napoléon le petit* : " I see," he had said, " Napoleon the Little, by Victor Hugo the Great." And the Court had broken into heroic mirth at

[1] Lettre à Madame de Girardin, 4th Jan. 1855.

this neat thrust, for the poet's fatuity and self-amplification were a legend. Let him laugh while he might! The end was not yet :

Ah, tu finiras bien par hurler, misérable !
... L'histoire à mes côtés met à nu ton épaule,
Tu dis, je ne sens rien ! et tu nous railles, drôle !
Ton rire sur mon nom gaîment vient s'écumer ;
Mais je tiens le fer rouge et vois ta chair fumer !

The Crimean War was not popular in France, but it strengthened the position of the Emperor, the ally of Queen Victoria, triumphant over the Tsar, and in the little island of Jersey, always military, aristocratic, and patriotic, the brilliant success of *Les Châtiments* did its author no good. The fame of the poems sped through Europe like wildfire ; copied in manuscript from surreptitious volumes dangerously smuggled into the Empire, Victor Hugo's iambics were alive on the lips of the Liberals ; old men, who were boys in those days, still remember how in every public school the borrowed notebook would circulate from desk to desk, while the enthusiastic lads learned by heart the wonderful satires which, turn by turn, are epic or ode, idyll or song. Let us be just and add that even the political opponents of Hugo admired the flame and fury, the life, the music, of a book unique in any language.

But in Jersey revolutionary poems were at a discount. " Napoléon le petit managed to turn me out of Brussels," wrote the poet to a correspondent : was Jersey a safer haven ? Unfortunately, all the French proscripts were not of Victor Hugo's calibre ; we know, on Juliette Drouet's authority, that some of them were very rough specimens. One of them, Félix Pyat, in the autumn of 1855 attacked Queen Victoria in a miserable little newspaper, *L'Homme*. Madame Hugo, in a letter to Madame Paul Meurice, admits that the article was " maladroit and equivocal." Jersey avenged the honour of the Queen by expelling the exile. Victor Hugo protested, and he in his turn received notice to quit. On the last day of October the poet and his household moved to Guernsey, which was to be their home for fifteen years. Victor Hugo left Jersey with regret. He had never taken root there (as he did at once in Guernsey),

had never felt sufficiently sure of the morrow to settle and
furnish a house, while Hauteville House in the sister island
(which he bought and arranged in his own romantic taste,
with carved oak and old tapestries, china, and heavy frames
of time - dulled gold) has remained associated with his
memory no less closely than his home in the place Royale.
But he had loved the beauty of Jersey.   The winter was
wild :

Le ciel pleuve, la mer gueule dans les rochers, le vent rugit
comme une bête, les arbres se tordent sur les collines, la nature
se met en furie autour de moi.[1]

But spring changed the wild western island to a dream
of Paradise.   " Jersey is Lemnos ! " cried our poet.   Summer
and winter alike there was quiet, and the sea :

Je travaille presque nuit et jour.   Je vogue en pleine poésie.
Je suis abruti par l'azur. . . . J'ai épousé la mer, l'ouragan, une
immense grève de sable, la tristesse, et toutes les étoiles de la
nuit.[2]

" I have wedded the sea ! "   It was on the sands of
Jersey that Victor Hugo learned to understand the beauty
of the sea.   True, he had loved the sea and sung the sea
before—never more musically than in the *Chants du
crépuscule* :

> Quand la nuit n'est pas étoilée
> Viens te bercer aux flots des mers ;
> Comme la nuit elle est voileé,
> Comme la vie ils sont amers.

He had set the sea to a song and had chosen the ocean
for an image. But his exact, acute, and plastic sense of
line and form led him to prefer the mountain.   Victor Hugo
was not a colourist.   Intensely sensitive to light and shadow,
to every detail of shape and silhouette, he rarely mentions
the precise colour of the objects he describes, and still more
seldom with any gusto or delight.   He saw a world sharply
outlined, and irradiated by light in every accident of its
relief.   The vague, dreamy, formless swell of greeny blue
or purply green had for him at first little sensual attraction.

[1] Lettre à Noël Parfact, 29th Oct. 1853.
[2] Lettre à Émile Deschanel, 14th Jan. 1855.

The sea was an image of the Infinite, and as such convenient. He was fifty years old before he really felt the lure of the Ocean—and then he sang it as no other poet, not even Swinburne, has sung it.

In Jersey, in Guernsey, the sea was his inseparable companion ; and he never wearied of the moods, the changes, the caprices, the grace, the grandeur of that moving immensity which, indeed, among all the spectacles of Nature, is the most akin to his own imagination—so much so that a French psychologist (Léopold Mabilleau) has attributed to the influence of the sea, reinforcing a tendency natural to our poet, the exasperated violence, the storms of wrath, and also that sudden widening of the mental horizon, which mark the productions of Hugo's genius during his residence in the Channel Islands. His prophetic fury, his apprehension of the Infinite, arose (says our philosopher) from the poet's contiguity to a melancholy ocean.

CHAPTER XX

CONTEMPLATION

EXILE is a lesser form of death, removing us in an instant from all our habits and associations, plunging us suddenly into a world unknown and formidable, of which, in the Hugos' case, they did not even know the language. Nothing to do but muse, marvel, meditate, think, remember! How brightly, against the dreary present, shone the splendid images of the past! In Guernsey the poet, if not his household, began at last to take root; but in the long wet winters of Marine Terrace, while, as yet, no project or interest had arisen to divert the thoughts of our outlaws, how tenderly, how sweetly, gleamed the phantom of Léopoldine constantly recalled!

> Nous avons pris la sombre et charmante habitude
> De voir son ombre vivre en notre solitude,
> De la sentir passer et de l'entendre errer,
> Et nous sommes restés à genoux à pleurer.[1]

Madame Hugo, in frail health, could not rouse herself from the dear, importunate obsession. In 1854 Madame de Girardin, visiting the Hugos in Jersey, had introduced the superstitions of spiritism and the practice of turning tables. The poor mother, whose faith in an after-life had never wavered, but who felt that between herself and her daughter, as between herself and her parents, the door was shut, now thought their communications were resumed, and asked no fairer horizon, no further society: Marine Terrace satisfied her, since even there she could catch the last vibration of the vanished voices. Table-turning became

[1] *Les Contemplations,* " Dolorosae."

a fever, a passion. On the 7th of March, Madame Hugo writes to a friend (Madame Paul Meurice), whose husband had recently lost both his mother and his brother :

Do you not converse with your mother ? I began, long ago, to hold conversations with my dear ones dead, and now the tables confirm me in my faith. . . . Is it not a divine benediction that you were initiated in our table-turning before your dear ones departed this life ? God, who loves you, wished you to understand that there is something behind the grave before He took them from you. It was not just a thing of chance. The tables have begun to answer the question that your husband sent, but the answer seems likely to be long ; already two *séances* have been occupied exclusively with it—with the exception of one answer to a question put by my husband. Charles has promised me another sitting for this evening, and I hope we shall continue with the answer that your husband requires.[1]

I think that, on the whole, this occupation was salutary for Madame Hugo. It gave her an object in life. The Hugos' tables were soon famous in Jersey ; hence much coming and going, much exchanging of tales of woe, many exercises in the faith, messages sent or received across the infinite abyss. But these practices, which may be a useful stimulant to a lymphatic imagination, are dangerous for the intenser vibrations of a poet. Victor Hugo had been slow to take fire, but he became no less ardent than his household, and we find him writing to Madame de Girardin, 4th January 1855 :

The tables tell us most surprising things. I wish I could tell you, and kiss your hands, feet—or wings ! Has Paul Meurice told you that a whole system of cosmogony that I have been brooding over—and have partly written out—during the last twenty years has been confirmed by the tables with magnificent enlargements ? We live in front of a mysterious horizon which changes all the perspectives of our exile ; and we think of you, to whom we owe the opening of this window.

The tables recommend silence and secrecy—except two details —important ones it is true—you will find nothing concerning them in *Les Contemplations*.

Naturally we ask : what was this system of cosmogony, this theory of the origin of the universe, confirmed by the tables ? And, full of curiosity, we turn to the *Contempla-*

---

[1] *La Vie d'une femme*, Gustave Simon, p. 307.

tions. We shall find nothing in the First Part, which is a collection of occasional poems—some of the rarest beauty and grace—written between 1830 and 1843. If this were a volume of criticism, and not a biography, I should linger on the extraordinary poetry of XXI. and XXII. in the first book—the earlier equal to anything in the Greek anthology, the second containing as it were in germ all the *Fêtes galantes* of Verlaine. But these marvels of lyrical perfection are not of the date nor of the sentiment of *Les Contemplations.* The First Part is divided from the Second by an abyss—the grave of Léopoldine.

Léopoldine is the muse of the Second Part. Léopoldine dead, Léopoldine buried. No mourner perhaps has ever recorded such terrible visions of the dead as they dwell imprisoned in their tombs. The poet's genius moves underground like Hamlet's mole. That way madness lies— and more than once we feel Victor's brotherhood to Eugène in this morbid visitant of the vault. Eugène's imagination lost him his reason. But Victor Hugo had a gift that saved him. He made poems of his nightmares ; he trans- figured the sombre stupor of his gloomy broodings and steeped them in the eternal light of Art. The mere beauty of form and rhythm kept him sane, although he stood on the edge of that bottomless pit in which lurk Pantheism and that which William James has called " the nightmare and suicidal view of life."

In his grief he looked on Creation and saw that it was evil. Life is the punishment of sin. Evil is matter, matter is Evil. Only there is a streak of soul in it, and thereby a possibility of redemption, for Soul is eternal, and Evil is not. A spark of soul fallen by its own fault into the world of substance becomes, according to the degree of its iniquity, a man, a bird, a beast, a fish, a tree, a stone.

On the coast of Guernsey these pensive pebbles, these stubborn rocks, haunted Victor Hugo with the sense of their antenatal criminality. What could they have done ? Were they Nero ? were they Borgia ? Certain masses of granite at Sark filled him with horror and pity. Their present being must surely expiate a previous fault, or aggra- vate it, for everything is in a state of flux ; everything changes, everything dies. Matter is death! And the universe is a whirling waste whose abyss is not less terrible than those surging waters which closed about the unholpen head of Léopoldine. " Hélas, tout est sépulcre ! . . . "

He feels as perhaps no poet ever felt before the helplessness of the individual in presence of the vast conflicting forces of the universe, and the stupor of that universe itself in front of eternity :

> J'ai vu dans les sapins passer la lune horrible,
> Et j'ai cru par moments, témoin épouvanté,
> Surprendre l'attitude effarée et terrible
> De la création devant l'éternité.[1]

But there is a Being which transcends the universe and fills eternity, an invisible, incomprehensible Spectator in whom alone is our hope. Thus, in the poem called *Melancholia*, the old horse flogged to death by a drunken master feels a vague presence consoling its agony :

> Son œil, plein des stupeurs sombres de l'Infini
> Où luit vaguement l'âme effarante des choses,

recognizes that compassionate Spirit,

> Et regarde Quelqu'un de sa prunelle trouble.

The same eternal witness consoles the deathbed of Jean Valjean. For sometimes a sudden *sursum corda* puts the human soul in communication with the Infinite. Our hand is held in an invisible grasp ; our mortal weakness feels itself sustained in the embrace of the Eternal. Prayer has thrown a bridge across the abyss and spanned the interval that separates the human from the divine.

Prayer is one of man's guardian angels. Another is pain :

> O douleur, clef des Cieux ! . . .
> L'expiation rouvre une porte fermée !
>
> Monter, c'est s'immoler. Toute cime est sévère.
> L'Olympe lentement se transforme en calvaire.
> Partout le martyre est écrit ;
> Une immense croix gît dans notre nuit profonde,
> Et nous voyons saigner aux quatre coins du monde
> Les quatre clous de Jésus Christ.[2]

---

[1] *Toute la Lyre*, I. " La Nature," vii.
[2] *Dolor*.

O Pain, thou Key of Heaven !
Atonement, key that opens a closed door !

Ascent is sacrifice ; the summits are austere.
Olympus changes, fades, till Calvary is here,
    Sun-scorched, or winter-iced.
The Cross immensely spreads, like a long shade unfurled,
Look !   At the four wide corners of the world
    Bleed the Four Nails of Jesus Christ.

In such a mood the poet could more calmly consider the death of his child, and, like Job, put his grief before the Eternal.

Le monde est sombre, ô Dieu ! l'immuable harmonie
    Se compose des pleurs aussi bien que des chants ;
L'homme n'est qu'un atome en cette ombre infinie,
    Nuit où montent les bons, où tombent les méchants.

Je sais que vous avez bien autre chose à faire
    Que de nous plaindre tous,
Et qu'un enfant qui meurt, désespoir de sa mère,
    Ne vous fait rien, à vous.

Je sais que le fruit tombe au vent qui le secoue,
    Que l'oiseau perd sa plume, et la fleur son parfum ;
Que la création est une grande roue
    Qui ne peut se mouvoir sans écraser quelqu'un ;

Les mois, les jours, les flots des mers, les yeux qui pleurent,
    Passent sous le ciel bleu ;
Il faut que l'herbe pousse et que les enfants meurent ;
    Je le sais, ô mon Dieu !

Dans vos cieux, au delà de la sphère des nues,
    Au fond de cet azur immobile et dormant,
Peut-être faites-vous des choses inconnues
    Où la douleur de l'homme entre comme élément.

Peut-être est-il utile à vos desseins sans nombre
    Que des êtres charmants
S'en aillent, emportés par le tourbillon sombre
    Des noirs événements.[1]

What accents, torn from the soul ! Despair and faith, bitterest irony, tenderest remembrance unite in this poem —the last page torn from the Book of Job ! How rash to attempt to render an echo of such a strain. And yet I am

[1] *A Villequier.*

convinced that it is only in verse, however inadequate, that
we can give at least a suggestion of the quality of a poet :

> O God, Thy world is dark ! The music of the spheres
>   Is made of sighs and sobs no less than songs, I think !
> Man is an atom lost in the endless Vale of Tears,
>   A night wherein the Good rise, and the Wicked sink.
>
> I know Thou hast no time, Creator that Thou art,
>   To hear us when we cry ;
> And that a child who dies, wringing a mother's heart,
>   Is nought to the Most High.
>
> When the wind shakes the bough, I know the fruit must fall,
>   I know the bird must lose the feather from its wing ;
> Creation is a wheel that, rounding on us all,
>   Grinds into dust at every turn some precious thing.
>
> Our months, our days, our tides, our tears, are things that pass,
>   Like clouds, 'tween sky and sod ;
> The grass grows ; children die ; I know it well ; alas,
>   I know it ! O my God !
>
> High in Thy Heaven, beyond the sphere of clouds and wings,
>   Where the dead blue extends, vast, without rift or rent,
> Perchance createst Thou unknown immortal things
>   Wherein the grief of man is a chief element ?
>
> Perhaps the immense designs of Thine unnumbered plans
>   Need that our darlings die,
> Drowned in the eddying dark—the black, wide whirl that spans
>   The whole space of the sky ?

There is more irony than faith so far in the poet's
resignation. He accepts the rod, but cannot say with
Dante : " In Thy will lies our peace." Still the progress of
the poems shows the gradual exhaustion of despair, the
submission of a broken heart. Renouvier, I think, was
right when he said that Victor Hugo, in his youth a Christian
from habit and custom ; after 1830, a Christian in language,
but not in thought ; became spontaneously and unconsciously a real Christian at the epoch of the *Contemplations*,
although a Christian heretic—a gnostic or a Manichee. He
never found it out, and, to the end of his days, had no
inkling of the nature of a religion which he considered the
original result of his own meditations.

So at last our poet arrives at a theory of the universe, a conception of the world which takes full account of the pain and evil inherent in it, and yet preserves a hope of progress, both for the individual and for the whole. This doctrine gilds, as with a ray of dawn, all Hugo's later works. Their infinite mansuetude, their boundless charity, prophesy a general redemption. The world is evil, but it shall one day be good. All things tend towards an ineffable climax.

ἄιλινον, ἄιλινον, ειπέ, τὸ δ' εὖ νικάτω.

In *Les Contemplations* our poet has not yet attained this beatitude. He dwells " dans l'effarement de l'Infini," still bewildered, affrighted, scared, by the immensity of the abyss, the gulfs of darkness, the dim colossal shadows that move in that obscurity :

O Nature, abîme ! Immensité de l'ombre—

But, sometimes in a huge cavern underground (as in the grottoes of Han), one may find an unexpected guide in the shape of a river, flowing towards the light ; so Hugo, in that world of gloom, discerns, like an ever-swelling stream, the mutual soul of man : " Comme un fleuve d'âme commune."

Une sorte de Dieu fluide
Coule aux veines du genre humain.[1]

The final philosophy of Hugo will be a sort of Messianism : a faith in the Mages, the Great Men, the sons of God, who are the successive redeemers of humanity. One such apostle outweighs many Borgias. For, in the eyes of Hugo, evil is a purely negative quality, a blank, a miss, a " manque à gagner." The good alone positively exists, and each great man, each poet, seer, sage, saint, or hero is a nugget of solid gold outweighing any quantity of those half-decayed dead leaves that we call criminals or tyrants, whose substance is but a show, who are but the trifles of time, unassimilable by eternity.

While, on his rock of Guernsey, Victor Hugo was re-inventing all the doctrines of the Albigenses, and seeking

[1] *Les Contemplations*, " Les Mages."

the phantom of Léopoldine in the past and the present, in this world and in the next, another daughter was fading almost unnoticed by his side. The coup d'État had surprised Adèle Hugo (the younger Adèle, " Dédé ") in her two-and-twentieth year, in the full bloom and gaiety of her girlhood, and had changed too suddenly all the circumstances of her lot. Hugo's two elder children, the radiant and gentle Léopoldine, the jovial, good-natured, idle, affectionate Charles, were out-going natures, easier to understand for a poet so tremendously occupied with his own speculations (even though an idolizing father) than the two younger ones, the delicate and pensive François, the translator of Shakespeare, and Adèle, whose frail health seems never to have recovered from the sad and stormy influences of her birth. The child of 1830 was a creature of much romantic grace, " belle comme une statue antique," says Alphonse Karr, but often capricious or discontented —perhaps a somewhat arid soul. For her, after Léopoldine's tragic end, no indulgence, no precaution had seemed too great. She had never been in contact with the realities of life until the moment came when they pressed on her too hardly. A few years later, in writing *Les Travailleurs de la mer* (of which the heroine, Déruchette, is evidently an image of Dédé), Victor Hugo sadly resumes the errors of such an education. In very truth, Adèle had been spoiled, rendered unfit for the give-and-take of ordinary existence. She thought everything due to her, and herself without a debt or a duty. A sweet-singing bird of a creature, a smiling nymph, a light-hearted chit of a girl—and then a broken lily.

It is impossible to read Madame Hugo's letters [1] without feeling very sorry for Adèle. At first she had borne with great spirit the sudden transplanting. " She does not mind giving up her balls," says her mother, " for she appreciates her father's aureole." At first, despite all the misery of breaking up the house and home, the spice of adventure and novelty had enabled the girl to accept cheerfully their stay in Jersey. In the middle of the last century Jersey was almost as much French as English—a quaint corner of

[1] Gustave Simon, *La Vie d'une femme.*

Normandy or Brittany washed a few miles out to sea.
And none of the Hugos had ever supposed that they would
make their abiding home in Jersey.   But in Guernsey they
were settled.   The years dragged on ; Adèle drooped and
pined ;   her father thought her selfish :   " Elle n'aime
qu'elle ! " he exclaimed angrily to his wife.   The girl was
ill.   Her father, all morning occupied among his books and
papers, absent in the afternoon on those long walks in
which he communed so fruitfully with Nature, dined several
nights a week with Madame Drouet and the exiles ; he saw
his household chiefly at the mid-day meal, which was always
cheerful and well attended ; or else when, as a carpenter,
joiner, and decorator, he needed the skilled assistance of the
bright, uproarious Charles, or the scholarly Toto ; at such
times, hearing Adèle's piano going for all it was worth, and
perhaps her fresh young voice singing " Bonny Dundee " or
the song from *Lucrezia Borgia*, he enjoyed the impression
that his numerous family was as happy and as busy as
himself.   He was creating for their use and pleasure a
sumptuous home.   True, he had asked the advice of none
of them when, seven months after their arrival in Guernsey,
he had bought the property called Hauteville House—a
picturesque old mansion, built a century before by an
English corsair, standing high and solid among its garden
terraces.   He was weary of furnished houses and that
" English comfort " which he found to consist in a mattress
as hard as a plank, scrappy sheets, straight-back chairs,
and bench-like ottomans.   He had just received the royalties
for the first two editions of *Les Contemplations*.   It was not
often that the money burned a hole in Victor Hugo's pocket,
but, like many parsimonious persons, he would sometimes
make a really magnificent purchase.   In Jersey a law of
the island forbade any foreigner to buy a freehold ; but
Guernsey, being farther from France, was less jealous of
the inroads of the alien.   Briefly, he bought Hauteville
House.   The family at first accepted the accomplished fact
with something better than resignation.   There was all the
discovery and invention and adventure of restoring and
furnishing the mansion, of planting the garden, which dis-
guised the monotony of their outlawed life on a very small

and foreign island. Madame Hugo, while admitting that she would have preferred Brussels, or even London, as a place of exile, celebrated the beauty of her new home, the splendour of the view, the youthful buoyancy and health of the poet, the good effect on the habits and disposition of her sons, of their austere and almost solitary existence :

Mon mari aime l'île, il prend des bains de mer à profusion. Ils lui sont très favorables, il est rajeuni et superbe. Il a produit de belles œuvres. . . . Il n'est pas détaché de la France, mais il a de l'éloignement pour la génération actuelle. . . . Ah, voyez-vous, on ne vit pas impunément pendant cinq ans, éloigné de son pays.[1]

In 1859 a general amnesty opened to the political exiles of 1852 the frontiers of France. Like Michelet, like Quinet, Victor Hugo, with admirable dignity, refused to countenance by his return that which he still thought iniquity. He remained on his rock mid-seas, aloof, irreconcilable. And it is certain that the constancy of his attitude, in almost as great a degree as the incomparable beauty of his literary production during this period, crowned him in the sight of the democrats of France their prince and their prophet. In such heroic circumstances distance does lend an enchantment. The littleness of everyday detail is eliminated, and the image of a great poet remains, seen on his rock, standing solitary in the storm, like Simon Stylites on his pillar, a witness to the things of the Spirit.

But such a conception is not possible to the members of a poet's household. In 1853 Madame Hugo had written that the grandeur of the " auréole " redeemed, in the eyes of her daughter, the hardships of their exile. But now that the exile was voluntary, the zeal of the wife and daughter began to relax. " I am doing my duty to God and to France ! " thought Victor Hugo ; and his wife said, " Are we doing our duty by Adèle ? " At Christmas 1856 the poor girl had a nervous breakdown, with symptoms of hypochondria and agitation. She had thrown herself into her music as into an abyss. She sang, she played, she composed songs without words (which Ambrose Thomas

[1] *La Vie d'une femme* : Lettre à Mme. Paul Meurice, 17th Oct. 1856.

declared not without merit) ; in the octaves of her piano
she created for herself an alibi, far from the dreary world
of Guernsey, where it rained every second day, where
nothing ever happened, where no one ever came ! For,
since the amnesty, even the exiles were less frequent visitors.
And this unreal life had strained too tight those fragile,
vibrant nerves, which are so dangerous when they accompany a half-fledged genius, a gift not quite complete. The
doctors forbade the piano : Adèle needed rest. Day by
day the poor child sank deeper into her gloomy reverie,
shutting herself in her room, musing on certain relics
(I know not what), which she would place before her and
gaze at in apathetic contemplation. For she, too, contemplated, though to less purpose than her father. Madame
Hugo fussed after her daughter ineffectually in tender
motherly alarm, and tried, in vain, to awake the anxiety of
her husband. Though they were housemates, she had
always preserved the habit of writing to him little notes on
matters of importance ; and these are some of many such
concerning the long illness of Adèle :

Our exile is a fact. We must endure it. This house is
bought and furnished at great expense—too great an expense.
Well, we must live in it, or, at any rate, make it our principal
home. But it is incontestable that we have acted as though
Adèle did not exist ! And who knows if the same thought has
not crossed the mind of Adèle ! And in that case is not the
child praiseworthy never to have made a grievance of it ?
Never to have uttered a complaint ?

You are her father. You ought to feel as anxious as myself
about Adèle. Here we live in a convent, and her mind preys
upon itself. She thinks, and thinks ; and her ideas are often
false, and get fixed, never being interrupted by any fresh current
from outside. That is the root of the matter. And it is just the
same with her odd habits. Her fads and fancies are never broken
by any unexpected event, and so they become inveterate. I do
all I can. I go into her room, and talk, and preach, and rummage
here and there, ferret about, and try to restore all her little
possessions each to its proper destination—and even take away
those that serve as an aliment to her queer ideas. It is just
labour lost. I find the same things in the same place next day,
though I am just as obstinate as she is. What she needs is a
change. Travel, amusement, life in common in an hotel or

lodgings would alter the current of her thought.   I know that a journey cannot transform a temperament, but these old-maidish habits might be broken—at any rate for a time.   My dear, I would borrow money rather than that Adèle should not have a change !

Victor Hugo needed a great deal of persuasion : he loved to have his family round him, and he saw himself vowed to loneliness ; he was parsimonious, and these journeys meant money ; he was proud of the dignity of his protestation, and his wife's visits to France would seem like meeting the Emperor half-way.   But things were at last arranged.   Madame Hugo's young sister, Julie Foucher —twenty years younger than Adèle—had recently married the engraver, Paul Chenay ; she offered her sister and her niece the use of her apartment in Paris, while she and her husband would come to Hauteville and keep the poet company.   Half-reconciled, Victor Hugo consented to this plan, and henceforth his wife and daughter will know more freedom and holiday—will visit Paris, London, Brighton. . . . Adèle seemed better for the change.   But the poet's mind misgave him, and we find him writing in his diary :

16th January 1858.

My wife and daughter left this morning at twenty minutes after nine for Paris.   They travel by Southampton and Havre. How sad.

CHAPTER XXl

THE ZENITH

THE poet seemed wrapped in his own imaginings as securely as a silk-worm in its cocoon, weaving the golden tissues that may drape a dull world and delight a million eyes. The things of his own household escaped him ; yet such an artist is really the least selfish of men, since the fruit of his labour is the inheritance of all, and Victor Hugo, in his own eyes, was not merely an artist but also a teacher, a man with a message. Like most of the Liberals of the middle nineteenth century, he was convinced that ignorance is the root of social misery :

We needs must love the highest when we see it.

He thought himself one of those Mages whose divinely appointed mission and ministry it is to diffuse the light. His desultory instruction and omnivorous love of reading had filled his brain with a strange jumble of errors and erudition. He was thoroughly grounded in nothing, had learned nothing with method and precision, though he was a fair Latinist and a regular communicant in the Classics, at an age when most men have forgotten their Virgil. He had an inkling of many odd and out-of-the-way subjects in literature and history ; his mind was an encyclopædia of picturesque inaccuracies. It is possible that this vast and vague assembly of facts and theories imperfectly appre-hended may favour the mythopoetic faculty, being fertile in those " féconds malentendus " which, according to Renan, form the origin of myths. But we like our artist to know his limitations. Victor Hugo, in his candour, looked upon himself as a man of science, a deep source of knowledge, whose obvious duty it was to refresh and nourish a nation, a democracy, if not a world. Well, that also was a fecund misapprehension. For perhaps only the conviction of a duty to perform, a mission to accomplish, could nerve a man for so immense a task as that which Victor Hugo set himself in his next volume, *La Légende des siècles*. This is a book of miniature or fragmentary epics—epic in their conception, miniature in size — illustrating the gradual evolution and expansion of the Human Soul throughout the succession of the centuries. *La Légende des siècles* is the Ascent of Man, who in the distant future shall realize his Ideal and attain his final millennium. It is doubtless the " cosmogonie " whose first adumbrations we sought in the *Contemplations*. But the key to his thoughts and their conclusion (though chiefly composed in these years of the closing 'fifties at Hauteville House) shall only appear, long after the poet's death, in the magnificent if shadowy fragments called *La Fin de Satan*, and *Dieu*. Almost every page of the first volume of *La Légende des siècles* is a triumph of art, and as we contemplate these admirable treasures— heirlooms of a race—κτῆμα ἐς ἀει—we marvel at the profusion of Hugo's genius on the verge of his sixtieth year ; for not only *La Légende des siècles*, with the final volumes which I have just indicated, but the most beautiful things in *Les Quatre Vents de l'esprit*, as well as the incomparable prose epic of *Les Misérables*, are the fruit of a few years between 1856 and 1862. The point of perfection, I think, is attained in the first volume of *La Légende*, by which, however, I mean the first volume as it appeared in 1859, and not as we find it in the editions of to-day ; for, unhappily (possessed by the demon of chronology and the sense of evolution), Hugo in his old age recast his work, arranging his little epics according to the date of their subject and not in the order of their composition ; so that the pearls of his initial venture are dispersed throughout the vague and misty seas of the effusions of his old age, while these, in their turn, submerge and scatter the earlier masterpieces, blurring the pure perfection of their line.

He who possesses the first edition of *La Légende des siècles*, as it came out in 1859, does indeed possess a treasure.

There is a sweetness of temper in its epic grandeur, something gracious and lovable in the sublime, such as we find sometimes in Homer or in Shakespeare's *Tempest*. Have I said too much ? Read *Booz endormi*, *Les Lions*, *Pauvres Gens*, and that astonishing prophecy of the aeroplane, *Plein Ciel* —to say nothing of the *Satyre* and the *Rose de l'Infante*. Were this a book of criticism, it would be interesting to compare this volume with Robert Browning's *Men and Women*, which, for its force, variety, and learning, it so often recalls—but with what a superfluity of beauty ! What an added harmony of music and vision.

Les Misérables, which appeared in 1862, is conceived in the same key as *La Légende* ; it also is a progression towards an apotheosis. But where the poem is legend or prophecy, the prose epic touches reality and moves in our sphere. Marius, the hero, is the contemporary, and indeed the double, of Victor Hugo—the son of a Royalist mother and a father who had served in Napoleon's armies, like General Hugo.

Marius, too, had been young in 1830, had lived on the barricades of a revolution, had married, after endless difficulties, the girl whom all his young will and passion were bent on obtaining. Marius is an image of Hugo's youth. But is Marius the hero of *Les Misérables*? No. Evidently their real hero is Jean Valjean, the convict, the criminal who steals the cherished treasure of his benefactor, who cheats the boy-sweep of his florin ; who then, repenting, is transformed into a man of honesty and honour. But an innocent man is accused of the theft which he had thought atoned for by years of charity. Jean Valjean gives himself up, and returns to his hell of a convict-prison. He escapes from that place of perdition, not reform, and again begins the upward struggle. He adopts a little girl, an orphan, the seven-year-old slavey of a shrew, educates her, wins for her a place in the sun, weds her to Marius, sets her safe above all chances and changes, rescues Marius himself when wounded to death on the barricade. And, having assured the happiness of these children of his choice, he dies neglected, heart-broken, consoled in his agony by a supreme witness, an invisible Comforter, the phantom of the benefactor whom, in his youth, Jean Valjean had betrayed.

There is, no doubt, a sort of moral paradox, an amplification like that produced by the fumes of opium, in this
conception of a hardened criminal shattered by remorse
because he has stolen two francs from a little boy, and giving
himself up to justice in order to save an innocent man
wrongly accused. Hugo is incurably sentimental. We
must accept him as he is. His virtuous thieves and angelic
prostitutes are, after all, but the transposition into modern
art of figures sufficiently familiar in the Gospels. Hugo was
as intimately convinced as any priest that the heart of man
is complex, never wholly good nor wholly bad, and that
there is no sin which may not be redeemed. In *Les
Misérables* he gives life and substance to those theories of
expiation and atonement which he has preached consistently
enough in his play of *Marion de Lorme* and in his poems of
Les Contemplations.

Jean Valjean is a double nature, such as suited the
genius of Hugo, that unrepentant Manichee : Jean Valjean
wears, as it were, two pouches ; in one he has the experience
of a convict, in the other the instincts of a saint ; and his
thoughts and deeds are extracted, as he goes through life,
sometimes from the one, and sometimes from the other.
Jean Valjean is a good man, on whom twenty years of a
convict prison have branded an indelible scar ; they did
nothing to redeem his soul, which he owed to the hazard of
a twenty hours' contact with a real saint, M. Myriel, Bishop
of Digne. When Jean Valjean stole the Bishop's plate,
there was something hidden with it in his sack, as surrep-
titiously as the silver cup in Benjamin's wallet ; and that
was Salvation. For kindness, charity, courtesy, though
betrayed, and finally a free forgiveness, accomplished that
which years of cruel repression had failed even to suggest.
In an earlier book—which all lovers of *Les Misérables* should
read—in *Claude Gueux*, Hugo had already incriminated the
injustice of human justice. Tolstoi, I think, must have
thought of *Les Misérables* when he wrote *Resurrection*.

In his former great novel, in that tragic, bitter, dilettante
Notre-Dame de Paris, Hugo, his heart wrung by the deep
disappointment of his marriage, had preached the hopeless
doctrine of Fatality. We are all, said he, subject to

Necessity. The device of that volume is : *Ananké.* But *Les Misérables* is a generous recantation, a palinody full of faith in the soul's liberty and in social progress. Ananké is the motto of an age gone by ; Fatality is a monster of the Middle Ages. Monsters evolve and develop into angels. From the dead cocoon of Necessity a soaring and glittering being issues, shedding hope and love from its radiant wings ; and Fraternity illuminates the Future. " Amour, tu es l'avenir ! " Hugo, in a rhapsody, celebrates the times when there shall be no more wars, no more classes sunk in misery, no more ignorance, no more crime, no more indigence.[1] Here Hugo wanders in Utopia ; but he does not ignore, in his novel, the terrible problem of crime. Besides Jean Valjean, the criminal-made, he sets Thénardier, the criminal-born, whom nothing can redeem ; who, when unexpected prosperity gives him, in a new country, a new lease of life, employs his unhoped-for capital as a fund to start himself in business as a slave-dealer. There is not one single noble instinct in Thénardier. He is the *mauvais pauvre*, worse even, as Hugo owns, and more redoubtable than the *mauvais riche.* And round Thénardier gravitates a system of thieves and bullies, criminal by a bent of their nature, from laziness, or brutality, or sheer malice, as well as from mere love of adventure. For nine-tenths of these, surely, there is little to be hoped in this world or the next. All we can admit is their annihilation, since Evil has no immortal soul. Hugo the novelist knows the depths of human nature more profoundly than Hugo the philosopher. The root of Crime is not mere Ignorance. There exists a mysterious natural depravity. Was not the vile Thénardier, who had studied to be a priest, less ignorant than Jean Valjean ? Was not the atrocious Clubin of *Les Travailleurs de la mer* better taught than the pure and admirable Gilliatt ? His crime is the result of a *préméditation scélérate*, and this malice prepense, which grows by what it feeds on, is not to be exorcised by a schoolmaster. " Science sans conscience," said Rabelais, " est la mort de l'âme." There are moral monsters still, and the problem of how to deal with them is still a mystery no mind has fathomed.

[1] *Les Misérables*, iii. 463, Edition Nelson.

Misérables is a word with two meanings, for *misérable* means " wretch," and also merely " wretched "—wretchedly poor. Victor Hugo had never been able to forget the condition of Lazarus at his gates ; pity for the poor no less than love of liberty had made him a revolutionary ; and the question of how to purify the dregs of society was seldom long absent from his mind. Something noble and magnanimous in his temper prevented him from acquiring the indifference of the pure artist, and at sixty years of age he rebelled as indignantly against injustice, oppression, or the hard and starving misery which infests the slums of great cities as any generous youth in his first fresh contact with reality. If I had to translate the title *Les Misérables*, I think I should call it : The Dregs of Society. In our common round of life we scarcely notice these dregs, fallen to the bottom ; the draught we drink is clear and sweet. But sometimes the Hand of God takes up the glass and shakes it rudely. Then there is a revolution and the dregs mix with the wine, and give their acrid flavour to the whole.

Les Misérables is a study of those first years after 1830, when the people of France, resenting the tricks of legerde-main, thanks to which Louis-Philippe had put their revolution in his royal pocket, broke out again and again in useless insurrections. But one of these riots was very nearly a real revolution—in June 1832. Hugo's letters written to Sainte-Beuve at the time show his sympathy with the students and workmen who dreamed of democracy ; he deplored the purely material prosperity which remained the sole ambition of the ruling middle class—" les misérables escamoteurs politiques." He trusted that the repression would not be too severe—" J'espère qu'ils n'oseront pas jeter aux murs de Grenelle les jeunes cervelles trop chaudes mais si généreuses " ; but he was not personally concerned in the revolt of 1832. He was too much absorbed by the success of *Notre-Dame de Paris* and the production of *Lucrèce Borgia*. It was his memories of the street-fighting of 1851 which enabled him in *Les Misérables* to vivify his picture of the life of a barricade, and to show that mutual exaltation, that more than individual existence, that incor-

porate and unanimous mind, in which a trench or a
barricade—any body of men so much in earnest as to make
light of death and pain—can live a sublimer life than their
separate components ever know. *Les Misérables* is an
epic of insurrection, the development of an obscure and
immanent force, that tends to the light, striving to destroy
the tyranny which would keep it plunged in the abyss.
Both the tyranny and the resurgent force are forms of
Ἀνάγκη, and are charged with the fetters of the Past. Their
clash is the conflict of two powers alike doomed to perish ;
for who lives by the sword shall perish by the sword ; but,
out of their ruined violence, a new order shall arise, which
shall not seek to repress or punish, but to reform and to
elevate ; which shall attempt not to grasp but to share, and
not to dominate but to love.

Such is the gospel of *Les Misérables* ; but a novel lives
less by its general ideas than by the characters which it
exhibits and the pictures it represents. Hugo has never
been so happy in his personages as in these volumes.
Marius and Cosette move through these scenes of riot and
upheaval haloed in a blue and tender gleam as wonderful
as that more golden haze which irradiates the figure of a
girl in Rembrandt's " Ronde de Nuit " ; for he sees them in
the light of his own youth—still infinitely fair and intimately
real, in spite of Life's disenchantment. Cosette is just a
girl in love—a type more than an individual—and she
has borrowed something from either of the two women
that Hugo loved with the two valves of his double heart.
Like Juliette, she has been educated in the Convent of
Petit-Piepus, and she has something of Juliette's headlong
unconsidered generosity and spontaneous grace. But she
is more like Adèle : " l'air si douce et si bonne." " Toute
la personne de Cosette était naïveté, ingénuité, transparence."
Like either of them, she was courageous—" elle avait un
fond farouche et brave." But it is not so much the woman
that we see as the charm that emanates from her, the
dawn-like, delicious, girlish radiance that suddenly trans-
fuses and transfigures the lean, lanky, sallow grasshopper of
a girl to whom Marius had paid scant attention. Cosette
is a haunting strain of music, an almond-branch in flower,

a delight we should be sorry to have missed. But Marius
is a person, for Marius is Victor Hugo, and the study of
Marius unbares the poet's heart. Here, for instance, is a
remark which we shall often recall. Marius has just learned
the possible background of disgrace which may tarnish his
marriage with Cosette ; and, recalling the past, he demands
severely of his own conscience, whether, in this great act
of his life, he had not thrown prudence to the winds ?

He acknowledged to himself that there was in his character
a chimerical and visionary element—a sort of inner cloud—which,
in paroxysms of passion or pain, suddenly dilated, until its ex-
panded volume invaded and subdued the other parts of his
personality, leaving him just a Conscience in a Mist.

And again the reiterated reference to the hesitations of
Marius, so scrupulous, so convinced, so obstinate, with such
an immense fund of resistance and constancy, who yet, in
moments when a sudden decision is imperative, finds that
he cannot *act*. Almost with a smile we watch our Marius
in the *masure Gorbeau* (while Thénardier prepares the
murder of Jean Valjean), and he—because Thénardier had
saved his father's life at Waterloo—is wishful to spare the
murderer as well as to rescue the victim, and so remains
irresolute, waiting for an hour, his loaded pistol in his
hand, and finally does nothing, " ayant vaguement espéré
le moyen de concilier deux devoirs." " A struggle between
conviction and gratitude." Half the public life of Hugo is
in those words. And again in Marius's terrible interview
with Jean Valjean on the morrow of his wedding : why
does he not put the two or three crucial questions which
he knows would clear all the shadows from his soul ? He
cannot.

In certain supreme conjunctions, which of us has not stopped
his ears so that he may remain deaf to the truth ? Love knows
those cowardly compromises—dreads the terrible light which
may linger in an infernal gleam about the brows of our Angel.

So Marius fears to learn the whole truth about Cosette,
just as Hugo clung obstinately to certain dear illusions
concerning the women he loved.

It is Jean Valjean, on the other hand, in the bitter disappointment of learning that he is no longer all in all to Cosette, who throws an unexpected ray on that disintegration of Hugo's own moral character which certainly ensued on his immense disenchantment of 1830 :

A soul sometimes falls to pieces (he says) under the influence of too violent a moral shock. Pierced by a sudden certainty that fills it with despair, a soul may be wounded to the very quick, and to such an extent that its conscience is struck with a sort of dissociation or paralysis from which it may never wholly recover ; for there is a degree in disenchantment which disconcerts the soundest virtue. Few men surmount such a crisis as firm in their sense of duty as they were before they experienced it.[1]

There are pages in *Les Misérables*—the charming idyll of Marius and Cosette in the Luxembourg Gardens ; the struggle in the soul of Jean Valjean when he hears that an innocent man has been arrested for his crime ; his dream ; his drive to Amiens ; and the scene in the Courts ; or again the magnificent recital of the suicide of Javert, with its view of Paris at night seen from the quai de la Mégisserie —there are pages which, I suppose, are unmatched in nineteenth-century fiction except perhaps by certain passages in the great novels of Tolstoi or George Eliot. And yet at this supreme point commences Hugo's decadence. For his age betrays him : that proliferation of tissue which is a sign of degenerescence, that senile amplification which more and more will gain upon our poet, are already incipient, though, in the immense complexity and variety of the novel, they seem less excessive than in such a simple tale as *Les Travailleurs de la mer*, his next romance.

A sea-captain of Guernsey, retired from active life but owner of his boat, the *Durande*, has invented a steam-engine, the marvel of those parts (the tale takes place early in the second quarter of the nineteenth century), considered, in fact, by many as a flying in the face of Providence, yet admitted to be convenient for the merchant-service between the Channel Islands and Saint Malo. Mess

---

[1] *Les Misérables*, t. iv. p. 48, Edition Nelson.

Lethierry calls his boat the *Durande* after his orphan niece, Durande (or Déruchette " for short "), and the niece and the steam-boat share his heart between them.

One day the *Durande* is wrecked at sea on a solitary shoal among the Dover rocks near Guernsey. The passengers are all saved, and, if it were only the boat, Mess Lethierry could repair the loss. But the engine ! A steam-engine in the Channel Islands in 1830 was not an object easy or perhaps even possible to replace. Mess Lethierry is over sixty ; he has no longer the same force and spontaneity of invention. He sees himself a ruined and broken-hearted man, for the boat has stuck in too dangerous and narrow a pass for a ship with its crew to approach in order to disengage it, or dismount and save the engine. One man alone in a small boat might dare it—if he were as good a smith as a sailor, and if he bore a charmed life to venture such a peril while the storm rages and dashes its waves over the breaking wreck. Ah, if such a hero existed . . . " I would marry him ! " cried Déruchette.

A pale haggard man steps forward at this moment. " You would marry him, Miss Déruchette ? " It is Gilliatt, their taciturn neighbour ; and of course he goes and gets the engine off the Dover rocks. Gilliatt, for a wonder, is not a monster, like Quasimodo and *L'Homme qui rit*, or a convict, like Jean Valjean ; and yet he is a hero, passionately in love with the pretty, irresponsible purity of an ordinary girl (for this is always the tragedy of romance as Victor Hugo sees it). He achieves the impossible to win her love—and does not win it after all ; it is always the same old tale. Not only does he disengage from its imminent peril the precious engine, which is the symbol of Progress, not only does he weather the lashing fury of the storm, but he fights with and vanquishes the *pieuvre*, the terrible, jelly-like, clinging polypus, whose envenomed tentacles and frail but irresistible feelers surround, imprison, blister, and strangle, in burning pain, their helpless prey. No doubt a polypus must always be an unpleasant antagonist, but Victor Hugo's enlarging eye has complicated the thing with the sea-serpent till the *pieuvre* becomes a symbol of all the lurking horrors that may lie in wait in the unlit corners of the universe, as well as of all that in nature is evil, irreclaimable, and native of the bottomless pit.

Les Misérables showed us the struggle of heroic manhood against the wrong and injustice that still linger in the social system; *Les Travailleurs* reveals the hero combating the forces of nature, triumphant over these, but vanquished by another fatality, an inner 'Ανάγκη : the passions of his heart. For, on his return to Guernsey, Gilliatt finds Déruchette lost in an ecstasy of love for a frailer being than he : the Anglican curate, Ebenezer Cawdry. The happiness he had fairly gained was not to be his. Heaven says, No !—*Non là-haut !* The passion of the strong is not to find its earthly close. And Gilliatt helps Déruchette to elope with her clergyman ; then, as he watches their ship sail out of sight, he lets the rising tide submerge him, till the waves ripple above his head.

Just as Jean Valjean, forsaken by Cosette, allows himself to perish of a broken heart ; just as Gilliatt is overwhelmed by the sea, so Gwynplaine, the hero of *L'Homme qui rit*, commits suicide, vanquished by Life which he seems in a fair fight to have conquered ; for we may triumph over the world without and succumb to the world within. The doctrine of Victor Hugo—notwithstanding that dawn of bliss gleaming on the far horizon—is, as regards the past and the present, infinitely sad.

That sense of forsakenness, of Heaven's bar against happiness, of the frailty and ingratitude that are the sole response a passionate heart may expect—that disenchantment which clouds all the sad conclusions of his novels, was doubtless increased by the solitariness of our poet's life. The charming and cheerful Charles had left him, had settled in Brussels, was ultimately to marry there ; he drew as with a magnet his mother in his train. One letter of Victor Hugo's, published in his correspondence, will show how he felt what, in his unconscious egotism, he considered the defection of this darling and delightful son.

HAUTEVILLE HOUSE, 1864.

Your letter does not answer the word that I clamoured from the very bottom of my heart : Come back !

We all miss you here ; I most of all, as you know well.   Come
back, come back !   Come back not only by the train and in the
body ;   return in heart and mind ;   bring to an end not only the
material separation which has kept us so long apart, but the
separation of our souls.   You have made me suffer deeply, poor
dear child, but I forgive you, for I love you, and when one loves
—what is the one thing impossible !   Not to forgive !

Yes, all my heart turns to you, my Charles, and calls you.
Come back !   Come back !   Alas, while you are suffering afar,
we too are suffering here—you know what anguish and anxiety !
I feel yours just as much as ours.   You see I was right ; all I
foretold has come to pass !   Ah, my God—to think of you so far
away, so sad !   What despair and despondency !   Come back,
come back—I can think and speak of nothing but your return !

Cruel anxieties, indeed, had saddened the household of
Victor Hugo.   Hauteville House sheltered no longer that
pleasant company whom we know so well from the
innumerable photographs, taken by Charles Hugo, at
present preserved in the Museum of the place des Vosges.
All that little world of 1857–60 rises before us as we look
at them.   The poet has not yet grown his beard.   Among
the shaggy martyrs of the Second Empire he is the one
clean-shaven man ; his powerful, bitter, disenchanted face
looks at us full of purpose and irony, and we can easily
imagine that, with the wisest intentions, he might be
unwittingly tyrannical.   The brown hair falls lank and long
from the crown of the head, leaving uncovered the enormous
forehead.   The line of the eyebrows is straight and severe
above the prominent frontal arch.   The finely carven lips
are parted and compressed in meditation and seem to say :
secretum meum mihi.   In the look of power, almost of
arrogance, there is a suggestion of Richard Wagner.   How
different he appears from the handsome, pleasant, gifted
members of his family, brilliant satellites who find their
source of life in him, while he, independent of them, obeys
a higher law.   Just to look at this old-fashioned album
suffices to penetrate us with a sense of the attraction and
also of the repulsion of genius, explains how they were
drawn irresistibly towards him only to feel him irremediably
of another essence than their own—not inhuman but un-
human, so that in the end the impossible intimacy mocked

their very souls and, one after another, they were driven from him and left him with his sole true kith and kin, the universe.

This middle-aged woman of unconscious grace, rather stout, but admirably proportioned, whose attitudes are always charming, looks like an Italian singer ; but it is Madame Victor Hugo. I have said an Italian singer, but there is a look of the priest, too, in the infinite indulgence of that charming mouth, with the little thoughtful commiserating pout of the lower lip. The forehead, as white as a half-moon, set in the curly hair, is still smooth and young ; the pointed fingers keep a caressing grace ; kindness, sweetness, but also a certain independence and aloofness, are evident in her glance. . . . This very handsome man is Charles, superb, radiant, attractive, evidently the beauty of the family. Beside him the thoughtful, rather saturnine face of François-Victor, whose mutton-chop whiskers and neater dress suggest some intellectual magistrate of the monarchy of July. Much younger-looking than her brothers, infinitely fragile and slight, with the loveliest slim arms and hands, a willowy figure, a pale long face set in the thickest braids of smooth black hair, here is Adèle, the unfortunate Adèle.

Balzac, who had seen her twenty years before as a child of fourteen at a dinner in the place Royale, had called her " la plus grande beauté que j'aurai vue de ma vie. Elle sera . . . enfin vous la verrez ! " [1] And he, who disliked and mistrusted Hugo, esteeming him " grand poète et petit farceur," was half inclined to give him his esteem on account of the rare beauty of Adèle. " C'est quelque chose de faire ses enfants beaux ! " " A Greek statue ! " cried A. Karr. The girl's riper years did not quite fulfil this promise, but her delicate slenderness, her great dark eyes, and the sad oval of her pensive face are infinitely distinguished.

The illustrious inhabitants of Hauteville House had many guests. From several of these, and especially from Paul Chenay and from Paul Stapfer,[2] we know the routine of the poet's life—how every morning he would rise early and work till eleven in his high " crystal chamber " on the

---

[1] *Lettres à l'étrangère*, 9 April 1843.
[2] *Victor Hugo à Guernesey.*

roof, a study singularly different from the over-decorated rooms below, for it was plain and bare, with no ornament save the great wide view of sea and sky, as plain as one of those perfect lines of the poet :

Le soleil s'èst couché ce soir dans les nuées,

or

Le clair-de-lune bleu qui baignait l'horizon,

which haunt one so much longer than the brilliant fanfares of the *Orientales*. At eleven an ice-cold douche would restore him to reality and prepare him for a hearty lunch. About two he would start for a long lonely stroll ; though sometimes young Adèle or Madame Drouet would accompany him, as a rule he would walk to the measure of his thoughts, " sorti pour rêver," as in the old days ; after which he would work until dinner-time, at which meal, whether it took place at Hauteville House or at Madame Drouet's, a large place was reserved for his friends.

M. Stapfer describes him, towards 1867, as an old man of sixty-five, straight and sturdy, a mantle thrown across his left shoulder, a large soft hat shading his eyes, his hands in his pockets, his shoulders well thrown back—no student's stoop—mincing delicately on the point of his admirable and well-shod feet, with a step as firm as a mule's. He was nearly always dressed in a plain straight morning coat, and though his clothes were often shabby, he looked well in them.

He would have had " le grand air " if he had been dressed like a beggar. The first impression (which never ceased during the three years that I frequented him) was that of an extreme civility of language and address. He was sometimes absorbed in his own thoughts, but never to the point of forgetting his politeness. He was ceremonious, *vieille France*, excessively courteous . . . never so delightful as in a *tête-à-tête*. Then the great man revealed himself in the pleasantest light, admirably natural, simple, amusing, witty, full of fun ; but as soon as there was an audience he would let himself be beguiled by his evil genius—the demon of display.

As the years went by, the various inmates of Hauteville House drifted hither and thither. The poet was more and more alone. Those days of the earlier sixties were gone by when Paul Chenay wondered that any household should be so busy : the poet in his look-out in the roof writing poetry ;   Charles   composing   a   novel ;   François-Victor translating Shakespeare ;   Adèle dreamily occupied with her music ;   Madame Hugo correcting the proofs of her biography ;   Madame Chenay copying *Les Misérables* ;   Paul Chenay himself engraving the Master's drawing of John Brown's body swinging from a tree l   Now they are far afield :   Madame Hugo in Paris, Charles in Brussels, Adèle where ?

Victor Hugo's distrust of his daughter's travels had been justified.   At first, these holidays had been successful. In 1862 (I think it was) Adèle had met in Brighton an English officer whom she had already remarked in Guernsey. The girl was attracted by him.   On her return home, with the cold bluntness that a very reserved person sometimes assumes to mask an inner trepidation, she signified to her father her intention of marrying this foreigner, this stranger : " Je veux me marier ; j'ai trente ans l " Victor Hugo was mortally offended.   Paul Chenay, who was his niece's confidant and a witness of the scene, has left in his libellous volume (*Victor Hugo à Guernesey*) his impression of the Master's implacable refusal.   Adèle was no less obdurate than he—no less resolved than Victor Hugo had been in the teeth of his mother's opposition some forty years before.   Silent, irreconcilable, Adèle nourished her love in solitude and melancholy.   Thereupon Madame Hugo was compelled to leave for Paris in order to see her biography through the Press.   It was the summer of 1863.   She expected to be away a few weeks at most, and left her daughter at Hauteville, where the presence of the Chenays rendered the situation less strained.   She enjoyed without too much anxiety her visit to her old haunts.   One day, accompanied by Charles, she made a pilgrimage to their old home in the place Royale.   She wrote to her husband :

Often, since we left it, I had seen it in my dreams with the squat arcades and the lofty windows of our apartment.   But the touch of reality saddened my dream.   We walked under the arcades, and, at the corner of the rue des Minimes, I recognized the pastrycook's where the children used to buy their cakes ; close

by was the lending library, and at the corner of the rue de
l'Écharpe, the old café. We passed the door of M. Jauffret's
School ; it looked quite unaltered ; we stopped at the little
door where I so often have rung the bell. And I thought of
M. and Mme. Jauffret, both dead, and of all this renewal of
things that makes them strange and foreign. A cemetery would
have seemed less sad.

When Madame Hugo returned on the 2nd of July she
found Hauteville House filled with tragic rumours. Adèle
had left her home to join her fiancé in London. Victor
Hugo, passionately angry, forbade the banns. The mother,
though heart-broken, pleaded her daughter's cause :

Adèle was a free agent (says Madame Hugo in one of her
little notes), she has transgressed no law by the marriage with
the man she loves. She might, perhaps, have put greater trust
in her parents. But if we may reproach her with a certain
lack of confidence, has she, on her side, nothing to upbraid us
with ? Has not her young life been sacrificed to a political
necessity ? Was she not unhappy—and still unhappier because
of our chosen place of exile ? Had she no right to a life of her
own ? You are indulgent, generous. You grasp my meaning.
These dear children have their irresistible impulses no less than
ourselves. We have not long to live. While we can, let us show
them sympathy and kindness.[1]

After some while the father let himself be gained over.
And indeed, with Juliette Drouet round the corner, what
right had he to resist ? He agreed to countenance the
marriage and put an announcement of the wedding in the
local newspapers, with a note to the effect that the young
couple had left for Nova Scotia early in October, where
Adèle's husband rejoined his regiment.

The worst was yet to come. The Hugos' announcement
provoked an immediate denial on the part of the family
of the young officer. No marriage had taken place ; no
engagement had ever existed, so they averred. While
Adèle continued to insist that she was married.

Years afterwards, on her return from Canada, in that
private asylum where the unhappy woman was to linger
till an extreme old age, Adèle maintained the assertion of
her marriage. It was probably the fiction of a dreaming

[1] Gustave Simon, *La Vie d'une femme*, p. 386.

brain. Timid and silent, she had brooded so long over her thwarted passion that the artist in her had made of it a phantasmal reality, in which she lived and moved. I have often wondered if Ernest Renan had her sad adventure in his mind when he composed his wonderful tale of the Hemp-Crusher's Daughter. It is, at least, with the sad long face of Adèle Hugo that I visualize " la fille du broyeur de lin."

CHAPTER XXII

THE CLOSE OF A CHAPTER

EARLY in January 1864, Madame Hugo left Guernsey. She could not bear the void of Hauteville House, the rooms that gaped with absence and emptiness, Adèle's piano, her pets. She had taken a sick person's dislike to Guernsey, and indeed she was already something of an invalid. The glorious eyes that had wept too much were blurred and vague ; she had begun to tell that rosary of minor miseries— palpitations, noises in the head, insomnia, sudden spasms— which, no less than her failing sight, announced the progress of a disease of the arteries. Always prone in her seasons of depression to fits of dreamy languor, these now became a sort of torpor, almost a somnolence, from which the mild, moist, relaxing climate had no spell to rouse her. Such a condition made it necessary that she should obtain better medical advice than could be procured on the island—or at least gave her an excuse for leaving it.

Madame Hugo did not consider herself indispensable at Hauteville now that Adèle no longer claimed her care. She left her young sister in charge. Madame Drouet was Victor Hugo's secretary, and that notable person would doubtless assist Madame Chenay and give an eye to the bills and the conduct of the servants during the absence of the real mistress of the house. " Je ne suis qu'une chétive doublure "—a mere understudy, wrote the poor lady pathetically in one of her letters. Her sons constantly claimed her presence. Charles was established in Brussels. François-Victor was obliged to go to Paris in order to see through the Press the first volumes of his translation of Shakespeare's plays—an important work and still, I believe, the best and completest version which has appeared in France. Victor Hugo introduced it to the French public by an extraordinary essay on *William Shakespeare* considered as a Mage—considered, in fact, as a sort of preliminary Victor Hugo. One wonders what the methodical François-Victor thought of this brilliant and fatuous improvisation. We have Baudelaire's opinion. He affirmed that the Almighty, in a mood of impenetrable mystification, had taken in equal parts genius and silliness from which to compound the brain of Victor Hugo, so that, by a natural consequence, his book on Shakespeare, like all his other books, abounded indiscriminately in beauties and tomfoolery—an inexhaustible treasure " de beautés et de bêtises."

What more natural than that Madame Hugo should accompany to Paris the delicate François-Victor, take care of him, and seek for her own ailments the counsel of a good oculist and a specialist for diseases of the heart ? Mother and son set out together. When the warm weather came they took a furnished flat at Auteuil, and in the autumn went to Brussels, where Charles was dreaming of a happy marriage. And Madame Hugo began to frame plans of a house in Brussels that would hold them all, offering to the poet congenial society and frequent visits from their friends in Paris, and promising her sons a natural career, impossible on that now-hated, if lovely, foreign island where Adèle's existence had been so strangely thwarted that the lonely unmated girl had lost her mind. Madame Hugo made every effort to attract her husband to Brussels. But, as regards the genius of Victor Hugo—or at any rate his prestige and his moral example—a cheerful and prosperous home in Brussels was not the equivalent of his " écueil en pleine mer," his wave-washed shoal ; he stood there with finer effect, not as a family man but as a witness, a hermit on his pillar, a Saint Simeon the Stylite ; the more remote, unfriended, melancholy his place of exile (and the fact of the sea-passage made Guernsey seem quite the unsuspected isle in far-off seas to the French public of the Second Empire), the more striking was the pattern he set of an irreconcilable protestation. Had he left the Channel Islands for a brilliant

capital easily accessible by rail, the symbol, the flag, of his
voluntary exile would certainly have been lowered. Unseen
on his far, wind-swept island, in his obstinate idealism he
appeared the voice of Conscience, the soul of Liberty ; and
Paris accepted from him a moral earnestness and a
grandiloquence which it would have found absurd in the
mouth of a citizen of Brussels.

It was natural that Hugo should think of his prestige
and his mission and that Madame Hugo should consider
her family, but the consequence was that they were often
apart. Madame Hugo returned to Guernsey for a few
weeks at the end of 1864, left again on the 18th of January
1865, and remained absent exactly two years—two years,
during which the poet finished and produced *Les Travailleurs de la mer*, and many poems. Save for a long visit
from his sister-in-law, Madame Julie Chenay, the poet was
chiefly alone at Hauteville House. We must imagine him,
living often in the past, resuscitating in a touching confusion
the images of the mother who had opposed his marriage
and the children she would so passionately have loved had she
known them—as in that little comedy, " La Grand'mère "—
written at this time—which opens the *Théâtre en liberté*. . . .
Mother, wife, and children were all scattered now, dead or
distant, half-estranged. . . . He would have been lonely
indeed without the faithful Juliette, whom he had established
in splendour in a new house on the hill, healthier and
handsomer than her old cottage, La Palue, whose damp
site had given her a long rheumatic fever. The decoration
of Hauteville-Féerie had been the business and the pleasure
of many months. It was, as Juliette remarked, the paradise
of rag-fair and the apotheosis of bottle-glass, with worm-
eaten, old oak chests suspended from the poles of long-
vanished sedan-chairs, and adorned by every variety of
bric-à-brac. The amusing lacquer work of the salon, Victor
Hugo's own contrivance, is still to be seen at the Musée
Victor-Hugo. By a delicate attention he had striven to
restore, for Juliette's bedroom, the image of the room she
had liked so much in her old Parisian flat in the rue Saint-
Athanase—and this chamber, at any rate, was a marvel,
with its hangings of crimson silk, brocaded with old gold ; the

embroidered peacocks in the panels of the walls, the Oriental
china on the antique carven cabinets ; and the dim Venetian
mirrors, hung at subtle angles, to disperse and multiply the
figures of these lovely things.   The democratic exiles, who were
Madame Drouet's sole society in Guernsey, were scandalized
at so much magnificence ; and one of these unbeloved and
unloving guests—these " proscrits barbus, crochus, moussus,
poilus, bossus, et obtus "—these " beaked and bearded,
musty, fusty, shaggy, blunt and hump-backed outlaws "
whom Juliette detested, and received perforce, told her
that he hoped she appreciated the Master's unseasonable
generosity in housing so handsomely " une dame de votre
âge."

Meanwhile Charles had married and had set up house
in Brussels at number 4 place des Barricades with Madame
Victor Hugo for his guest ; and the mother, though her
health grew steadily worse, though her eyes became so
dim that she could seldom read or write, forgot her own
troubles in the childlike happiness of the young couple.
Charles was forty, but apparently not destined to grow
up, a cheerful, radiant creature.   Alice, said her mother-
in-law, was " a dear little girl, with the gaiety of a little
bird."   They were full of fun and frolic.   Then there were
the preparations for their baby—and then the " joli sourire
du citoyen Georges " when he arrived upon this earthly
scene.   In June 1866 Victor Hugo came to Brussels, and
as he held in his arms the first-born of his eldest son he
did not say his " Nunc Dimittis," for he felt his whole
being still so full of vigour and purpose that he supposed
they two might live to carve out the future together—
almost contemporaries.   " Mon mari reste jeune," wrote
Madame Hugo some months later, " d'une vigueur exception-
nelle.   Il est heureux et glorieux, ce qui est ma grande joie."

Although nearing her end, Madame Hugo, in her desire
to attract her husband to the house in Brussels, spared no
pains to gather round her the friends of other days.   In
1865 and 1866 she welcomed to her hearth another voluntary
exile, another French poet, banished from France for no
political disagreement with the Government (for if ever a
man was in favour of authority and the rule of a social

élite it was Charles Baudelaire) but through some whimsical
fancy of his own.   Although a secret antipathy divided
them, the two poets had a high opinion of each other's
verbal genius, though I fancy Hugo pitied the morbid
mind diseased of his younger admirer, while Baudelaire
could scarce contain his contempt for Hugo's humanitarian
prolixities.   He preferred Madame Hugo.   The Master's
vaticinations disgusted the fastidious Baudelaire ;   Charles
Hugo's brilliant fireworks fatigued him, and he was bored
by the drier humour of François-Victor.   To the younger
ladies of the circle he paid no attention, " Il gardait ses
lèvres pincées, son regard aigu, sa dédaigneuse politesse,
soigné de sa personne, net et muet."   Only the serene and
gentle welcome of his hostess aroused in him a feeling of
contentment and cordiality, until sometimes, at the end
of the evening, completely thawed (and oblivious of Victor
Hugo's distaste for music), he would seat himself at young
Madame Charles Hugo's piano and play scene after scene
of *Tannhäuser* to the sightless invalid.   And he enjoyed,
perverse creature that he was, the pleasure he gave her
when he sang the praises of " that great poet . . . Sainte-
Beuve " and the indignation of Hugo and his sons. . . .

Despite her cheerfulness in her affliction, despite the
comparative happiness which she appeared to enjoy in
Brussels, none the less Hugo was cruelly moved to see
his wife so evidently doomed—and to blindness, worse than
death.   He insisted that she should go to Lille in order to
consult a famous oculist, but there was nothing to be done
for the eyes, which were but one symptom of the general
state.   Hugo, all his life, had lived in terror lest his own
sight should fail him.   But the blow had fallen on Adèle.
At Brussels that summer, in the wing which his children
had added to their house for him, Hugo began a novel,
L'Homme qui rit.   The heroine is blind—a beautiful, gentle,
blind girl, dark and pale, with whom the hero has been
brought up from childhood.   She has never seen the
deformity of her lover, neither his physical nor his moral
defects, though he has forsaken her for another more
brilliant woman ;   when he returns, it is too late.   She dies
in his arms and he throws himself into the sea in despair.

There is no absolute connexion between this story and the feelings of Victor Hugo when he found his wife almost sightless and condemned to death—but I think we feel in it the alarmed, the terrified beating of his heart. Adèle had been the companion, the witness of all his life, the love of his youth ; she still was, shall I say, the very dearest sister ? Aware of her approaching end, full of indulgence, she insisted on drawing into her home-circle the half-reluctant Juliette Drouet, and on her return to Guernsey in January 1867 for the first time set foot in her husband's unlawful Eden and called at Hauteville-Féerie on Madame Drouet, whom she had often received in her drawing-room in Brussels. In 1867, in March, she left the island for a last joy : in honour of the Great Exhibition, which filled Paris with foreigners, the Imperial Government removed the embargo laid on the production of all Victor Hugo's plays and permitted the revival of *Hernani*. Hugo was alarmed by his wife's proposal. Any emotion was dangerous in her condition ; he feared, too, that should the play be made the occasion of a manifestation against the exiles, Madame Hugo would not be able to contain her resentment. He would have preferred a dignified abstention, but he had all his household against him. The invalid's eyes were rather stronger, " Dussé-je les reperdre," she cried, " j'irai à *Hernani* ! " After a long rest at Brussels she set out with her sons, and recovered something of the flame and energy of 1830. Those who saw her in 1867 found her transformed, transfigured ; she wrote exulting : " Je vais assister à la distribution des billets—car je suis chef de bande." She promised to be calm before the paid hiss of the Imperial police. But there were no hisses—*Hernani* was. received with triumph, with frantic applause, and by the young with a sort of solemn enthusiasm. " Victor Hugo is our religion," said one of the students to the poet's wife. And he, in Guernsey, caught from Madame Hugo's glad and almost girlish letters an echo of their brilliant and romantic youth—the theatre ringing with applause, and his young wife (as the Duchesse d'Abrantès had seen her) " si belle, si jolie, si parfaite, et lumineuse de bonheur," with a wreath of white roses in her dusky curls.

Hernani revived more than literary memories. Madame Hugo, during her stay in Paris, tried to patch up an old quarrel.   Already, while at Auteuil in 1864, she had received the visit of Sainte-Beuve—a visit half-unwillingly, ungraciously accorded, for the great critic was expecting to be made a Senator of the Empire and feared the effect of any acquaintance with the family of so conspicuous an exile.   Still, the visit had been paid ; rare but friendly letters had been exchanged, and in 1867 Madame Hugo writes to her husband, " Je t'assure que dans une de ses lettres il me parle de toi d'une façon émue."   She would fain have left behind her on all sides peace and goodwill, but in this direction her efforts came to nothing.

That year again Victor Hugo spent the summer with his family in Brussels, busy on *L'Homme qui rit.* Your true Hugolatrer has a singular tenderness for this novel, in which Hugo, after a manner which suggests that of Il Greco in some of his most famous pictures, sacrifices the sense of form and reality to the desire for expression and spiritual significance.   But I am a " Hugoïste " rather than a " Hugolâtre," and I admit that this novel is spoiled for me by the excess of Hugo's defects : the strange marriage of the emphatic with the vague ; the abuse of amplification and antithesis ; the harsh contrasts—on one hand the monstrous, on the other the ideal ; the extraordinary mixture of pedantry and ignorance in his display of erudition.   But it is only the surface that is affected or ridiculous.   That Lord David Dirry-Muir when he disguises himself as a common sailor should take the name of Tom —Jim—Jack, is ridiculous ; but Hugo has clearly seen the love of adventure in an English aristocrat, and I admire his conception of Lord David, who passes half his life before the mast as a mere Jack Tar and half as the most brilliant member of the House of Lords.   To call an official a Wapentake is as comic as if he were to call the man a Parish ; yet Hugo has very well seen the medley of the modern with the mediaeval that characterizes England in the eyes of a thoughtful French observer.   There are too many monsters, too much eccentricity, too much cruelty, too many passages of jerky, half-suffocated, and yet interminable eloquence. But, when all is said and done, *L'Homme qui rit*, though the least to be recommended of Hugo's novels, on account of its unnaturalness and forced effects, is none the less a fine study of the Aristocratic bias and the failure of an élite, unbalanced by a conscious lower class, to make a nation.

1868 was a year of mourning. In April the baby at Brussels died, and " came again," as Victor Hugo said in his mystical fashion, in August, when was born that second Georges who (with a sister who came into the world a year later) was to be the delight of our poet's old age and his master in the gentle art of being a grandfather. Victor Hugo had arrived in Brussels at the end of July in answer to his wife's pressing appeal.

And as for me (she had written) when I hold you again, I shall cling to you so fast, without with your leave or by your leave,—I shall be so gentle and so sweet that you will never have the courage to desert me. For the end of my dream is to die in your arms.

The baby was born on the 16th of August. With all her dear ones round her and the little lost babe " returned," Madame Victor Hugo was at her happiest. She seemed unusually well on the 24th. She went a long drive with her husband and her sons ; on the 25th she was struck by a fit of apoplexy. On the 26th she died—and died as she had wished—in Victor Hugo's arms.

Victor Hugo never travelled without Madame Drouet. She had her lodging hard by. The woman who had so long filled unofficially the place of the less-regarded wife appeared, in the shock of death, to regret her rival. At least the sudden end appalled her—for there was but three years' difference in their ages—and her true affection for the poet made her also tremble for his grief. She found words of real feeling to mourn " cette angélique et sublime femme qui resplendit maintenant dans le monde des âmes " ; she recalled the protecting kindness that Madame Hugo had extended to the beloved, unlawful Hagar : " sa grande et généreuse bonté qui était pour moi la réhabilitation délicate et discrète " ; she prayed that the dead woman's memory might be, like her "exquise personne," gentle, charming, and beneficent ; and the day that she re-entered the drawing-room where the mistress was represented by an empty chair, tears came into Juliette's eyes—" for I thought I saw her smile at me from Heaven, as she used to look up and smile whenever I crossed her threshold." But, before sunset on the day of the funeral (which, with her customary tact and dignity, Madame Drouet refused to attend), we find her reminding Victor Hugo that now, at last, they possessed " le droit de nous aimer à ciel ouvert " and could defy the malignity of men. Doubtless, she supposed that " the discreet and delicate rehabilitation " due to the dead wife would be perfected by a tardy marriage. But the prudent poet, having been for some five-and-thirty years in full possession of his lady-love, turned a deaf ear. A sort of piety forbade him to replace the wife of his youth. But a deeper reason was that strange mingling, that almost quakerish mixture of spiritual ideality with anti-formalism, which more and more became the religion of Hugo's old age. What had a priest (or, for that matter, a mayor) to do with the secret and eternal fusion of immortal souls ? The bare idea filled him with a spasm of fierce anti-clerical resentment. And one day he wrote under one of Juliette's photographs : " Je t'aime, cinquante ans d'amour, c'est le plus beau mariage."

One chapter was ended. Another was soon to close. In October 1868 Victor Hugo returned to Guernsey accompanied by his Egeria. They continued to reside, the one at Hauteville House, the other at Hauteville-Féerie, meeting every day, lunching and dining together. Juliette, supreme at last, prayed that this life might continue for ever—their exile never find a close. " If I dared," she wrote, " I would beseech Heaven to prolong our sojourn here till the end of our days." Guernsey, she assured the poet, was " the antechamber of Paradise." But Victor Hugo was not persuaded. He was anxious and restless as he had never been before. As sea-gulls cry and fly when the storm is impending, something in his soul felt the convulsion of Europe approach. In August 1869, with Madame Drouet, Charles Hugo, and Paul Meurice, he made a long excursion on the Rhine, so full of memories for him, and which he had already so marvellously illustrated with pen and pencil. He had for some years back visited the great river every summer—in 1862, 1863, 1864, 1865—haunting those eastern frontiers of France whence, on his father's side, he drew his origin ; that limit-land of Germany where Napoleon's memory still lingered, where his own father's name was still remembered ; that *Rhénanie* which combines the sweetness and genius of France with the solidity of German thoroughness. " Le Rhin est beaucoup plus français que ne le pensent les Allemands," the poet had written in 1840 in his preface to his volumes on the Rhine. " La rive gauche du Rhin est restée française, tandis que la rive droite, naturellement et nécessairement allemande, est devenu toute prussienne." The clash was at hand : Would the left bank of the Rhine revert to France ? Or would the Prussians who overran Rhenania invade the peaceful mountains of the Vosges ?

CHAPTER XXIII

THE EXILE'S RETURN

IT is not with impunity that a sovereign retains in his mind the aims and experience of a conspirator. Napoleon III. was less an Emperor than a theorist in politics ; he had a dream as dear to him as the well-being of his people. Arch-nationalist and international, his heart beat for the unity of Italy ; he sympathized with Bismarck in planning the resurrection of a German Empire. He saw Europe as a senate of mighty nations crowned and serene. He abetted and connived at all the schemes for Prussian predominance : yes, strange to say, until 1866 the French Emperor's sympathies lay with Prussia. As the price of his acquiescence in her aggrandizement he hoped to obtain the left bank of the Rhine, or at least the annexation of Belgium. Then, with the Prussian victory at Sadowa, came the awakening. Austria was stunned ; the balance of power was destroyed ; and Napoleon got nothing. Bismarck had fooled him. To the north-east and at the south-east of his frontiers the Emperor had placed two strong united powers. These had only to coalesce with Spain, with Belgium, to reproduce the terrible supremacy of Charles Quint which it had cost France two hundred years of constant effort to overthrow. Once more she might find herself grasped on every side in the paralysing grip of her enemy. When Bismarck proposed to place a Hohenzollern upon the throne at Madrid, Napoleon rebelled.

France—at least intellectual and Imperial France—had shared all the delusions of her Emperor :

Let Germany become united ! (About had declared in 1860).

France has no dearer wish. She loves the German people with
a disinterested friendship. An Italian nation of twenty-six
million to the south ; a German nation of thirty-two million to
the east : France does not fear them.

Four years later, Victor Duruy protested :

We have had your German Rhine, and though you have
garnished it with bristling fortresses whose cannon are turned
towards France, we do not wish to possess it again. The time
for conquests is past. There shall be no more conquests save
by the free consent of nations.

But after Sadowa, France awakened from her dream, and
it was in a mood of profound unrest and rancour that she
contemplated the work of her sovereign—the Rhenish
provinces swarming with Prussian troops ; Italy strong,
and estranged by reason of Napoleon's vacillating policy
in regard to Rome, intangible Rome. Even Belgium
suspicious and unneighbourly because of that awkward
hint about a possible annexation—which had alienated
England. No friends, and what an enemy !

Then war broke out, war that must speedily mean
either a defeat for France, which would destroy the Empire,
or a victory for the armies of Napoleon that would establish
him triumphant on his throne. Which did our poet desire ?
France merited a victory ? the Empire deserved defeat ?
In a flash Victor Hugo felt that he loved his country more
intensely than he hated the oppressor. His prayer was
that the French armies might prosper and speedily occupy
the left bank of the Rhine :

I want the Rhine for France, because we must try to make
the French group as strong as possible, both materially and
intellectually, in order that it may counterbalance, in the Parliament of the United States of Europe, the German group, and
that it may impose the French language on the European
federation.[1]

Early in the month Victor Hugo left Guernsey for
Brussels. In case of a defeat, he could be in a few hours
at the gates of Paris, with his two sons, all three of them
with their rifles on their shoulders ready to march off to

[1] Lettre à D'Alton-Shée, 2nd Aug. 1870. Correspondance.

the ramparts with the Garde Nationale—the militia of the
city.   In case of a French victory, he would retire with his
family to Hauteville House.   Which should it be : Paris
again, and national disaster ?   Or exile renewed in the
triumph of France ?   He waited in much anguish of mind.
" Je me sens à la fois Européen et Parisien." [1]

Sedan decided the future.   The Republic was proclaimed
on the 4th of September ; on the 5th, at four in the afternoon,
Victor Hugo crossed the frontier with Madame Drouet,
Madame Charles Hugo and her children.   The scene was
touching, though, according to his wont, a little theatrical
or at least representative.   The " sublime Exile " asked
to receive the wine and the bread of France, and treading
French soil for the first time in nearly twenty years, partook
of what to him was in truth, in its degree, a Holy Com-
munion.   When he had eaten, he begged Madame Drouet
to keep him safe the crust of that bread ; and covering
his face with his two hands he remained silent a long moment
in the attitude of a man who prays, or who is dazzled by a
sudden effulgence of light.   Tears dropped slowly through
his fingers. . . .

They were at Paris by half-past nine at night.   An
immense crowd was packed all round the railway station,
singing the *Marseillaise* and the *Chant du départ*, crying
" Vive Victor Hugo ! " as though the old poet brought them
hope and victory in his baggage.   Four times he had to
stand up in his carriage and speak to the people of Paris,
who accompanied him to the house of his friend Paul
Meurice, where the poet took up his quarters.   The drive
from the Gare du Nord to the avenue Frochot, less than
a mile away, had occupied two hours.   In Paris the poet
found not only thronging friends, but his two sons who had
gone before him.

On the 18th of September the siege began.   And we can
follow that siege almost day by day in the admirable volume
of notes and impressions called *Choses vues*, a volume
surprising indeed as showing how clear, precise, restrained
the Mage, the Bard, could reveal himself when he chose
to observe reality.   On the morning of the 7th of October,

[1] A Paul Meurice.   Correspondance.

Hugo, walking on the boulevard de Clichy, noticed a balloon tethered at the end of a street leading to Montmartre. He went up to look at it, and found not one but three, a large yellow balloon, a smaller white one, and quite a little one ribbed yellow and red.

The crowd murmured, "Gambetta's off!" And there, in a group by the big yellow balloon, stood Gambetta. He was wearing a thick greatcoat and a close sealskin cap; he sat down on the kerbstone to draw on a pair of fur-lined boots. He then took off a leather bag or knapsack which he was carrying slung over his shoulders, and got into the carriage of the balloon, while a young airman tied the precious wallet safely to the ropes, above Gambetta's head. It was half-past ten, a fine morning, with a light breeze from the south, and a flood of gentle autumn sunshine. Suddenly the big yellow balloon rose in the air, with Gambetta in it, and two men beside him; then the white balloon went up with three passengers also, one of them waving a tricolour flag. Above Gambetta's head, from the ropes of the yellow balloon, there floated a long pennon red, white, and blue. And the crowd cried "Vive la République! . . ." So the Dictator left Paris for Tours, invested with a power which was perhaps illegal but supreme, in order to organize in the provinces the reconstruction of a Government of National Defence.

Already in mid-October the cold of that dreadful winter had begun. Food was rationed. Fuel scarce and dear. And Victor Hugo's heart swelled with pity for the poor. He begged the Government to issue a decree of municipal relief. "It will cost us more than three-quarters of a million!" murmured the Minister.

"Well, well," said Hugo, "take them from the rich and give them to the poor." And he had his way.

No butter, no cheese, no eggs, no milk, and horse for the family joint! The nurture of little Georges and little Jeanne became a question which shared Victor Hugo's thoughts with his patriotic preoccupation. For himself he had the true French hardiness and indifference to personal comfort, and he rather enjoyed a horse-sausage whose maker had advertised it as a "saucisson chevaleresque."

Meanwhile all Paris is reading *Les Châtiments*, no longer contrabands ; one of the new cannons for the city ramparts is baptized *Les Châtiments* ; another is called *Victor Hugo*. All sorts of honours and presidencies are pressed on the poet, who wisely refuses, remaining the adviser, the prophet, the Bard—not the Executive Government. But we see that he enjoys his popularity, and then, on the 9th of November, he notes a more momentous piece of news : " To-day little Jeanne began to talk ! " She goes on from strength to strength, and, seven days later, we read in the poet's diary : " She crawls about on all-fours—beautifully."

Victor Hugo's diary is full of projects and occupation ; but the special one he came to Paris to perform remained impossible ; he never shouldered his rifle on the ramparts. Both his sons were enrolled in the Garde Nationale. Early in December, when their battery was told off for a sortie, the poet announced his intention of going with them, so to speak, " over the top." But on the eve of the encounter the whole battalion came to Victor Hugo's door, and the officer, mounting the stairs, read the following address : " The Garde Nationale of Paris forbids Victor Hugo to take part in the sortie ; any one can take part in a sortie, and only Victor Hugo can do the task of Victor Hugo."

New Year brought cold and hunger : " What we eat is no longer horse—it is the Unknown ! perhaps dog ? perhaps rat ? My digestion begins to suffer." The Prussians send six thousand bombs a day against Paris. The warming of the two rooms in the pavillon de Rohan where Hugo had his offices costs ten francs a day. The bombardment increases in fury, and Victor Hugo amuses himself in compiling the following statistics—which will remind the Parisians of our times of their experiences in 1918 :

First week in January, twenty-five thousand Prussian projectiles, at an average cost of 60 francs for every stroke of the cannon. Expense to the Prussian army, one million five hundred thousand francs. Result to the population of Paris, twelve killed ; average cost of a Parisian victim, six thousand pounds sterling.

In January the coal gave out, and a very troublesome minor misery was the impossibility of washing the dirty linen. The laundries struck work. There was nothing to burn, nothing to eat.

On the 28th of January the miserable city accepted its defeat. An armistice was declared. A National Assembly was to be held at Bordeaux to elect a government and to treat of peace. On the 8th of February Victor Hugo had been elected Member for Paris, the second out of forty-three Delegates, by more than two million votes. He left, with all his family, for the capital of the Gironde on the 13th of February 1871. The siege of Paris was ended ; his troubles had begun.

Paris, famished and shivering ; Paris without a shirt, with the German bombs bursting in the wards of the hospitals ; Paris had been a cheerful, hopeful sojourn compared to Bordeaux when Thiers and Jules Favre returned from Versailles with the terms of peace. Had France possessed a single army capable of continued resistance, it would have been impossible to accept those brutal clauses. But, in order to avert a second Sedan, the whole Army of the East had crossed the frontier and taken refuge in Switzerland ; Bourbaki, the General, had ended his days in despair with a bullet in his brain. And the greater part of France, with Thiers, feels that peace, however scandalous, was inevitable—otherwise the whole country, like Bourbaki, must perish in a moment of glorious despair. When the terms of peace were read out in the Assembly of Bordeaux— the secession of Alsace and Lorraine, the Prussians in occupation until the indemnity of five milliards of francs— £200,000,000 — should be paid — there was a moment of despair, after which the greater part of the Chamber accepted the bitter cup. But a residue declared themselves ready rather to begin the war over again, and resist to the death, and conspicuous among these were the Members for Paris— those who had suffered the siege and paid in their persons. Nor was any of them more ardent than Victor Hugo. Since they had to accept the hideous treaty—" le traité ! Shylock—Bismarck "—he demanded at least that an Assembly compelled to such a shameful act should resign *en masse* and leave new Delegates, unhampered by a patriotic crime, to deal with the destinies of the country. But few followed him

so far. Still, it was in a fever of emotion, almost of indignation, that these poets or patriots listened to the prudence
of Thiers—who knew, who could prove a further resistance
impossible—when he bade them behave " like sensible men
and not like children." The feeling was the stronger that
the Mayor of Strasbourg, present at Bordeaux, had died the
day before, broken-hearted ; his emotion at learning the
terrible news had snapped an artery. Seldom has history
recorded a more tragic moment than that First of March,
when, after the vote for Peace had been carried by a
majority of 340, the Members for Alsace and for Lorraine,
no longer Frenchmen, rose and left the Hall, declaring null
and void a treaty that disposed of them and their country
without their consent. With them went Gambetta, who,
having been elected both for Paris and Strasbourg, had
chosen the victim-city. With them also, among a little
company of Radical Delegates, went Victor Hugo, ever
faithful to the Rhine.

An experience of three weeks had sufficed to show Victor
Hugo how hard it is to reconcile ideas and realities : to
preach peace and goodwill among men and yet to avenge a
martyred country. Every day had brought its disenchantment. One of the sharpest, and that which chiefly decided
him to send in his resignation as Member of the National
Assembly, was the refusal of the Right to recognize Garibaldi
as a delegate of the French people. Garibaldi had been
elected for Paris at the same time as Victor Hugo, Ledru-
Rollin, and Louis Blanc. Of all the foreign friends of France
he was the only one to strike a blow in her favour, rushing
to the rescue with his little band of heroes. But after all
he was not French, and it was natural that in so critical a
moment, when the whole future of France was in question,
Frenchmen should be consulted first of all.

Anyhow, on the 8th of March, Victor Hugo definitely
resigned his mandate. He was beginning to feel how those
twenty years of absence and exile divided him from his
contemporaries. The men of the Right, with their traditions
and prejudices, appeared to him but dark and dusty brains.
Alas, the men of the Left, positive and often free-thinking
beyond the verge of atheism, seemed to him equally

oblivious of the Truth. The great current of Evolution, of Darwinism, carried them on far from all his beacons. Victor Hugo began to feel at last that despite his vigour he was no longer young, no longer in tune with his times, in fact a " vieille barbe de '48."

It was in this mood that he envisaged his return to Paris. On the 13th of March he lunched at Charles's table with his two sons, his daughter-in-law and the children. In the afternoon François-Victor left for Paris. Victor Hugo and his daughter-in-law proceeded to a restaurant where the poet was offering a farewell dinner to some friends. Charles was late—unaccountably late. Then there was a mystery of hushed voices, the father was called to the door: Charles was dead! The driver, on arriving at the restaurant, had opened the door of his cab, and had seen the young man lifeless, huddled in a corner, struck by some sudden apoplexy or aneurism, blood still streaming from his nose and mouth. Charles had been suffering from a mild form of bronchitis for some weeks—they had spoken of a season at Arcachon, but without much anxiety. . . . Charles, the handsome, buoyant, radiant Charles! His father's reserve of happiness; he who, with his young family about him, seemed like a sapling oak, its boughs full of nests; Charles, who had shared all his father's political hopes and illusions. The sunshine was darkened in the poet's sky.

Of the poems of Hugo's old age, I think the most beautiful are those addressed to this dear dead son in *L'Année terrible*, especially the verses beginning " O Charles " (for there are several lyrics inspired by his bereavement). Who can read without emotion this return of an old man on his past, as he looks on the orphaned children of his son, playing at his feet ?

> Soyez joyeux, pendant que je suis accablé :
> A chacun son partage.
> J'ai vécu presque un siècle, enfants ; l'homme est troublé
> Par de l'ombre à cet âge.
>
> Est-on sûr d'avoir fait, ne fût-ce qu'à demi,
> Le bien qu'on pouvait faire ?

A-t-on dompté la haine, et de son ennemi
   A-t-on été le frère ?

Même celui qui fit de son mieux a mal fait ;
   Le remords suit nos fêtes.
Je sais que si mon cœur quelquefois triomphait,
   Ce fut dans mes défaites.

En me voyant vaincu je me sentais grandi,
   La douleur nous rassure.
Car à faire saigner je ne suis pas hardi—
   J'aime mieux ma blessure.

   .   .   .   .

Moi-même un jour, après la mort, je connaîtrai
   Mon destin que j'ignore,
Et je me pencherai sur vous tout pénétré
   De mystère et d'aurore.

Je saurai le secret de l'exil, du linceul
   Jeté sur votre enfance,
Et pourquoi la justice et la douceur d'un seul
   Semble à tous une offense.

   .   .   .   .

Je saurai pourquoi l'ombre implacable est sur moi,
   Pourquoi tant d'hécatombes,
Pourquoi l'hiver sans feu m'enveloppe, pourquoi
   Je m'accrois sur des tombes.

Despite the halts, the hesitations, the ellipses of these verses, what a profound sincerity, what a grave and rolling music is here. I would fain try to reproduce a faint, a faltering echo of the sense and of the sound—for this is one of the last of Hugo's great lyrics ; a fragment of it, rather, cut ruthlessly from the middle, patched here and there, a shred or pattern of the perfect vesture :

Play, children, though my brows are overcast. . . .
   Since I, a child, was glad,
Nearly a hundred years, children, have passed.
   At my age men are sad.

Have we done well ? Paid even half our debt ?
   Left half our stains effaced ?
I know that if my heart was ever great,
   'Twas when I stood disgraced.

Vanquished, I felt new vigour in my need
   And knew the pang divine.

I am not bold to make another bleed ;
  Nay, let the wound be mine !

.   .   .   .   .   .

Well, after death, the meaning shall be plain,
  So long occult, withdrawn ;
And I shall bend above you, dears, again,
  Mysterious as the dawn.

Knowing wherefore I dragged those banished years,
  And why your father's shroud
Fell on your cradle ; why the Just appears
  Barabbas to the crowd.

Then I shall solve the riddle, seize the truth
  My starving spirit craves :
Why, like a lonely cypress, all my growth
  Is rooted in these graves.

(I did not invent that cypress ; it appears in the next stanza, which, alas, I have no space to quote, though the whole poem is admirable.)

The body of the unfortunate and charming Charles Hugo was taken to Paris, and buried there, with all the vain honours of a public funeral, on the 18th of March, against the sinister background of a rising revolution. For it was on the 18th of March that the Commune of Paris rose in insurrection against the Peace. Three days later the poet left for Belgium with the young widow and her babies. In Brussels he thought he had a sure asylum—in Brussels, his first refuge in 1852, Brussels where Charles's home awaited them.

His heart torn between his paternal grief and the misfortunes of his country, Victor Hugo did not see how well a season of silence would have become him. With Paris in flames, he offered his house as a sanctuary to the Communards who had escaped in time from the terrible repression of the armies at Versailles. And Brussels feared the hospitable septuagenarian, as though he were a firebrand in its midst ! On the night of the 27th of May a hostile and aristocratic mob stormed and raved before the house of the place des Barricades, stoning the windows, barely missing the cradle where slumbered little Jeanne, feverish and ill that night as it happened.

Nothing can describe the emotion of the old poet when he saw baby Georges take the hand of baby Jeanne and calm her terror. He was alone in the house with these children, their mother, and three maids. A voice called "Assassin! Down with Victor Hugo!" and that sinister "*A Mort!*" the dreadful roar of a French-speaking crowd. Some men brought a beam from a mason's yard. Voices called for a ladder. But, before the preparations of the besiegers were complete, after two hours of their attack, the dawn broke—for on the eve of June the nights are short—the daybreak, with its sudden sobering clarity and cool grey light, its normal activities, rumbling of carts, assurance of help and law. The crowd awoke from its fury like a man from an evil dream, and disappeared as swiftly as it had gathered, while the nightingale ceased singing, which all night long had trilled from some neighbouring garden, undisturbed, a music as indifferent as the stars.

We know all these details from several poems written in the heat of the poet's emotion and collected in *L'Année terrible*, in *Toute la lyre* and *L'Art d'être grand-père*. This midnight attack left on his mind an ineffaceable impression. He had thought himself in Belgium a man of mark. As a householder, and one of the considerable shareholders of the National Bank—for his popularity and a wise choice of investments had enriched Victor Hugo—he had thought himself safe. But two days after the onslaught of the mob, he received notice to quit—that is to say, a decree of expulsion.

The poet, for one wild moment, thought of quitting this inhospitable world, of fleeing—not, like Molière's Alceste, to some

> endroit écarté
> Où d'être homme d'honneur on ait la liberté,

but farther still, to those stars who in so many exiled nights at Guernsey had been his friends and counsellers:

> Fier, devant la tourbe immonde,
> Il rit, puisque le ciel s'offre à qui perd le monde,
> Puisqu'il a pour abri cette hospitalité,
> Et puisqu'il peut—ô joie! ô gouffre! ô liberté!

Domptant le sort, bravant le mal, perçant les voiles,
Par les hommes chassé, s'enfuir dans les étoiles.[1]

But a moment's reflection showed him that, however suitable for a poet, this solution was not practicable for the father of a family, so that, instead of starting alone for Sirius, he took some half-dozen tickets for Vianden in the neighbouring state of Luxembourg. Vianden must be a quaint and charming little town if we judge it by Hugo's drawings—picturesque studies, in sepia and ink and chalk, of old black and white houses, steep banks, poplared rivers. It lies in a wooded country on the edge of the Forest of Arden. The calm of this quiet neutral place was healing to Hugo's lacerated heart—a sort of peaceful Limbo. There also he had the joy of welcoming his friend Paul Meurice, liberated after three weeks' detention as a Communard by the forces at Versailles—" tout notre petit groupe a brusquement rayonné au milieu du grand deuil où nous sommes, patrie et famille." [2]

François-Victor had joined his father ; the children played and flourished under the great trees. Victor Hugo prepared for the press his volume *L'Année terrible*. Madame Drouet congratulated herself on the absence of Parisian sirens and enjoyed the interlude.

But winter saw them all back in Paris, first of all established in a flat at Auteuil, and then, in 1874, in an airy apartment at No. 66 rue de La Rochefoucauld, almost at Montmartre. On the 2nd of January 1872 Victor Hugo read *Ruy Blas* to the actors of the Odéon Theatre who were about to represent the play. And he writes in his note-book :

J.J. (Juliette) was present. On the 2nd of January 1833—just nine-and-thirty years ago to-day—she was present when I read *Lucrèce Borgia* to the company of the Théâtre Saint-Martin, now burned and destroyed—O memories !

But despite these memories, in Paris, Juliette, old and infirm, felt herself scarcely alert and quick enough to parry all the young and lovely rivals who thronged about her

---

[1] Expulsé de Belgique, *L'Année terrible*.
[2] A Paul Meurice. Correspondance.

poet, whom some magic had preserved in a regrettably miraculous youth. With what tender pertinacity she sang the charms of Guernsey, the wonders that the fresh sea air might accomplish for the failing health of François-Victor, the development of little Georges and little Jeanne! Perhaps the poet too, in his noisy rue de La Rochefoucauld, regretted sometimes the grand wide prospect, the ocean winds, the spacious sunsets of old Hauteville House. In August 1872 they all set out on that journey in a mood of homecoming, and remained for the space of a year in that happy sojourn, once the place of exile—Saint Simeon's pillar—but now regarded almost as an enchanted refuge, an island of the Blest, where the wicked cease from troubling and the weary are at rest!

CHAPTER XXIV

THE LAST SHEAF OF HARVEST

A YEAR of mourning in the peace of loneliness ; a year of rest, of truce, and holiday—for in a life as arduous as Hugo's, the twelve months which produce that vast novel *Quatre-vingt-treize* appear a time of leisure ; a year filled with the most fervent of those ancillary *amours* which are the regrettable side, the ungraceful shadow, of a noble poet's sad senility ; a year also in which, day by day, he watches the last of his children still seated by his fireside grow frailer and frailer. In August 1873 the whole household returns to Paris : the poet, François-Victor, Madame Charles and her children, and, of course, Juliette Drouet, to whom, despite his passing infidelities, Hugo is ever more and more closely and indissolubly attached, vowing her an unalterable adoration, and finding in her not merely a Baucis, but a sister-soul, a *dimidium animae*.

Hugo, I think, was perhaps happier in Guernsey, with his stars and his tides, his lonely wanderings, his books and his babies. But he had a cult for Paris. During the dreams of nineteen years of exile, Paris had shone transfigured in his mind : Paris,—not merely the city of Notre Dame and of the Feuillantines, in every part of which he had resided, every quarter of which he knew by heart throughout the sequence of the centuries ; not merely the city where he had loved and thought and suffered, but a sort of Jerusalem the Golden, object of a religion, symbol of light, liberty, and progress :—Paris had become one of those immense idols which his imagination, idealizing as a philosopher's and as concrete as a little child's, loved to construct and to bow down before—we see their statues in his spirit's temple,

each majestic in its shrine : Paris, Napoleon, the People—
objects of deep devotion and adoration, only subsidiary to
that diviner faith which transcends all religions in Hugo's
soul : the faith in the ultimate goodness of the Infinite.

Paris is not Allah ; but Paris is his Mecca ; and to Paris,
ruined by the assault of Versailles and the arson of the
Commune, the poet and his household hie, where speedily
sorrow overtakes them, for at Christmas - time poor
François-Victor died. It was not the sudden, heart-tearing
loss of Charles. We remember how, thirty years before,
Sainte-Beuve, writing to his friends of Lausanne, had spoken
of the sad state of " le pauvre enfant Toto," his lungs
decidedly diseased. François-Victor had lived to middle
manhood ; had completed his life's work, the translation
of Shakespeare ; had kept his father faithful company.
The old man could scarcely have expected more for this
fragile darling. But now he felt all the loneliness of his
old age. Ruins within, ruins without : his hearth deserted,
Paris in ashes, a new generation risen whose gods were not
his God—*Omnia vidit eversa.*

> Que te sert, ô Priam, d'avoir vécu si vieux !
> Tu vois tomber tes fils, ta patrie et tes Dieux !
>
> Un vieillard est souvent puni de sa vieillesse
> Par le peu de clarté que le destin lui laisse.
> Survivre est un regret poignant, presque un remords,
> Voir sa ville brûlée et tous ses enfants morts
> Est un malheur possible—et l'aïeul solitaire
> Tremble, et pleure de s'être attardé sur la terre.[1]

> O Priam, of what use was it to live so long !
> To watch your children die and see your country's wrong !
>
> An old man pays ofttimes the price of his old age
> In that dim dusk which Fate leaves him for heritage.
> Survival, like the shame of guilt, bows down his head.
> To see one's city burned and all one's children dead
> Is possible. The lonely grandsire, desolate,
> Trembles, and dreads the years he yet may have to wait.

Something still remained : a persistent hope in the
future of France, in a possibly distant but glorious *revanche*

[1] *Toute la lyre,* t. ii.

and the pleasure of seeing Paris day by day, like the phoenix, revive from her ashes. And, for the personal life, were there not Georges and Jeanne, and that immortal Juliette, Madame Drouet ? The poet decided to keep house with his daughter-in-law and her babies. In 1875 he rented two large flats at No. 21 rue de Clichy. On the fourth floor he installed himself with Madame Charles Hugo and the children. In the flat below, Madame Drouet, the most ingenious of housekeepers, reigned over the dining and reception rooms.

More and more the presence of the children will make itself felt, not only in the poet's life, not merely in the poems which evoke their charming figures : *L'Art d'être grandpère* after *L'Année terrible*, *Toute la lyre*, but in the final volumes of the *Légende des siècles* and in *Quatre-vingt-treize*. In this novel Victor Hugo, still haunted by his divided sympathies of Bordeaux and the Commune, has described a Civil War—the war of the Revolution in Vendée, the heroic campaigns of 1793. And the two valves of his heart beat for the two hostile armies. The Chouans had been the heroes of his childhood ; his mother, as a girl of fifteen, had been out with Madame de la Roche-Jacquelein :

> Paysans ! paysans ! hélas !   Vous aviez tort,
> Mais votre souvenir n'amoindrit pas la France ;
> Vous fûtes grands dans l'âpre et sinistre ignorance.[1]

In *Quatre-vingt-treize* Victor Hugo fights on the side of the Blues, of the soldiers of the Revolution, but his heart is very tender for the brigands of the woods and hedges ; and the story, which centres round the siege of an old feudal tower, a fastness of the Chouans, shows the same loyal spirit of disinterested chivalry reigning in either camp. But the true heroes of the tale are neither Chouan nor Bleu ; they are three little children, almost babies, three little orphans the age of Charles's nestlings. Three ! you will say ; there were only two. No, there were three. In Victor Hugo's eyes they were always three. There was that first Georges, who died at Brussels :

[1] *La Légende des siècles*, Jean Chouan.

Vous n'avez pas cru
Que j'oublierais jamais le petit disparu ? [1]

And so there are three babies shut up in the tower to which
the Republicans set fire : two boys and a girl. Of course
they are rescued. There are a good many divagations in
Quatre-vingt-treize, and we may have a poor opinion of the
Dumas-like dialogues between Danton, Robespierre, and
Marat in Paris ; but, so soon as the reader reaches the
forests of Vendée, he will find himself enveloped in an
extraordinary poetry : freshness of morning woods, fierce-
ness of forest-fighting, pathetic unconsciousness of childhood, which comes (unscathed as Shadrach, Meshach, and
Abednego) out of the very flames of battle. There is perhaps
some senility in the exasperated tenderness of these visions
of infancy—something morbid, wet with the dropping of
warm tears—but such a pang of sincerity is felt in the
poet's fears for the thousand perils to which unprotected
childhood is exposed, that he touches not merely our
imagination but our heart. Never has Hugo spoken more
simply out of his own experience. For, in these latter
days, the well-being of his small grandchildren was perhaps
the only preoccupation that struck through his superficial
sage serenity to the very marrow of his soul ; and, as time
went on, as it became evident that the pretty and girlish
Madame Charles Hugo would probably marry again, many
a chill fear filled the old poet with forebodings. He could
not hope to live till the children should be grown. And,
in November 1875, we find him writing that heart-breaking
Petit Paul of the third *Légende des siècles*, where a little
orphan boy, ill-treated by the stepmother who is jealous
of him, creeps one night to the grave of the old grandfather
who had adored him, and is found there in the morning,
dead, frozen, safe. In 1877 Hugo publishes *L'Art d'être
grandpère*, in which baby-worship reigns supreme, which is
sometimes, I must own, a little maudlin, but none the less
sincere : a pathetic endeavour to surround the two children
with an aura of poetry which shall render them sacred
beings—make them, as it were, the Wards in Chancery of
Parnassus—sure of efficient protection whatever may be

[1] *L'Art d'être grandpère,* " Un Manque."

their orphaned state. It was about this time that their mother remarried. Her position in Hugo's ambiguous house had not been simple : the daughter of the house, she was not the mistress of it ; nor was the omnipotent Juliette Drouet connected with her by any avowable tie. Her youth, her delicate self-effacement, and Juliette's ineffable tact had combined to gloss over the situation ; but it was difficult. Charles Hugo had been in his tomb several years when the young widow gave her hand to the radical politician Lockroy, a handsome, careless, gifted creature, who, as member of the Constituent Assembly at Bordeaux, had witnessed the tragic funeral of Charles Hugo, the despair of his girlish widow. There was nothing of Mr. Murdstone in the high-spirited Lockroy, and Hugo, who was just, made no objection to the marriage—

> Car à faire saigner je ne suis pas hardi—
> J'aime mieux ma blessure.

All he asked was that his son's orphans should not be taken from him.

Meanwhile *Quatre-vingt-treize* had, if possible, increased the popularity of Hugo in Paris. The book, with its subtle apology for civil war, or a strife in which both parties— being equally French—are almost equally superior to the mean of humanity, though one set may be in the right and the other in the wrong ; *Quatre-vingt-treize*, in which the chivalrous old Vendéan Marquis represents the idols of Hugo's youth just as the Republican leader embodies his modern ideals, was admirably calculated to please a public heartily ashamed of the Commune and its repression, and eager to make peace with a general amnesty all round. In January 1876 Hugo was elected a Senator of the Department of the Seine. His adventures at Bordeaux and in Belgium had pretty well robbed him of his political illusions and he no longer attempted the part of Gwynplaine ; but he attended the Senate with great regularity, and took an efficient if effaced share in its debates. Above all, he sat there as the visible representative of liberty and progress.

Although more than forty years divide those times from these, there are still living in Paris a good many persons of

my acquaintance who remember the Victor Hugo of that
period. First of all, I would quote, from her *Souvenirs
autour d'un groupe littéraire*, the impressions of that charming
writer, Madame Alphonse Daudet.

How should I forget that first visit of all to the flat in the
rue de Clichy—the modest apartment, so disproportionate to the
glory of its great inhabitant, which, in the estimate of his contemporaries, no palace could contain ! He rises from his seat by
the fireside, opposite the armchair of his old friend Madame
Drouet (the whilom Juliette of the Gaieté Theatre), and I am
astonished to find him so short in stature, although soon enough,
when he greets me and talks to me, I find him great, very great,
and very intimidating ! And this timidity is no fugitive emotion ;
I shall never overcome it ; it will always suffuse me in front of
Victor Hugo, a result of the immense admiration, the reverence,
as for some absent divinity, which my parents had inculcated
in my young soul for the poet of genius. So that my voice
will always tremble when I answer his affable remarks ; and,
ten years later, I shall look up astonished when I hear other
women talk to him familiarly of their housekeeping, or the
futile habits of their lives. . . .
At this moment of his return Victor Hugo was dazzling in
conversation—so many memories, evoked and narrated with
such inexhaustible animation, when politics did not monopolise
the talk. He welcomed his guests with the most charming
courtesy, with in his manners something noble and dignified,
with the kindly smile of a grandfather under those thick locks
which I have seen whiten through all the shades of white to the
virgin snow of the octogenarian.

The noble head, the courtly grace of manner, the rough
and thickset figure are revived more than once in the discourse of my friends. " I thought he was a mason," said
Mademoiselle Hélène Vacaresco, who, as a promising poetess
of ten or twelve, was bidden repeat her stanzas to Olympio.
" And you will never forget that you have recited them to
Victor Hugo," he said with kind solemnity, laying his hand
on her head.

Le père Hugo (writes Flaubert in his letters to George Sand)
est un charmant bonhomme, lorsque la galerie politique lui
manque. . . . Avant hier il m'a cité par cœur du Boileau et
du Tacite. Cela m'a fait l'effet d'un cadeau, tant la chose est

rare. D'ailleurs, les jours où il n'y a pas de politiciens chez lui, c'est un homme adorable.[1]

The *Journal* of the Goncourts, Jules Claretie's *Souvenirs*, the amusing *Au hasard de la vie* of Lockroy—most of the memoirs and diaries of the times afford us similar snapshots of our poet, now on the pinnacle of fame.

At nearly eighty years of age he still spent his mornings in writing, his afternoons in reverie and exercise. He would walk for two hours (frequently accompanied by a stout old lady with very white hair, Madame Drouet) and in the evenings he would receive his friends, according to his custom for the last fifty years. His table every night was spread for twelve : six members of his household and as many guests, whom he would welcome with that sweet and royal grace of address which never failed him. Juliette Drouet, her delicate features shaded by two madonna-braids of snow-white hair, presided at his table, still preserving some relic of her former beauty, and a certain theatrical and superannuated elegance of attire which Madame Daudet noted with affectionate amusement. Despite her seventy odd years she was still a very active mistress of her house, writing not only all the invitations, but answering a great part of Hugo's immense correspondence—especially the feminine part, of which she continued to be inordinately jealous. It was she who arranged in all their details these nightly dinner-parties. To this end Hugo allowed her (as M. Guimbaud tells us in his book) a hundred francs a day for the table and nearly half as much for wine. These are not the accounts of Harpagon. But Victor Hugo was not really a miser, despite the popular legend (which liked him no less for the " old-gentlemanly vice ") ; he was methodical, not avaricious. He gave away a tenth of his expenditure, not in riotous guineas to prodigal poets, but in definite subscriptions. " My fortune has got out of hand," he complained to his friend, Paul Meurice ; " if I occupied myself with it, it would engage my whole attention, and I would rather give my attention to my work." So, in the poet's extreme old age, Paul Meurice

[1] 26th May and 2nd Dec. 1871.

took upon himself the voluntary service of a faithful
steward, and I doubt if Victor Hugo knew the exact figure
of his revenues.

While Victor Hugo left his friend to administer his
fortune, he occupied himself with the disposal of an
immense accumulation of manuscripts, to which he was
constantly adding. In literature as in life the methodical
poet's watchword had been: waste not, want not; and
despite the serried volumes of his published works, his portfolios were full to overflowing. Portfolios indeed! They
were large and solid safes! At Hauteville House, during the
years of exile, Victor Hugo had written assiduously—what
interest was there to divert him from his work? He composed even in the intervals of his fitful slumbers. His bed
was surrounded with a sort of low dais, on which were laid
pencils and sheets of paper ready to be superscribed with
any stanza, happy line, or brilliant image that might occur
to the poet in the watches of the night. When morning
came these were carefully sorted and arranged in one or
other of the several iron chests which surrounded the glass
look-out which he called the Crystal Chamber. In Paris,
in the, avenue de Clichy (according to the account of his
secretary, M. Richard Lesclide [1]), the poet's study was
carpeted with a litter of papers through which one walked
as through snow. "When the writing-table was over-
burdened, a sheaf or so of manuscript would fall on to the
floor—and the Master forbade any attempt to put things
tidy." "I burn nothing," he would say, "posterity can
burn what it likes." Towards 1876, as full of vigour and
energy and charm as in his youth, he thought the day had
dawned at last for introducing some sort of order into this
embarrassing wealth of hoarded treasure.

It was of course impossible to publish all these glorious
arrears at once. No one ever understood the staging of his
genius better than Victor Hugo. He reserved for his post-
humous glory certain volumes of whose effect he was sure,
vintage of the comet-year, poems chiefly written between
1850 and 1860, which, though in part unfinished and fragmentary, contain passages of the most magnificent effect—

1 *Propos de table de Victor Hugo.*

such are the poem called *Dieu* and, perhaps, in a less degree
La Fin de Satan. The strange apocalypse with which the
first of these poems opens ; the symbolic beings who
interpret the idea of the Divinity : owl, bat, crow, vulture,
eagle, griffin, Angel, Spirit of Light ; the sense of the
chaos and disorder of the elements ; the horror of mineral
and animal existence ; the sacred shudder provoked by
the mystery of the Infinite ; the adoration of Jesus
crucified ; the belief in the Soul's passage and progress
from form to form till it attains the ideal sphere ; no less
than the splendid roll of the verse, all clearly mark that
the poem called *God* was written during the period of *Les
Contemplations* ; but, if the first fabric and the most beautiful
images belong to that time, Hugo had frequently added to
the later parts, which abound in references to his final
theories of infinite indulgence and pardon for all, with pity,
far more than power, as the supreme attribute of a Being

Qui n'a qu'un front : Lumière ! et n'a qu'un nom : Amour !

A volume : *Les Quatre Vents de l'Esprit*, which came out
in 1881, shows, at any rate for the lyric part, what sheaves
the poet still could glean from the harvest of his early
autumn. Yet, by a sort of miracle, in this winter of his
extreme old age, his genius had not deserted him. That
grand little epic *The Cemetery of Eylau*, a classic in France,
where, I suppose, every schoolboy knows it more or less by
heart, was composed in Victor Hugo's seventy-third year, on
the 28th of February 1874. Several others in the volume which
includes it [1] are still later in date. Some of these certainly
are lachrymose in their excessive tenderness ; but, even in his
young days, there had appeared from time to time, in Hugo's
grand and, on the whole, gloomy genius, an odd streak of
the maudlin, never more evident than, for instance, in *Les
Feuilles d'automne*, in such a poem as " La Prière pour tous."
The goody-goody and the Chadband-like were one strange
point of his multi-faceted, mighty, innumerable genius. It
is natural, after all, that they should be more evident in
the works of the septuagenarian, but they are not, as we
might suppose, a new symptom connoting his senility.

[1] *La Légende des siècles*, tome iii.

Of all these poems, I imagine that those which Hugo himself preferred were those which I should like to call his gnostic poems—full of his mystic doctrine of expiation and immortality, of divine indulgence, of death-bed repentance, of liberty, progress, and duty. Violently anti-papist and anti-clerical, he is not anti-religious. In the French sense of the word he is a spiritualist—an inveterate believer in the soul. With all his heart he believes in the existence of a God and realizes the goodness of that incomprehensible source of being. But he is not a Christian. He thinks the world evolves towards a glorious goal but that its path is veiled in mystery and shadow. Religion is the *sursum corda* of one who walks in the night, and all revealed religions are alike harmonious dreams. Still he believes in Life, infinitely larger than our existence — Life which transcends our visible universe—which mounts from the stone to the tree, from the brute to the savage, from man to an unknown destiny, until at length, after centuries of varied incarnations, the individual soul shall be absorbed in the Eternal Splendour.

CHAPTER XXV

THE BUDDHA ON THE BRACKET

In that salon of the rue de Clichy—which the poet ended by arranging so picturesquely that Banville declared him the first of French upholsterers—Hugo reigned the uncontested king of poetry. On his return from exile he had found certain Pretenders installed upon Parnassus with aspirations to a crown of their own. There was Mallarmé. There was Leconte de Lisle. The latter especially was inclined to give trouble and to consider himself—or be considered by his disciples—in the light of a rival power. But the sweep and perfection of Hugo's verbal genius dazzled his adversaries as completely as his friends. There is an amusing account [1] of the act of contrition of Leconte de Lisle. He was invited to dinner with his wife and chief disciples, and received with noble magnanimity by the Master, as Napoleon might have welcomed at his court some mediatized sovereign duly reduced to subjection. It is a glimpse of the routine of those dinners of the seventies : the ladies low-necked, the men in frock-coats and black ties ; when all were assembled, but only then, the doors were flung open, and Victor Hugo, in his morning coat, would appear. The guests rose to their feet, and the poet, advancing towards the standing ladies, would pay to each his courtly word of greeting and homage, take her hand and raise it to his lips. If it was not " le dernier salon où l'on cause," Hugo's salon was the last regal Drawing-room of Democracy.

In 1878, one warm evening at the end of June, after one of these copious repasts to which the poet's formidable appetite never failed to do honour, Victor Hugo began

[1] In Fernand Calmette's *Leconte de Lisle et ses amis*.

discussing Voltaire and Rousseau with Louis Blanc. And
the two old friends and fellow-exiles thrust and parried
with so much verve and fire, such eloquence and vigour,
on this old-fashioned theme that at last Victor Hugo was
observed to turn pale. He faltered, he stumbled ; the
doctor, hastily summoned, opined that there was a congestion
of the brain. The attack was slight, a mere warning. A
prolonged rest in the country might avert all evil conse-
quences. A week later, on the 4th of July, the poet set
out for Hauteville House, accompanied by Madame Drouet,
by the Lockroys with little Georges and little Jeanne, by
his two secretaries, as well as his friend Paul Meurice with
his wife—that charming, original Madame Meurice whom
Baudelaire described as " an Artist fallen into Democracy
like a butterfly into a bowl of gelatine."

They returned to Paris on the 10th of November,
determined to inaugurate a quieter existence. Victor Hugo
at last consented to leave the noisy house at the corner
of the rue d'Athènes and the rue de Clichy ; he moved into
a long, old-fashioned villa—which I can just dimly remember
—on the avenue d'Eylau, some way beyond the Arc
de l'Étoile. In 1880 the avenue Victor Hugo (as it is called
to-day) was still a retired and tranquil spot. Here he hoped
to be more or less secured from the constant irruption of
visitors and sightseers from every quarter of the globe.
It was a long, old-fashioned cottage, no grander, not much
larger, than that which he had occupied in the rue Notre-
Dame des Champs ; the sitting-rooms were on the ground
floor, with two stories and an attic above. Juliette occupied
the first floor, the poet the second ; the Lockroys with the
children were housed close at hand. In this new setting
the old existence was resumed—all the poets of Paris
frequented the salon of Victor Hugo. But, wrote Madame
Daudet, observing with her keen young eyes :

In health and in mental vigour the grand old man had gone
one step lower down the final stair. He still loved to receive
his friends, and one of the charms of that open house was its
boundless hospitality. Still round the table (which the poet's
grandchildren decorated at one end with their childish beauty)
the guests turned to the Master and sought in his glance the

order of the day ; from time to time he would still open a vein
of reminiscence, so living, so picturesquely recounted, that we
were dazzled the whole evening long.   Madame Drouet, . . . her
delicate features drawn into that dolorous effigy which the
painter, Bastien-Lepage, has preserved for us, still presided at
his dinner-table   And, in these latter times, the Master would
look sorrowfully at her noble and ravaged countenance as ·she
sent away dish after dish untasted.

"Madame Drouet ! You are eating nothing ! You must
eat. A little courage ! "

Eat—she was dying ! [1]

A cancer of the stomach was slowly destroying her tissues,
leaving intact the energy and fire of a nature which could
not give way. At her age (she was born in 1806) the
processes of disease are slow and less painful than in youth.
Still, the faithful housekeeper, so bountifully providing for
her guests, was menaced by starvation. Yet the invalid
would not resign her office, her privilege, of nurse. At the
least cough or headache of her octogenarian lover, she
would leave her room and pass the night in a little cabinet
on the second floor opening out of the poet's bedroom. Did
he but stir, she was there with a warm drink or an extra
covering. Every morning it was she who drew the curtains
from Victor Hugo's window, roused the old man with a kiss
on the forehead, lit his fire, prepared the two fresh eggs
that formed his breakfast, read him the papers, brought
the letters, and kept him as long as possible in his room,
knowing that, once dressed and downstairs, he would spare
himself no fatigue. Senate, Academy, visits — who knows
perhaps some desperate flirtation — would call him from
her side. For at nearly eighty years of age Juliette Drouet
still was jealous, and her white-haired poet still susceptible
to beauty. More than ever he was an Olympian, superior
to mortal men, claiming as his due the praise of poets, the
beauty of women, the charm of childhood. What power
had she over such a being ? A man of genius, freed from
the bondage of accepted opinion, having long outlived more
than one creed and conviction, he looked at life through
no eyes but his own, went his own way, nor cared to follow

---

[1] *Souvenirs autour d'un groupe littéraire.*

other men's examples. The rules that guide the multitude were to him, as they were to Socrates, mere Lamiae—bugbears to frighten children with. And (sometimes with sad results) he invented his own morality. His daily round, however, was simple and normal. The poet's afternoons began, almost invariably, with a ride on the top of an omnibus from Passy to the Bourse, where he would eat a *baba au rhum* in a certain confectioner's shop. This economical drive replaced the constitutional walk of former years. Victor Hugo was several times a millionaire (in francs) and could well have afforded a brougham. But his tastes were democratic and popular, he liked the omnibus ; and he was well aware that the omnibus liked him—that this little daily jaunt contributed immensely to his favour in the eyes of the people of Paris. " Victor Hugo n'est pas fier ! " Monarch and idol of the literary world, he was also the pride of his city. He was the great survivor. Lamartine, Alfred de Vigny, Musset, Théophile Gautier, Dumas, Balzac, Michelet, Sainte-Beuve, Mérimée, George Sand were dead. He alone remained of a generation of giants. And he, too, had been dead for nearly twenty years (for is not banishment a form of death to a Parisian ?), but he was risen from the grave and might be seen on the roof of " Passy-Bourse." He looked hale and hearty, with his sturdy figure, fresh face, abundant white hair and beard, and beautiful, steady, deep-blue eyes. Father, mother, brothers, sons, had died comparatively young, but the genius which still inspired him continued to preserve Victor Hugo.

> Il a le front pensif de l'homme qui persiste.
> Il est vieux, seul, vaincu, proscrit. Il n'est pas triste.
> On sent qu'il porte en lui la cause juste. Il croît,
> A mesure que l'ombre autour de lui s'accroît
> Je vois dans sa prunelle augmenter la lumière.[1]

Still, that seizure of the summer of 1878 had left him with one infirmity : he had become very deaf. The give-and-take of friendly intercourse was no longer for him. And this privation added to the intellectual loneliness of Hugo's old age. He had never been more passionately acclaimed.

[1] *Margarita.*

In 1882 two of his plays were produced on the stage—the charming little piece *Margarita*, and *Le Roi s'amuse*, while a third, admittedly unactable, but delightful at least in its love scenes, fell from the Press : the tragedy of *Torquemada*. All were successful, though there was really nothing in common between the poet and his public. His moral and religious ideas were more akin to the *Apology of Socrates* than to the positive materialism of the " Strug-for-lifers " (as Daudet called them) of 1880 ; his classical culture was opposed to the scientific spirit of the age ; and even his practice and theories in art were wholly different from the impassible precision of a Leconte de Lisle, the concise objectivity of a Heredia, or the hermetic and musical esoterism of Mallarmé. These were all artists to the core ; because of the splendour of his genius they hailed Victor Hugo as their Master, but they did not follow in his path. He reigned over them, admired and disregarded, as the Buddha on his bracket presides over some busy studio where men smoke and talk, develop their ideas, and take no account of the golden idol's Buddhism. He is there for his beauty, not for guidance.

At least throughout this year, 1882, Victor Hugo enjoyed the faithful companionship of Juliette Drouet. I find in Juliette's letters the record of a visit which they paid to Saint-Mandé on the 21st of June, she bound to the grave of her daughter, Claire Pradier, he to the doctor's house where poor Adèle, barely less entombed, dwelt in perpetual retirement. They returned from this pious pilgrimage, says Juliette, if not consoled, " which never can be in this world," at least resigned to accept the will of God. Five months later, on the 22nd of November, she accompanied him to the first night of the revival of *Le Roi s'amuse*. That was the last time she crossed their threshold. She faded out of life on the 11th of May 1883.

The atmosphere of tender flattery and absolute devotion with which she had surrounded Victor Hugo during fifty years was suddenly exhausted ; he was left, so to speak, to pant in an airless world. Several pages in his brother-in-law's — Paul Chenay's — volume give a sad picture of the wifeless, childless, old man, still attended with every

care and homage, but no longer fanned by that breath of
intimate love which his nature and his genius had always
craved. Some years before, in 1876, on the tomb of Madame
Louis Blanc, in rendering his homage to that devoted
companion of an exile, he had insinuated an allusion to his
own life with Juliette.

He was her glory ; she was his delight. She fulfilled the
great, the obscure function of woman, which is Love. . . . Man
strives, endeavours, invents, creates, sows and reaps, destroys
and builds, thinks, fights, meditates ; woman loves. And what
does she do with her love ? She makes the strength of man.
The worker needs a life associated with his own. The greater
he, the gentler must be his helpmate.

Louis Blanc was the apostle of the ideal. He was the
philosopher whose mantle covers a magistrate of the people ;
he was a great orator, a great citizen, an honest and combative
thinker, a historian who ploughs through the Past the furrow
of the Future. And his life was full of trouble and insult.
When Louis Blanc, in his struggle for the Just and the True,
outraged by public hatred, had well employed his day and
laboured through the storm unmoved at his heroic duty, he
turned towards his humble, noble wife, and rested in her smile.[1]

Victor Hugo could no longer rest himself in the smile
of his companion—that tender, confident, flattering smile.
An element as necessary to his existence as air or food or
sleep had failed him. And he was very old. The end was
at hand. Sometimes, especially in these latter days, his
mind, familiar with the funerals of his nearest and dearest,
turned to the great ceremony which will be his. It will
be a lay funeral, of course—one of those great gatherings
of the Democracy where his voice alone, soon to be stilled,
had ventured to speak of immortality, of God, despite the
disapproving glances, the evident constraint and uneasiness
of his embarrassed hearers. No voice will be raised in
prayer above his open grave, and yet who more than he has
believed in prayer ? Who has more faithfully affirmed

> Que tout cet inconnu qui m'entoure est vivant ;
> Que le Néant n'est pas et que l'Ombre est une Âme ?

He would have liked a prayer. . . .

[1] *Actes et paroles* : Depuis l'exil.

Oui, je trouverais bon que pour moi, loin du bruit,
Une voix s'élevât et parlât à la nuit !
Je le voudrais, et rien ne me serait meilleur
Qu'une telle prière après un tel malheur—
—Ma vie ayant été dure et funèbre, en somme.[1]

The volume in which this poem appeared, in 1883, was the last published in Hugo's lifetime. He would not encroach on that store of noble works, so human, so divine : *Choses vues*, *Dieu*, *Le Théâtre en liberté*, *Toute la lyre*, etc., which were to prolong his life as a poet when death should already have removed the man. Deaf, lonely, but great, surrounded by the tender veneration of a nation filially proud of his grand old age, he survived two years. The poets of France no longer called him the Master ; they called him *le Père*. Sainte-Beuve had lived to hear the students of the Latin Quarter hail him familiarly as " l'Oncle Beuve " ; but all that was noblest and finest in France greeted Hugo, with a more reverent emotion, as " Father."

His final fading out of life in May 1885 was a European preoccupation.

Not only in literary and political circles, not only in Paris, but all over France, in the academies and also in the workshops, in the salons and in the garrets, there was but one universal anxiety : Victor Hugo is dying. Victor Hugo is dead. No one remembered the ministerial crisis, or the question of Tonquin, or Afghanistan, or the Salon, or M. Zola's *Germinal*. The one subject of conversation was Victor Hugo's health and the gap his death would leave in our national life. Neither Thiers nor Gambetta had thus engrossed the public mind, and his funeral can only be compared to the return to France of Napoleon's ashes.[2]

Victor Hugo died at one o'clock in the afternoon on Friday, 22nd May 1885. He had written in his will : " I believe in God. I refuse the service of all the Churches ; I beg a prayer from every soul." And he had asked for a pauper's funeral. But the humble bier was installed under the Arch of Triumph veiled in crape. The coffin was raised on a lofty dais, and the green flames of great bronze

---

[1] *Légende des siècles*, iii., " Les Enterrements civils."
[2] Gabriel Monod, *Portraits et souvenirs*.

lamps flared eerily round it and were reflected in the breastplates of the mounted cuirassiers, who brandished other torches, as they strove to keep in place the crowd that, in rushing tides and surges, beat all night long against the flanks of their horses.

I can remember confusedly that heroic funeral. I was in Venice when Victor Hugo died, and came posting to Paris, to the house of a lady who, some years before, had been my governess. She lived in the avenue d'Eylau and took the keen interest of a neighbour in the ceremony. On the eve we sallied forth to see by night the catafalque under the Arch of Triumph, and when the great day arrived we were early on the Champs Élysées. We had the good chance to discover and hire a four-wheeled cab from some station, stranded in the crowd, unable to stir, whose flat roof, railed round for the security of luggage, made an admirable vantage-point. The sight was magnificent ; the throng, the mass, immense. All the great bodies of the nation : Army, Parliament, Senate, Academy, honoured the poet who had been the symbol of the Republic. As far as the eye could reach the crowd extended. Banner after banner, wreath after wreath, delegation after delegation passed by. And the humble hearse of the pauper in the midst of this national magnificence seemed an antithesis in Victor Hugo's vein. The hours went by: three hours, four hours, five hours. The endless procession showed no falling-off, though, little by little, its character had changed. The Friendly Society of Ménilmontant, the Free-Masons of Montmartre, the Gymnasts of Belleville (in their tights), Ba-Ta-Clan, " les Béni-bouffe-toujours." And I wondered how many of these manifestants had read *Les Feuilles d'automne* or could quote a stanza from the *Contemplations*. It was very hot on the top of the cab; we were hungry, tired to death. I began to cavil and question, murmuring grimly that this gigantic festival would have satisfied the Master's love of display, his morbid taste for popularity at any price. It was like a page torn from a volume of *L'Homme qui rit* ! His emphatic genius, his cyclopean humour, his vague humanitarianism, his socialistic fervours, his eye for effect, his talent for staging an enormous scene,

became more apparent to me than his deep, epical simplicity
of feeling, his cosmic grandeur, his marvellous music, and
that great fraternal heart filled to the brim with pity and
hope.   At this point some one in the crowd exclaimed,
" Il serait content, le Père ! "   It was my thought—how
much better expressed !   All his children had conspired to
do him honour and he loved even the least.   A nation is
not only composed of its constituted bodies — they may
be the spine, the brain ; but the life-blood of a country is
the mass of the people—just this popular throng.   Yes !
even the " Béni-bouffe-toujours." *Sinite parvulos* . . .
He would have loved them—with his great, mobile, ardent
vibrating soul, which, his life long, had rung and quivered,
and clamoured like a mighty musical bell in answer to all
the passions of France.

> Oh ! c'est alors qu'émus et troublés par ces chants
> Le peuple dans la ville et l'homme dans les champs . . .
> C'est alors que les bons, les faibles, les méchants,
> Tous à la fois, la veuve en larmes, les marchands . . .
> Et le croyant soumis prosterné sous la tour,
> Écoutent, effrayés et ravis tour à tour,
> Comme on rêve au bruit sourd d'une mer écumante,
> La grande âme d'airain qui là-haut se lamente.[1]

On the morrow of the death of Victor Hugo a light
cloud passed across his solar glory.   Men were tired of
calling Aristides the Just.   He had left the stage free for
lesser men, the pupils of Baudelaire and of Sainte-Beuve :
Parnassians and Symbolists on the one hand, on the other
Intimists, like the delicious Verlaine and the insipid
François Coppée.   And these too had their day.

Meanwhile the works of Victor Hugo still came pouring
from the Press—the brilliant *Choses vues*, the exquisite
Théâtre en liberté, the admirable rhythms of *Dieu* and *La
Fin de Satan*.   The Frenchman, who, to the very fibre of
his soul, is an artist, could but marvel at their technique
while admitting an evident exaggeration in their feeling.
Still, the prosperity of Rostand (who is, as it were with a
bar sinister and under the rose, the poetic heir of Victor
Hugo) revived in the public a romantic taste.   Then war

---

[1] *Feuilles d'automne*, " A Louis B."

broke out. Only one voice in France could utter all we felt, *had* uttered it, had voiced all the courage, intensity, fury, patience, and burning pity of our souls :

La grande âme d'airain qui là-haut se lamente !

And France, more than ever entranced, enchanted, listened in gratitude and glory to the voice of her unique, supreme lyric poet—Victor Hugo.

BIBLIOGRAPHY

Œuvres Complètes de Victor Hugo.
Victor Hugo, par un témoin de sa vie.
Correspondance de Victor Hugo.
VICTOR HUGO. Lettres à la fiancée.
L'Enfance de Victor Hugo. Par GUSTAVE SIMON. Hachette, 1904.
SAINTE-BEUVE. Poésies complètes.
    Le Livre d'amour.
    Le Cahier.
    Portraits contemporains.
Sainte-Beuve amoureux et poète. G. MICHAUD.
Le Roman de Sainte-Beuve. Par GUSTAVE SIMON. Ollendorff, 1906.
LÉON SÉCHÉ. Sainte-Beuve : son esprit ; ses mœurs. Deux volumes.
    Mercure de France, 1904.
La Vie d'une femme. Par GUSTAVE SIMON. Ollendorff, 1914.
Les Amours d'un poète. Par LOUIS BARTHOU. Documents inédits.
    (Revue de Paris. Juillet, août, septembre, octobre.) 1918.
Correspondance inédite de Sainte-Beuve avec M. et Madame Juste Olivier.
    Mercure de France, 1904.
Le Livre du bord. Par ALPHONSE KARR. T. 3.
BALZAC. Lettres à l'étrangère.
LOUIS GUIMBAUD. Victor Hugo et Juliette Drouet. Lettres inédites.
    Blaizot, 1914.
JUANA RICHARD LESCLIDE. Victor Hugo intime. 1907.
EDMOND BIRÉ. Victor Hugo après 1830.
EDMOND BIRÉ. Chateaubriand, Victor Hugo, H. de Balzac. E. Vitte,
    1907.
PAUL CHENAY. Victor Hugo à Guernesey.
PAUL STAPFER. Victor Hugo à Guernesey.
LÉOPOLD MABILLEAU. Victor Hugo. Hachette.
FERNAND GREGH. Victor Hugo. 1902.
CHARLES RENOUVIER. Victor Hugo : Le Philosophe.
    Victor Hugo : Le Poète. Deux volumes.
MADAME ALPHONSE DAUDET. Souvenirs autour d'un groupe littéraire.
    Fasquelle, 1910.
PAUL AND VICTOR GLACHANT. Essai critique sur le théâtre de Victor
    Hugo. 1902.
RICHARD LESCLIDE. Propos de table de Victor Hugo.
APPONYI, COUNT RODOLPHE. Journal. Plon, 1913–14.
BALABINE, VICTOR DE, COUNT. Journal. Émile-Paul, 1914.
EDMOND DE GONCOURT. Journal.
ÉDOUARD LOCKROY. Au hasard de la vie.
CHARLES BAUDELAIRE. Lettres de. (Édition Crépet.)
EUGÈNE CRÉPET. Charles Baudelaire : Étude biographique.

FLAUBERT, GUSTAVE. Lettres à George Sand.
FERNAND CALMETTE. Leconte de Lisle et ses amis.
GABRIEL MONOD. Portraits et souvenirs : Victor Hugo.

Paintings, drawings, engravings, photographs, manuscripts, and albums, preserved in the Musée Victor Hugo in Paris.

INDEX

THE END